CHINA: POWER AND PERILS

STRATFOR
221 W. 6th Street, Suite 400
Austin, TX 78701

Printed in the United States of America

The contents of this book originally appeared as analyses
on STRATFOR's subscription Web site.

ISBN: 1453866078
EAN-13: 9781453866078

Publisher: Grant Perry
Editor: Michael McCullar
Project Coordinator: Robert Inks
Designer: TJ Lensing

CONTENTS

CHAPTER 3: POLITICS

CHAPTER 4: SECURITY

CHAPTER 5: INTERNATIONAL RELATIONS

ILLUSTRATIONS

CHINA TERRAIN

Copyright STRATFOR 2010   www.STRATFOR.com

INTRODUCTION

The growth of the Chinese economy and the emergence of China onto the world stage have appeared as the latest examples of the Asian economic miracle. China has racked up year after year of double-digit or near double-digit growth; its gross domestic product is close to surpassing that of Japan to become the second largest in the world; Chinese consumption of commodities impacts global pricing; Chinese companies are competing with other multinationals; and Chinese firms are buying up land and projects around the world. China's political assertiveness is expanding to match, and the Chinese military is taking a more active role in international peacekeeping operations, joint training and exchanges across the globe.

But the perception of strength masks a deeper insecurity. China has followed a basic economic model that focuses on the flow-through of money, a model that looks at growth, rather than profits, as the key measurement. This model, like a Ponzi scheme, works extremely well in good economic times, but it breaks down rapidly under crisis. Beijing has stashed away a substantial reserve fund, but the global economic slowdown of the late 2000s has forced the government to shift to massive stimulus spending and has revealed the inherent risks in its export-based economy.

These risks come as no surprise to the Chinese government. For years, leaders in Beijing have been advocating a shift from an export-based economy to one with a heavier focus on domestic consumption. Beijing also wants to break away from profitless growth, to rein in inefficiencies and redundancies in the industrial sector and to expand infrastructure and economic activity inland. As with any country, these changes are neither easy nor quick. But the Chinese government, while mouthing the need for change, also has remained constrained by fear that any rapid policy adjustment could trigger a domino effect of pent-up social pressures that could lead to long-term instability in the country. Beijing's unease over the Chinese economy and society has led to a very cautious government — one that is often slow to respond and does the minimum necessary to assuage perceptions while avoiding social dislocation on a large scale.

History shows that the unification of China into a single country requires a strong, centralized leadership. But the maintenance of that country requires the steady expansion of a bureaucracy that reaches down to the lowest levels. Over time, this bureaucracy gains in real strength, while the center loses its authority. So long as there is no serious crisis, the illusion of central control is maintained, as the benefits to the regions offered by the central government outweigh risks to their own local interests. But in times of stress, the balance between center and region can grow strained quickly: If the central government needs to shift resources to a less-developed area, it often does so at the expense of the more-developed area; if there is a call to rectify redundancies in a certain industrial sector on a national level, regional interests resist. Historically, this has led to warlordism, export-oriented regions siding ultimately with their foreign benefactors over the central Chinese government, the rise of resistance from the majority rural population — and, in extreme cases, to the collapse of dynasties.

The Chinese may be nearing one of these turning points. Economic policies are held hostage by fears of social unrest and by resistance from regional and local interests. At the same time, the Chinese government feels it needs to maintain the flow of money and technology from its export sector to fund development of the rural and newly urbanized regions to avoid the rise of the disgruntled peasant.

Maintenance of the export-based economy, the redundancies in Chinese industry and the emerging Chinese consumer class are forcing Beijing to reach farther and farther abroad for its raw materials and markets. This exposes China's economic security to more and more risks the farther the effort extends. This expansion also has required a change in China's political and security interactions. China is pursuing influence, if not control, over its perceived sphere of interest while stretching tenuously beyond, through the Indian Ocean to the Middle East and Africa, and more recently flirting with Latin America.

The more China reaches outward to ensure its own domestic concerns, the more it butts up against other regional powers — or against the global interests of the United States. In the end, given its geographic location, China is a land power; its interests are foremost centered on its own population and on potential challenges from its numerous land borders. Supporting a navy that runs headlong into the strategic concerns of the United States may be, in some ways, a required natural extension of China's economic opening and reform, but it is also a major challenge for China to overcome. Beijing's current solution is to try to appear to be a global power while also claiming the status of a developing — and thus non-threatening — nation. It is a tightrope that is appearing more and more frayed.

In short, China may be reaching a point of crisis — a point where it must make decisions about its economic, social and political balances or have such decisions forced upon it because of internal or external crises. Into this comes another leadership change: 2012 marks the first unknown in Chinese leadership since Deng Xiaoping, who hand-selected both former President Jiang Zemin and Jiang's successor, Hu Jintao, thus ensuring a relatively stable two decades of political transition. The 2012 leadership change, the rise of the so-called fifth-generation leaders, has no such built-in continuity and authority. Certainly, China's current leaders have worked toward a consensus, and cooperative leadership based on a balance of factional interests is taking shape, but rule by debate and consensus is not always the best way to deal with crises.

As China edges closer to the leadership transition, it faces myriad challenges, despite an outward appearance of economic strength and political confidence. Understanding these problems, and the way the Chinese government itself views its situation and approaches decision-making, is critical to being able to predict and prepare for the China of the next decade.

Rodger Baker, VP, Strategic Intelligence
STRATFOR
Austin, Texas
Oct. 4, 2010

A NOTE ON CONTENT

STRATFOR presents the following articles as they originally appeared on our subscription Web site, www.STRATFOR.com. These pieces represent some of our best analyses of China's economics, politics and international relations since June 2002, organized under chapter headings and presented in the order in which they were published. Since most of the articles were written as individual analyses, there may be overlap from piece to piece and chapter to chapter, and some of the information may seem dated. Naturally, many of the observations herein are linked to a specific time or event that may be years removed from China's situation today. However, STRATFOR believes bringing these pieces together provides valuable insight and perspective on a significant global player.

CHINA AS AN ISLAND

RUSSIA

KAZAKHSTAN

MONGOLIA

Beijing ★

Shanghai ●

CHINA

Chengdu ●
Chongqing ●

PAKISTAN

INDIA

MYANMAR

Hong Kong ●

TAIWAN

NORTH
KOREA

SOUTH
KOREA

JAPAN

Pacific
Ocean

0 mi   500   1,000
0 km

Copyright STRATFOR 2010   www.STRATFOR.com

CHAPTER 1:
THE GEOPOLITICS OF CHINA

June 15, 2008

Geography

Contemporary China is an island. Although it is not surrounded by water (which borders only its eastern flank), China is bordered by terrain that is difficult to traverse in virtually any direction. There are some areas that can be traversed, but to understand China we must begin by visualizing the mountains, jungles and wastelands that enclose it. This outer shell both contains and protects China.

Internally, China must be divided into two parts: the Chinese heartland and the non-Chinese buffer regions surrounding it. There is a line in China called the 15-inch isohyet, east of which more than 15 inches of rain fall each year and west of which the annual rainfall is less. The vast majority of Chinese live east and south of this line, in the region known as Han China — the Chinese heartland. The region is home to the ethnic Han, whom the world regards as the Chinese. It is important to understand that more than a billion people live in this area, which is about half the size of the United States.

The Chinese heartland is divided into two parts, northern and southern, which in turn is represented by two main dialects, Mandarin in the north and Cantonese in the south. These dialects share a writing system but are almost mutually incomprehensible when spoken. The Chinese heartland is defined by two major rivers — the Yellow River in the north and the Yangtze in the South, along with a third lesser river in the south, the Pearl. The heartland is China's agricultural region. However — and this is the single most important fact about China — it has about one-third the arable land per person as the rest of the world. This pressure has defined modern Chinese history — both in terms of living with it and trying to move beyond it.

A ring of non-Han regions surround this heartland — Tibet, Xinjiang province (home of the Muslim Uighurs), Inner Mongolia and Manchuria (a historical name given to the region north of North Korea that now consists of the Chinese provinces of Heilongjiang, Jilin and Liaoning).

These are the buffer regions that historically have been under Chinese rule when China was strong and have broken away when China was weak. Today, there is a great deal of Han settlement in these regions, a cause of friction, but today Han China is strong.

These are also the regions where the historical threat to China originated. Han China is a region full of rivers and rain. It is therefore a land of farmers and merchants. The surrounding areas are the land of nomads and horsemen. In the 13th century, the Mongols under Genghis Khan invaded and occupied parts of Han China until the 15th century, when the Han reasserted their authority. Following this period, Chinese strategy remained constant: the slow and systematic assertion of control over these outer regions in order to protect the Han from incursions by nomadic cavalry. This imperative drove Chinese foreign policy. In spite of the imbalance of population, or perhaps because of it, China saw itself as extremely vulnerable to military forces moving from the north and west. Defending a massed population of farmers against these forces was difficult. The easiest solution, the one the Chinese chose, was to reverse the order and impose themselves on their potential conquerors.

There was another reason. Aside from providing buffers, these possessions provided defensible borders. With borderlands under their control, China was strongly anchored. Let's consider the nature of China's border sequentially, starting in the east along the southern border with Vietnam and Myanmar. The border with Vietnam is the only border readily traversable by large armies or mass commerce. In fact, as recently as 1979, China and Vietnam fought a short border war, and there have been points in history when China has dominated Vietnam. However, the rest of the southern border where Yunnan province meets Laos and Myanmar is hilly jungle, difficult to traverse, with almost no major roads. Significant movement across this border is almost impossible. During World War II, the United States struggled to build the Burma Road to reach Yunnan and supply Chiang Kai-shek's forces. The effort was so difficult it became legendary. China is secure in this region.

Hkakabo Razi, almost 19,000 feet high, marks the border between China, Myanmar and India. At this point, China's southwestern frontier begins, anchored in the Himalayas. More precisely, it is where Tibet, controlled by China, borders India and the two Himalayan states, Nepal and Bhutan. This border runs in a long arc past Pakistan, Tajikistan and Kyrgyzstan, ending at Pik Pobedy, a 25,000-foot mountain marking the border with China, Kyrgyzstan and Kazakhstan. It is possible to pass through this border region with difficulty; historically, parts of it have been accessible as a merchant route. On the whole, however, the Himalayas are a barrier to substantial trade and certainly to military forces. India and China — and China and much of Central Asia — are sealed off from each other.

The one exception is the next section of the border, with Kazakhstan. This area is passable but has relatively little transport. As the transport expands, this will be the main route between China and the rest of Eurasia. It is the one land bridge from the Chinese island that can be used. The problem is distance. The border with Kazakhstan is almost a thousand miles from the first tier of Han Chinese provinces, and the route passes through sparsely populated Muslim territory, a region that has posed significant challenges to China. Importantly, the Silk Road from China ran through Xinjiang and Kazakhstan on its way west. It was the only way to go.

There is, finally, the long northern border first with Mongolia and then with Russia, running to the Pacific. This border is certainly passable. Indeed, the only successful invasion of China took place when Mongol horsemen attacked from Mongolia, occupying a good deal of Han China. China's buffers — Inner Mongolia and Manchuria — have protected Han China from other attacks. The Chinese have not attacked northward for two reasons. First, there has historically not been much there worth taking. Second, north-south access is difficult. Russia has two rail lines running from the west to the Pacific — the famous Trans-Siberian Railroad (TSR) and the Baikal-Amur Mainline, which connects those two cities and ties into the TSR. Aside from that, there is no east-west ground transportation linking Russia. There is also no north-south transportation. What appears accessible really is not.

The area in Russia that is most accessible from China is the region bordering the Pacific, the area from Russia's Vladivostok to Blagoveshchensk. This region has reasonable transport, population and advantages for both sides. If there were ever a conflict between China and Russia, this is the area that would be at the center of it. It is also the area, as you move southward and away from the Pacific, that borders on the Korean Peninsula, the area of China's last major military conflict.

Then there is the Pacific coast, which has numerous harbors and has historically had substantial coastal trade. It is interesting to note that, apart from the attempt by the Mongols to invade Japan, and a single major maritime thrust by China into the Indian Ocean — primarily for trade and abandoned fairly quickly — China has never been a maritime power. Prior to the 19th century, it had not faced enemies capable of posing a naval threat and, as a result, it had little interest in spending large sums of money on building a navy.

China, when it controls Tibet, Xinjiang, Inner Mongolia and Manchuria, is an insulated state. Han China has only one point of potential friction, in the southeast with Vietnam. Other than that, it is surrounded by non-Han buffer regions that it has politically integrated into China. There is a second friction point in eastern Manchuria, touching on Siberia and Korea. There is, finally, a single opening into the rest of Eurasia on the Xinjiang-Kazakh border.

China's most vulnerable point, since the arrival of Europeans in the western Pacific in the mid-19th century, has been its coast.

Apart from European encroachments in which commercial interests were backed up by limited force, China suffered its most significant military encounter — and long and miserable war — after the Japanese invaded and occupied large parts of eastern China along with Manchuria in the 1930s. Despite the mismatch in military power and more than a dozen years of war, Japan still could not force the Chinese government to capitulate. The simple fact was that Han China, given its size and population density, could not be subdued. No matter how many victories the Japanese won, they could not decisively defeat the Chinese.

China is hard to invade; given its size and population, it is even harder to occupy. This also makes it hard for the Chinese to invade others — not utterly impossible, but quite difficult. Containing a fifth of the world's population, China can wall itself off from the world, as it did prior to the United Kingdom's forced entry in the 19th century and as it did under Mao Zedong. All of this means China is a great power, but one that has to behave very differently from other great powers.

Geopolitical Imperatives

China has three overriding geopolitical imperatives:

1. Maintain internal unity in the Han Chinese regions.

2. Maintain control of the buffer regions.

3. Protect the coast from foreign encroachment.

Maintaining Internal Unity

China is more enclosed than any other great power. The size of its population, coupled with its secure frontiers and relative abundance of resources, allows it to develop with minimal intercourse with the rest of the world, if it chooses. During the Maoist period, for example, China became an insular nation, driven primarily by internal interests and considerations, indifferent or hostile to the rest of the world. It was secure and, except for its involvement in the Korean War and its efforts to pacify restless buffer regions, was relatively peaceful. Internally, however, China underwent periodic, self-generated chaos.

The weakness of insularity for China is poverty. Given the ratio of arable land to population, a self-enclosed China is a poor China. Its population is so poor that economic development driven by domestic demand, no matter how limited it might be, is impossible. However, an isolated China is easier to manage by a central government. The great danger in China is a rupture within the Han Chinese nation. If that happens, if the central government weakens, the peripheral regions will spin off, and China will then be vulnerable to foreigners taking advantage of Chinese weakness.

For China to prosper, it has to engage in trade, exporting silk, silver and industrial products. Historically, land trade has not posed a problem for China. The Silk Road allowed foreign influences to come into China and the resulting wealth created a degree of instability. On the whole, however, it could be managed.

The dynamic of industrialism changed both the geography of Chinese trade and its consequences. In the mid-19th century, when Europe — led by the British — compelled the Chinese government to give trading concessions to the British, it opened a new chapter in Chinese history. For the first time, the Pacific coast was the interface with the world, not Central Asia. This in turn massively destabilized China.

As trade between China and the world intensified, the Chinese who were engaged in trading increased their wealth dramatically. Those in the coastal provinces of China, the region most deeply involved in trading, became relatively wealthy while the Chinese in the interior (not the buffer regions, which were always poor, but the non-coastal provinces of Han China) remained poor, subsistence farmers.

The central government was balanced between the divergent interests of coastal China and the interior. The coastal region, particularly its newly enriched leadership, had an interest in maintaining and intensifying relations with European powers and with the United

15-INCH ISOHYET AND CHINA POPULATION DENSITY

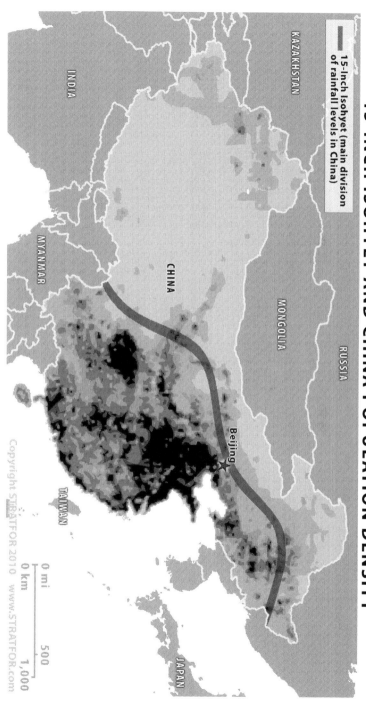

15-Inch Isohyet (main division of rainfall levels in China)

KAZAKHSTAN

INDIA

MYANMAR

CHINA

MONGOLIA

RUSSIA

Beijing

TAIWAN

JAPAN

0 mi   500   1,000
0 km

Copyright STRATFOR 2010   www.STRATFOR.com

States and Japan. The more intense the trade, the wealthier the coastal leadership and the greater the disparity between the regions. In due course, foreigners allied with Chinese coastal merchants and politicians became more powerful in the coastal regions than the central government. The worst geopolitical nightmare of China came true. China fragmented, breaking into regions, some increasingly under the control of foreigners, particularly foreign commercial interests. Beijing lost control over the country. It should be noted that this was the context in which Japan invaded China, which made Japan's failure to defeat China all the more extraordinary.

Mao's goal was threefold, Marxism aside. First, he wanted to recentralize China — re-establishing Beijing as China's capital and political center. Second, he wanted to end the massive inequality between the coastal region and the rest of China. Third, he wanted to expel the foreigners from China. In short, he wanted to recreate a united Han China.

Mao first attempted to trigger an uprising in the cities in 1927 but failed because the coalition of Chinese interests and foreign powers was impossible to break. Instead, he took the Long March to the interior of China, where he raised a massive peasant army that was both nationalist and egalitarian and, in 1948, returned to the coastal region and expelled the foreigners. Mao re-enclosed China, recentralized it and accepted the inevitable result. China became equal but extraordinarily poor.

China's primary geopolitical issue is this: For it to develop it must engage in international trade. If it does that, it must use its coastal cities as an interface with the world. When that happens, the coastal cities and the surrounding region become increasingly wealthy. The influence of foreigners over this region increases and the interests of foreigners and the coastal Chinese converge and begin competing with the interests of the central government. China is constantly challenged by the problem of how to avoid this outcome while engaging in international trade.

Controlling the Buffer Regions

Prior to Mao's rise, with the central government weakened and Han China engaged simultaneously in war with Japan, civil war and regionalism, the center was not holding. While Manchuria was under Chinese control, Outer Mongolia was under Soviet control and extending its influence (Soviet power more than Marxist ideology) into Inner Mongolia, and Tibet and Xinjiang were drifting away.

At the same time that Mao was fighting the civil war, he was also laying the groundwork for taking control of the buffer regions. Interestingly, his first moves were designed to block Soviet interests in these regions. Mao moved to consolidate Chinese communist control over Manchuria and Inner Mongolia, effectively leveraging the Soviets out. Xinjiang had been under the control of a regional warlord, Yang Zengxin. Shortly after the end of the civil war, Mao moved to force him out and take over Xinjiang. Finally, in 1950 Mao moved against Tibet, which he secured in 1951.

The rapid-fire consolidation of the buffer regions gave Mao what all Chinese emperors sought, a China secure from invasion. Controlling Tibet meant that India could not move across the Himalayas and establish a secure base of operations on the Tibetan Plateau. There could be skirmishes in the Himalayas, but no one could push a multidivisional force across those mountains and keep it supplied. So long as Tibet was in Chinese hands, the Indians could live on the other side of the moon. Xinjiang, Inner Mongolia and Manchuria buffered China from the Soviet Union. Mao was more of a geopolitician than an ideologue. He did not trust the Soviets. With the buffer states in hand, they would not invade China. The distances, the poor transportation and the lack of resources meant that any Soviet invasion would run into massive logistical problems well before it reached Han China's populated regions, and become bogged down — just as the Japanese had.

China had geopolitical issues with Vietnam, Pakistan and Afghanistan, neighboring states with which it shared a border, but the real problem for China would come in Manchuria or, more

CHINA PROVINCES AND BUFFER REGIONS

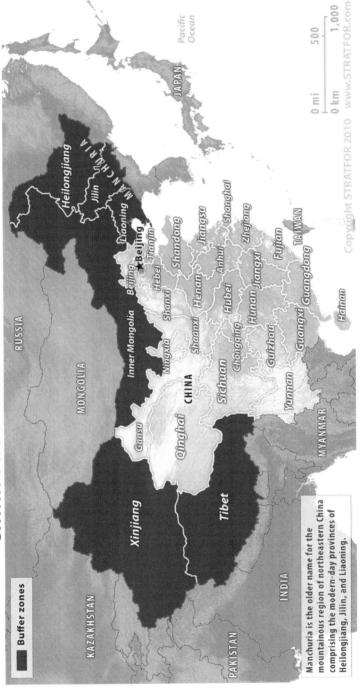

Buffer zones

Manchuria is the older name for the
mountainous region of northeastern China
comprising the modern-day provinces of
Heilongjiang, Jilin, and Liaoning.

Copyright STRATFOR 2010   www.STRATFOR.com

precisely, Korea. The Soviets, more than the Chinese, had encouraged a North Korean invasion of South Korea. It is difficult to speculate on Josef Stalin's thinking, but it worked out superbly for him. The United States intervened, defeated the North Korean Army and drove to the Yalu, the river border with China. The Chinese, seeing the well-armed and well-trained American force surge to its borders, decided that it had to block its advance and attacked south. What resulted was three years of brutal warfare in which the Chinese lost about a million men. From the Soviet point of view, fighting between China and the United States was the best thing imaginable. But from STRATFOR's point of view, what it demonstrated was the sensitivity of the Chinese to any encroachment on their borderlands, their buffers, which represent the foundation of their national security.

Protecting the Coast

With the buffer regions under control, the coast is China's most vulnerable point, but its vulnerability is not to invasion. Given the Japanese example, no one has the interest or forces to try to invade mainland China, supply an army there and hope to win. Invasion is not a meaningful threat.

The coastal threat to China is economic, though most would not call it a threat. As we saw, the British intrusion into China culminated in the destabilization of the country, the virtual collapse of the central government and civil war. It was all caused by prosperity. Mao had solved the problem by sealing the coast of China off to any real development and liquidating the class that had collaborated with foreign business. For Mao, xenophobia was integral to national policy. He saw foreign presence as undermining the stability of China. He preferred impoverished unity to chaos. He also understood that, given China's population and geography, it could defend itself against potential attackers without an advanced military-industrial complex.

His successor, Deng Xiaoping, was heir to a powerful state in control of China and the buffer regions. He also felt under tremendous pressure politically to improve living standards, and he undoubtedly understood that technological gaps would eventually threaten Chinese national security. He took a historic gamble. He knew that China's economy could not develop on its own. China's internal demand for goods was too weak because the Chinese were too poor.

Deng gambled that he could open China to foreign investment and reorient the Chinese economy away from agriculture and heavy industry and toward export-oriented industries. By doing so, he would increase living standards, import technology and train China's workforce. He was betting that the effort this time would not destabilize China, create massive tensions between the prosperous coastal provinces and the interior, foster regionalism, or put the coastal regions under foreign control. Deng believed he could avoid all that by maintaining a strong central government, based on a loyal army and Communist Party apparatus. His successors have struggled to maintain that loyalty to the state and not to foreign investors, who can make individuals wealthy. That is the bet that is currently being played out.

Geopolitics and Current Position

From a political and military standpoint, China has achieved its strategic goals. The buffer regions are intact and China faces no threat in Eurasia. It sees a Western attempt to force China out of Tibet as an attempt to undermine Chinese national security. For China, however, Tibet is a minor irritant; China has no possible intention of leaving Tibet, the Tibetans cannot rise up and win, and no one is about to invade the region. Similarly, the Uighur Muslims represent an irritant in Xinjiang and not a direct threat. The Russians have no interest in or capability of invading China, and the Korean Peninsula does not represent a direct threat to the Chinese, certainly not one they could not handle.

The greatest military threat to China comes from the U.S. Navy. The Chinese have become highly dependent on seaborne trade, and the U.S. Navy is in a position to blockade China's ports if it wished. Should the United States do that, it would cripple China.

Therefore, China's primary military interest is to make such a blockade impossible.

It would take several generations for China to build a surface navy able to compete with the U.S. Navy. Simply training naval aviators to conduct carrier-based operations effectively would take decades — at least until these trainees became admirals and captains. And this does not take into account the time it would take to build an aircraft carrier and carrier-capable aircraft and master the intricacies of carrier operations.

For China, the primary mission is to raise the price of a blockade so high that the Americans would not attempt it. The means for that would be land- and submarine-based anti-ship missiles. The strategic solution is for China to construct a missile force sufficiently dispersed that it cannot be suppressed by the United States and with sufficient range to engage the United States at substantial distance, as far as the central Pacific.

This missile force would have to be able to identify and track potential targets to be effective. Therefore, if the Chinese are to pursue this strategy, they must also develop a space-based maritime reconnaissance system. These are the technologies the Chinese are focusing on. Anti-ship missiles and space-based systems, including anti-satellite systems designed to blind the Americans, represent China's military counter to its only significant military threat.

China could also use those missiles to blockade Taiwan by interdicting ships going to and from the island. But the Chinese do not have the naval ability to land a sufficient amphibious force and sustain it in ground combat. Nor do they have the ability to establish air superiority over the Taiwan Strait. China might be able to harass Taiwan, but it will not invade it. Missiles, satellites and submarines constitute China's naval strategy.

For China, the primary problem posed by Taiwan is naval. Taiwan is positioned in such a way that it can readily serve as an air and naval base that could isolate maritime movement between the South China Sea and the East China Sea, effectively leaving the northern Chinese coast and Shanghai isolated. When you consider the Ryukyu

Islands that stretch from Taiwan to Japan and add them to this mix, a non-naval power could blockade the northern Chinese coast if it held Taiwan.

Taiwan would not be important to China unless it became actively hostile or allied with or occupied by a hostile power such as the United States. If that happened, its geographical position would pose an extremely serious problem for China. Taiwan is also an important symbolic issue to China and a way to rally nationalism. Although Taiwan presents no immediate threat, it does pose potential dangers that China cannot ignore.

There is one area in which China is being modestly expansionist: Central Asia, particularly Kazakhstan. Traditionally a route for trading silk, Kazakhstan is now an area that can produce energy, badly needed by China's industry. The Chinese have been active in developing commercial relations with Kazakhstan and in developing roads into Kazakhstan. These roads are opening a trading route that allows oil to flow in one direction and industrial goods in another.

In doing this, the Chinese are challenging Russia's sphere of influence in the former Soviet Union. The Russians have been prepared to tolerate increased Chinese economic activity in the region while being wary of China's turning into a political power. Kazakhstan has been European Russia's historical buffer state against Chinese expansion and it has been under Russian domination. This region must be watched carefully. If Russia begins to feel that China is becoming too assertive in this region, it could respond militarily to Chinese economic power.

Chinese-Russian relations have historically been complex. Before World War II, the Soviets attempted to manipulate Chinese politics. After World War II, relations between the Soviet Union and China were never as good as some thought, and sometimes these relations became directly hostile, as in 1968, when Russian and Chinese troops fought a battle along the Ussuri River. The Russians have historically feared a Chinese move into their Pacific maritime provinces. The Chinese have feared a Russian move into Manchuria and beyond.

Neither of these things happened because the logistical challenges involved were enormous and neither had an appetite for the risk of fighting the other. We would think that this caution will prevail under current circumstances. However, growing Chinese influence in Kazakhstan is not a minor matter for the Russians, who may choose to contest China there. If they do, and it becomes a serious matter, the secondary pressure point for both sides would be in the Pacific region, complicated by proximity to Korea.

But these are only theoretical possibilities. The threat of an American blockade on China's coast, of using Taiwan to isolate northern China, of conflict over Kazakhstan — all are possibilities that the Chinese must take into account as they plan for the worst. In fact, the United States does not have an interest in blockading China and the Chinese and Russians are not going to escalate competition over Kazakhstan.

China does not have a military-based geopolitical problem. It is in its traditional strong position, physically secure as it holds its buffer regions. It has achieved its three strategic imperatives. What is most vulnerable at this point is its first imperative: the unity of Han China. That is not threatened militarily. Rather, the threat to it is economic.

Economic Dimensions of Chinese Geopolitics

The problem of China, rooted in geopolitics, is economic, and it presents itself in two ways. The first is simple. China has an export-oriented economy. It is in a position of dependency. No matter how large its currency reserves, how advanced its technology or how cheap its labor force, China depends on the willingness and ability of other countries to import its goods — as well as the ability to physically ship them. Any disruption of this flow has a direct effect on the Chinese economy.

The primary reason other countries buy Chinese goods is price. They are cheaper because of wage differentials. Should China lose that advantage to other nations or for other reasons, its ability to export would decline. Today, for example, as energy prices rise, the cost of production rises and the relative importance of the wage differential decreases. At a certain point, as China's trading partners see it, the value of Chinese imports relative to the political cost of closing down their factories will shift.

And all of this is outside of China's control. China cannot control the world price of oil. It can cut into its cash reserves to subsidize those prices for manufacturers, but that would essentially be transferring money back to consuming nations. It can control rising wages by imposing price controls, but that would cause internal instability. The center of gravity of China is that it has become the industrial workshop of the world and, as such, it is totally dependent on the world to keep buying its goods rather than someone else's goods.

There are other issues for China, ranging from a dysfunctional financial system to farmland being taken out of production for factories. These are all significant and add to the story. But in geopolitics we look for the center of gravity, and for China the center of gravity is that the more effective it becomes at exporting, the more of a hostage it becomes to its customers. Some observers have warned that China might take its money out of American banks. Unlikely, but assume it did. What would China do without the United States as a customer?

China has placed itself in a position where it has to keep its customers happy. It struggles against this reality daily, but the fact is that the rest of the world is far less dependent on China's exports than China is dependent on the rest of the world.

Which brings us to the second, even more serious part of China's economic problem. The first geopolitical imperative of China is to ensure the unity of Han China. The third is to protect the coast. Deng's bet was that he could open the coast without disrupting the unity of Han China. As in the 19th century, the coastal region has become wealthy. The interior has remained extraordinarily poor. The coastal region is deeply enmeshed in the global economy. The interior is not. Beijing is once again balancing between the coast and the interior.

The interests of the coastal region and the interests of importers and investors are closely tied to each other. Beijing's interest is

16

in maintaining internal stability. As pressures grow, it will seek to increase its control of the political and economic life of the coast. The interest of the interior is to have money transferred to it from the coast. The interest of the coast is to hold on to its money. Beijing will try to satisfy both, without letting China break apart and without resorting to Mao's draconian measures. But the worse the international economic situation becomes the less demand there will be for Chinese products and the less room there will be for China to maneuver.

The second part of the problem derives from the first. Assuming that the global economy does not decline now, it will at some point. When it does, and Chinese exports fall dramatically, Beijing will have to balance between an interior hungry for money and a coastal region that is hurting badly. It is important to remember that something like 900 million Chinese live in the interior while only about 400 million live in the coastal region. When it comes to balancing power, the interior is the physical threat to the regime while the coast destabilizes the distribution of wealth. The interior has mass on its side. The coast has the international trading system on its. Emperors have stumbled over less.

Conclusion

Geopolitics is based on geography and politics. Politics is built on two foundations: military and economic. The two interact and support each other but are ultimately distinct. For China, securing its buffer regions generally eliminates military problems. What problems are left for China are long-term issues concerning northeastern Manchuria and the balance of power in the Pacific.

China's geopolitical problem is economic. Its first geopolitical imperative, maintain the unity of Han China, and its third, protect the coast, are both more deeply affected by economic considerations than military ones. Its internal and external political problems flow from economics. The dramatic economic development of the last generation has been ruthlessly geographic. This development has benefited the coast and left the interior — the vast majority of Chinese — behind. It has also left China vulnerable to global economic forces that it cannot control and cannot accommodate. This is not new in Chinese history, but its usual resolution is in regionalism and the weakening of the central government. Deng's gamble is being played out by his successors. He dealt the hand. They have to play it.

The question on the table is whether the economic basis of China is a foundation or a balancing act. If the former, it can last a long time. If the latter, everyone falls down eventually. There appears to be little evidence that it is a foundation. It excludes most of the Chinese from the game, people who are making less than $100 a month. That is a balancing act, and it threatens the first geopolitical imperative of China: protecting the unity of the Han Chinese.

CHAPTER 2: ECONOMY

Riding the Rural Tiger
March 8, 2006

Chinese President Hu Jintao and Premier Wen Jiabao have been touting the "New Socialist Countryside" initiative. The initiative is being painted as a priority for reducing China's widening rural/urban gap in the near term and for creating a more sustainable and robust economic future in the long term. The problems of rural economic reform, the social gap and rural unrest rank high on the agenda of China's central leadership and in the current session of the National People's Congress (NPC). Potential solutions to these problems form the heart of China's 11th five-year economic plan (2006-2010).

Over the past quarter century, China has made remarkable economic progress. By all accounts, its cities are booming: The bicycle-clogged alleys of the past are now traffic-clogged avenues, and construction cranes rise within cities as part of a seemingly endless rejuvenation and modernization campaign. Statistically speaking, China has never been stronger; gross domestic product (GDP) has risen from $200 billion in 1978 to $2.7 trillion in 2005. Foreign trade last year reached $1.4 trillion, with a trade surplus of nearly $102 billion. Exports accounted for 18 percent of the 9.9 percent GDP growth China reports for 2005. In the same year, the country utilized some $60.3 billion in foreign direct investment and sent $6.92

billion overseas in non-financial-sector investments. Foreign currency reserves at the end of 2005 registered $818.9 billion, rivaling Japan's.

But the growth has been anything but even. Urban growth continues to outpace rural growth, despite income increases across the board. In 2005, per capita disposable income reached $1,310 in urban areas, compared to just $405 in rural net income. Income disparity in 1984 was about a 2 to 1 ratio; now it is 3 to 1. Overall, the poorest 10 percent of China's citizens hold only 1 percent of the nation's wealth, and the wealthiest 10 percent claim 50 percent of the money. Even in urban areas, there are massive disparities: The poorest 20 percent of urban dwellers control just 2.75 percent of private income; the top 20 percent control 60 percent of the total.

The gaps manifest in other ways as well. China's registered urban unemployment stands at 4.2 percent, but rural unemployment — which isn't measured officially — is anecdotally much higher, and even Beijing admits that some 200 million rural workers have migrated to cities recently in search of employment. That represents a substantial portion of the total rural population, which numbers 800 million to 900 million. In the cities, these migrants are treated as second-class citizens at best. In the countryside, they fare little better: Measures of education and health care are substantially lower. Moreover, there has been little legal recourse for farmers, who technically don't even own the land they work, when local officials confiscate the land for new industrial and housing projects.

The central government is well aware of these problems and, perhaps ironically, began issuing public cautions about social and economic tensions years before the international business community bothered to notice. Unrestrained economic growth no longer is viewed as a viable or sustainable option, and Beijing has begun to reassert more centralized control over economic development, with a particular emphasis on reducing the rural-urban gap.

But in seeking to address this problem, Beijing has exposed a deeper issue: endemic corruption and self-interest at the local and provincial levels of government. It is where economic disparity and government corruption intersect that social clashes occur most often.

Geography of Corruption

More than 25 years after its launch by Deng Xiaoping, China's economic reform and opening program has reached a critical juncture. Economic reforms have outpaced social and political reforms, and historical strains between the coast and inland regions, between urban and rural and between the educated and less educated are threatening the fabric of social stability and the central government's ability to rule. It is easy to see the frayed edges: Local protests turn violent where urban development projects eat away at the rural land. As the social instability moves closer to the coastal cities, there is a risk that China's competitiveness as an investment destination will be harmed, thereby triggering a spiral of economic and social degradation. Social instability also lays bare the growing rift between the central government and the local and regional leaders.

From a historical perspective, China's apparently stunning economic success stems from the pursuit and implementation of the quintessential Asian economic plan, which can be summed up as "growth for the sake of growth." Japan, South Korea, most of the Southeast Asian "tigers" and China all facilitated their economic "miracles" by focusing on the flow-through of capital without regard for profits. As long as money was flowing in, there could be jobs. As long as there were jobs, there was a stabilizing social force. There was also an overall rise in personal wealth, though rarely was it evenly spread.

The coastal provinces and cities became the focal points for international investments in manufacturing, as investors exploited preferential government policies and cheap labor. The rural areas — traditionally the backbone of China's economy — and the petroleum and heavy industry of the northeast (which had been core to early Communist Chinese economics) faded in relevance. Though Beijing occasionally promoted more inland development and investment opportunities, geography and a lack of infrastructure made these unappealing to investors. The concentration of wealth in the coastal regions was a source of minor social tensions, but restrictions on internal migration kept a buffer between rural and urban populations, and social frictions remained comparatively low. These restrictions, however, have been only selectively enforced as of late, and many are being lifted.

The booming coastal economies created clear opportunities for corruption. As provincial and local leaders became the gatekeepers for foreign investments, they also became mini-emperors of their own economic fiefdoms. Collusion and nepotism — always a part of Chinese political society — became even more entrenched as the money flowed in. With the central government fixated on growth, the best-performing local leaders were rewarded. The more foreign capital they were able to attract, the greater their personal influence and takings. These officials were measured not on efficiency or profitability but on total flow-through of capital, rates of growth, employment and social stability.

This partly explains why attempts by the previous government to address the unequal development in China failed. Each time former President Jiang Zemin or former Premier Zhu Rongji tried to adjust policies and financial flows to the interior, there were strong objections from the wealthier coastal provinces. When they launched anti-corruption campaigns, the graft their investigators uncovered was deep and wide, and in some cases even threatened to reach up to the top echelons of power — at times implicating Jiang himself. This only further entrenched the problem and removed incentives for Jiang and Zhu to act; after all, both were part of the so-called Shanghai clique and derived their political support from the coastal regions.

Under these two leaders, the government was much more successful in reducing the independence of the military, as neither Jiang nor Zhu had significant ties into the institution. But because the economic and political elite in the coastal regions were the source of the central leadership's power, they were able to repel reforms sought by the central government.

This all changed with the coming of Hu and Wen, both of whom are from rural areas. Wen, a perennial political survivor known for his ability to connect with the "common man," has been practically deified among rural dwellers because of his 10-year-old coat. That the premier still wears the same coat after 10 years is a clear sign (according to ample coverage by the news media and blog sites) of his care for the people, rather than for himself.

Herein lies the secret of Hu and Wen's strategy to regain control over the local and regional governments and Party officials. Whereas Jiang and Zhu tried using anti-corruption campaigns — only to end up implicating themselves and their core supporters — Hu and Wen are moving to harness the power of China's rural masses. Depending on which Chinese official you believe, this is a mass of humanity numbering from 700 million to 950 million people. Even at the low end of the estimates, however, rural-dwellers make up more than half of China's population — and greatly outnumber the 300 million middle- and upper-class Chinese living mainly in Beijing and the coastal cities.

Harnessing the Masses

Chinese leaders have a long history of using the masses as weapons when challenges to central authority arise — from the attempts to harness the Boxers at the turn of the 20th century to Mao's communist revolution to the Cultural Revolution. In each case, the process was chaotic and the outcomes were uncertain. Though Mao eventually succeeded in rallying the rural populace to effect his communist revolution, it simply served as a starting point for a new Chinese system. The use of the Boxers led to the dissolution of the Chinese dynastic system, and the Cultural Revolution wiped out whatever economic gains had been made, leaving China to start nearly from scratch once again.

What Hu and Wen intend to do is rally the masses to pressure local leaders into returning authority to the center. From this, centralized economic direction will, they hope, lead to more equalized development without significantly undermining the country's growth (though a slight slowing will be expected). Ultimately, the causes of social discontent would be mitigated and social frictions reduced as money is shifted to the interior.

This is a rather risky proposal, but China's core leadership sees this as the least distasteful among a poor selection of options. The initiative is being presented not as a disruptive social revolution but as the duty of those who got rich first to assist those who trail them. The initial details of the official plan include greater spending in rural areas on infrastructure, education, healthcare and agriculture, with funding coming primarily from the urban centers. The plan already is meeting with mixed reactions from China's regional leaders — and while the NPC is expected to approve the plan, that does not mean it is well liked.

However, as the government's core leadership has pointed out ad nauseam over the past year, the Chinese economy is in a fragile state, and the rural/urban inequalities threaten to undo everything China has built up since the economic opening and reform program began. Unless the central government regains complete control over economic strategy and tactics, there is a fear that China ultimately would fracture into competing regions, largely independent of any central authority — a sort of economic warlordism reminiscent of the final days of previous Chinese dynasties.

Beijing's choice, then, is between taking no action against local governments out of fears of triggering massive capital flight or inadvertently crippling investment and export activity, or rallying the rural masses — which would be another avenue toward recentralizing control.

Thus, the central government has made a point of publicizing ever-more-dire statistics concerning rural and urban unrest. The Ministry of Public Security reported 87,000 cases of public disturbances in 2005, up from 74,000 in 2004 and 58,000 in 2003. (The numbers are high, but the definition of "disturbance" remains ambiguous.) The ministry has also warned of an imminent "period of pronounced contradictions within the people" in which "unpredictable factors affecting social stability will increase." Meanwhile, Wen has repeated that the cause of many protests is the confiscation of rural land for development and industrial projects — projects that often are linked to corrupt local officials or are local initiatives that don't match the central priorities.

The message to the local leaders, of course, is that China's masses are on the move. In discussing the rural/urban gap, Chen Xiwen, deputy director of the Office of the Central Financial Work Leading Group, noted recently (and somewhat ominously) that 200 million farmers have left the countryside; Chen warned that "to increase the living standard of these farmers, China should spare no efforts to build the new socialist countryside." In essence, Beijing is threatening the local leaders with the specter of a rural rising. The class struggle is on, and the farmers far outnumber the city dwellers. The implicit message is that, for the safety of the city, the farmers must be funded and rural areas built up.

At the same time, Beijing is looking at a wholesale change in the local leadership, beginning with the Party secretaries and chiefs of China's 2,861 counties. New regulations — not altogether welcomed by the existing Party cadre — will require new county-level Party secretaries and chiefs to be around 45 years old and possess at least a bachelor's degree. These individuals would be less likely to have already built up their personal economic connections and be more beholden to the central government for legitimacy and support. Beijing is also increasing supervision and admonition of Party and government officials.

But to make these changes last, Beijing needs to give the lower cadre some incentive to follow the central government's demands — even if it means a reduction in local investments or a rise in local unemployment. Beijing must ensure that local officials are more closely tied to the central leadership in Beijing than to foreign investors and shareholders in Japan or the United States. For this, Beijing needs to make it utterly clear what risks the local government leaders face. Threats of prosecution and even the token executions of some officials have not worked, but the potential for more and larger social uprisings might.

This means Beijing needs to allow, if not subtly encourage, more localized demonstrations, and that apparently is where Hu and Wen intend to go. The central government's response to stories of rural unrest has remained rather low-key thus far. In reference to the Dongzhou protests in December 2005, where at least three were killed when local security forces opened fire on the crowd, officials on the sidelines of the NPC session recently made it a point to say the officers in question are under detention and did not follow orders. In other uprisings, there even have been suggestions of sympathy from the center. In the cost-benefit analysis, Beijing apparently has determined that the risks of allowing the current trend of growing regionalized power to continue outweigh the risks of trying to manipulate popular sentiment against local officials.

This, perhaps more than anything, underscores the severity of the economic and governing problems facing China's central leadership. The strategy of unleashing the rural masses, allowing and even subtly encouraging protests could quickly get out of hand. However, given the wide array of localized concerns, there is a natural disunity that could be expected to constrain protesters — keeping demonstrations locally significant but nationally isolated. So long as protesters don't join across provinces and regions, so long as no interest is able to link the disparate demonstrations, the central leadership will retain some leeway to implement its policies.

But as history bears witness, any attempt to harness protests and mass movements is a very risky strategy indeed.

Why China Needs U.S. Debt
Feb. 13, 2009

China does not see any choice but to keep buying U.S. government debt, Luo Ping, a director-general at the China Banking Regulatory Commission (CBRC), told a New York risk-managers conference

Feb. 12. The Financial Times quoted him as saying: "Except for U.S. Treasuries, what can you hold? Gold? You don't hold Japanese government bonds or U.K. bonds. U.S. Treasuries are the safe-haven. For everyone, including China, it is the only option." Even if the dollar depreciates because of Washington's financial bailouts, he added, China has no other options.

Luo is acknowledging something of an open secret. Despite occasional hints (or threats) that China might attempt to bankrupt the United States by suddenly selling all of the U.S. debt it holds, that really is not an option. China would be economically destroyed in the process, unless there was some alternative place for Beijing to invest. For a number of reasons, there is none.

Over the past two decades, the United States and China have developed a special relationship based on the safety of U.S. debt. In essence, the United States gives China access to the wealthiest consumer market in the world, which in turn soaks up China's massive output of consumer goods. This not only provides income for Chinese exporters but also helps ensure social stability in China by providing employment — which is Beijing's primary economic policy goal. China in turn invests its large trade surpluses, earned in U.S. dollars, into U.S. Treasury debt (e.g., 30-year bonds or 10-year notes). This allows China to store its earnings in one of the largest and most liquid financial markets in the world without needing to convert between currencies. Meanwhile, the recycling of surpluses into Treasury instruments helps to bankroll continued U.S. spending. It is vendor financing on a global scale.

This relationship has fueled unprecedented booms in both U.S. consumer spending and Chinese industrialization. Even in the midst of recession, China continues to sock away savings — but now, because of the financial crisis, questions are being raised as to whether U.S. Treasury debt is the best vehicle for storing those funds.

Simply put, it costs a lot to buttress a collapsing financial market. As the cost of U.S. financial bailouts piles up, Washington's balance sheet is deteriorating. Since the credit crisis began in the fourth quarter of 2007, bailouts have put U.S. government commitments at nearly $9 trillion. To be sure, this is more akin to a line of credit than a tally of real spending — though the actual federal outlays to date, around $3 trillion, represent roughly 20 percent of U.S. gross domestic product (GDP). At any rate, the stakes are high and investors are nervous.

China is the largest holder of U.S. government debt, so it is no wonder that Yu Yongding, the head of China's World Economics and Politics Institute and a former adviser to the central bank, on Feb. 11 said that because of its "reckless policies" the United States should "make the Chinese feel confident that the value of the assets at least will not be eroded in a significant way." His remarks were meant to impress upon Washington that, as the primary financier of U.S. debt, China holds considerable power in the relationship.

In general, as a country's balance sheet comes under increasing strain, investors tend to sell that country's assets and move their funds to places with more attractive fundamentals (such as a trade or budget surplus). But the notion that U.S. debt is becoming a questionable asset and is about to be dumped by investors has not proved true. Instead, money from all over the world has been flooding into American markets, sending the dollar to its highest levels — and bond yields to their lowest — in years.

U.S. Treasuries remain the primary vehicle for investing surpluses, and for Chinese surpluses in particular. The reasons are many. For one thing, few other countries have debt markets large enough to support the level of investment China needs to make. The U.S. debt market is larger than the three next largest combined. In fact, only Japan has a debt market larger than that of the United States — but because Japan's debt represents some 170 percent of its GDP, it has a credit rating no better than that of the better-run states in sub-Saharan Africa. The U.S. Treasury debt market, while large, represents only about half of U.S. GDP — a much more manageable fraction.

Of the top ten largest debt markets, the four that are in the eurozone — Germany, France, Italy and Spain — could provide

28

viable alternatives for China. But these also pose problems. Much like Middle Eastern oil states, China not only receives most of its income in dollars but also effectively pegs its own currency on the dollar. This means that for the Chinese, savings and investments held in dollar-denominated assets are relatively safe, stable and accessible. From Beijing's perspective, it makes little sense to convert surplus dollars into euros only to grow more exposed to currency fluctuations. (And even that assumes that one trusts the financial governance of other states – for example, Italy.)

If Beijing does not view euro-based debt as a viable alternative to the United States because of currency stability, it has even less confidence in other top-ten debt markets, which are denominated in even less-stable currencies. The markets for the Brazilian real, the South Korean won, and even the Canadian dollar and British pound are simply too fractured and volatile to provide the level of safety that the U.S. dollar does. And in any case, all of these markets are much too small to absorb Chinese trade surpluses month after month. Only the regular issuance of multibillion-dollar debt tranches by the United States, fueled by U.S. budget and trade deficits, can suffice.

If government paper cannot fill its needs, China could turn to commodities — if anything, perhaps gold could provide a viable store of value without subjecting China to the fiscal swashbuckling of a foreign government. But even here, the size of the gold market could not support Beijing's investment needs. Even if China were somehow able to absorb the total annual output of the world's gold mines — roughly 80 million troy ounces — doing so would both collapse global debt markets and send gold prices to stratospheric heights (not exactly a welcome scenario for a country utterly dependent upon international trade). And for all that, China could sock away the same amount of value after only about three months of trading with the United States.

Ultimately, steering funds clear of American debt markets is not desirable — or even possible — for the Chinese. Luo, the CBRC official (who is known for his colloquial style), stated Beijing's viewpoint about as plainly as it can be put during his speech in New York, saying: "We hate you guys, but there is nothing much we can do."

The Economic Recession in China
May 7, 2009

China registered 6.1 percent gross domestic product (GDP) growth for the first quarter of 2009, down from the 6.8 percent growth rate for the fourth quarter of 2008. While this may appear fairly robust compared to the 6.1 percent decline in GDP registered in the United States for the same quarter (a number that was a slight improvement over the 6.3 percent decline in the fourth quarter of 2008), comparing these numbers is not comparing apples to apples. The United States, along with many other countries, notes GDP changes from quarter to quarter (the Q1 number is in comparison to the preceding Q4), whereas China counts changes year on year (Q1 is in comparison to the previous Q1).

By some estimates, as measured comparable to the U.S. system of accounting, China's economy sunk to zero growth in Q4 2008, or even went negative — and that decline continued into Q1 2009. But even looking just at the year-to-year numbers, Chinese economists have quietly admitted that at least 4 percentage points of their growth figure are attributable to government stimulus monies, and that economic growth was really in the 1 or 2 percent range, far below government targets. Other observers of Chinese statistics agree with the 4 or so percentage points attributable to stimulus, but also suggest that some 2 or 3 percentage points are also exaggerations reported up the chain from lower levels of the bureaucracy to avoid falling too short of central government expectations, meaning that growth again was at zero or negative in the first quarter.

Amid a global economic crisis, even zero percent growth is not all that bad. But it is a significant problem for the Chinese leadership, which has placed excessive importance on the specific growth numbers, in part due to concern that a flagging economy could stir social instability and in part due to Communist Party legitimacy being linked to economic growth these days.

Beijing's response has been a reversion to the tried-and-true methods of:

- Supporting export industries.

- Encouraging, via rewards or threats, the maintenance of employment levels by companies (even if this is unprofitable, contributes to overproduction and delays or avoids the weeding out of the weak and inefficient in the Chinese economy).

- Large-scale state spending (directly from government coffers or indirectly through a loan surge from major state-backed banks) designed to boost infrastructure development and underwrite a rise in domestic consumption of large items like automobiles and major appliances.

These measures may give Beijing some control over China's looming unemployment problem, which is something officials fear but are still far behind in addressing, with social security and health care initiatives still largely in the formative stages, rather than well developed in preparation for the combination of a sustained economic slowdown and an aging population. But Beijing largely has stalled or reversed initiatives from the past several years that were designed to reform the economy into a less redundant, more efficient and flexible system better able to adapt to global change. In short, China's short-term solutions to the global economic crisis are buying time, but they are delaying, if not undermining, real structural change. And that could portend a bigger Chinese crisis in the coming years.

The Chinese Bank Spending Spree

In the first quarter of 2009, Chinese banks went on a massive state-mandated lending spree. The so-called big three — the Industrial and

Commercial Bank of China (ICBC), the China Construction Bank (CCB) and the Bank of China (BOC) — issued some 4.58 trillion yuan ($670 billion) in new loans during that quarter. Much of this purportedly was issued for major infrastructure projects as part of the government's $586 billion stimulus package, though anecdotal reports suggest much went to state-owned enterprises (SOEs). The SOEs may have used the loans for market speculation, paying off earlier loans or maintaining payroll during the economic downturn rather than spending capital improvements and efficiency programs.

The first-quarter loans accounted for more than 90 percent of the initial government yearly loan targets, prompting concerns that after the initial flood of loans, liquidity would dry up for the rest of the year. But Chinese officials have now said new loans will not stop at the 5 trillion yuan (about $732 billion) target, and it has been suggested that total lending may be closer to 8 trillion or 9 trillion yuan (about $1.1 trillion or $1.3 trillion) for the year, and initial estimates put April new lending at 400 billion to 600 billion yuan (about $58 billion to $87 billion).

While lending has helped Chinese companies maintain employment levels during the economic slowdown, it also brings about renewed risks to the Chinese banking sector and undermines earlier nascent moves to try to drive Chinese businesses to be more profitable and efficient rather than to rely on state bailouts and loans to stay afloat. As the big three were issuing record quantities of new loans in the first quarter, their net profits were falling; the CCB reported an 18.2 percent decline for the quarter, and the BOC reported a 14.1 percent decline. Only the ICBC reported a net growth in profits (of some 6.2 percent), but according to the bank, this was due to a significant hike in fees and a dip in operating costs.

For each of the big three, loan interest makes up by far the bulk of operating income (79.5 percent for the ICBC, 77.5 percent for the CCB and 73 percent for the BOC). And the banks are noting narrowing margins on loan interest as the cause for their net profit declines. It is also likely that hidden within these numbers is a growing problem of loan repayment, particularly given reports of thousands of companies that have been shutting their doors since the fourth quarter of 2008 or turning unprofitable in the current economic environment.

While the lending spree is designed to give the economy a boost and maintain a system flush with liquidity to avoid the U.S.-style economic crunch, it is also increasing the risks of nonperforming loans (NPLs). This risks weakening the banks, which already were bailed out more than a decade ago to the tune of some $325 billion in transfer of bad debt to asset management corporations, thus cleaning the banks' balance sheets.

It also reduces the pressure on Chinese companies (particularly state-owned companies) to reform their business practices and become more efficient and profitable rather than rely on government loans and incentives to operate. In addition, with most loans targeting state firms, China's private companies remain on the back burner. This is another reversal of earlier initiatives to push for a greater role for the private sector aimed at making the system more susceptible to market forces, and thus more likely to weed out inefficient and outdated companies.

Avoiding the Oversupply Issue

One issue the government keeps coming back to (and keeps running away from just as quickly) is the massive oversupply of production in certain sectors of the Chinese economy. Much of the Chinese economy is made up of redundant, small, inefficient production facilities, the remnants of the old Mao-era encouragement of self-sufficient provinces and cities. Many of these redundancies remain because while inefficient on a national scale, they still provide employment, tax revenues and economic output numbers for the provincial and local officials. Few are willing to see their local industries shuttered to satisfy a national need to become more streamlined and efficient for the long run.

The new pressures building on China's banks could not come at a worse time. In the mid-1990s, the run-up of bad debt was beginning to cause significant problems for the Chinese financial sector, and a bailout program was launched in 1999. The government took mounds of bad loans from the Chinese state banks, transferring them to new firms called asset management corporations (AMCs). In exchange, the AMCs issued bonds worth the full face value of the NPLs back to the banks, despite the fact that the NPLs were worth — at most — one-third of that. In one wave of the accounting wand, the state banks went from being anchored down by dud assets to being flush with cash.

Those bonds provided a huge boost to the banks' balance sheets, as they were backed by China's central bank, the People's Bank of China, and so were as good as cash when determining how healthy the institutions were. This made the Chinese banks rather attractive with their initial public offerings, gaining foreign investment and expertise and limiting competition in the Chinese banking sector as it opened due to World Trade Organization regulations.

But the NPLs were never disposed of. These AMCs were supposed to follow the model of previous "bad bank" programs, disposing of the bad debt by forcing indebted firms to pay up or — if push came to shove — liquidating the firms for whatever salvageable assets might be sold off to pay the debt. But closing firms down, obviously, would mean adding to the ranks of the unemployed. So the AMCs instead simply held the bad debt — for 10 years — while the state banks used their shiny new cash-equivalent bonds to issue even more loans.

As 2009 rolls on, this strategy is coming back to haunt the government. The NPL bonds are structured so that the AMCs only need to pay interest, not principle and interest as with normal bonds. With the bond rates at approximately 2 percent, this has been a barely manageable task. (Remember, the AMCs have been disposing of very few actual dud companies, so their income has been tiny, though supplemented by some good assets also transferred at the time of their creation.) But all of the bonds in question are 10-year bonds, with the entire value of the principle due around the end of the year. Because very few NPLs actually have been disposed of, and because

NPLs generally are worth less than one-third of their face value, the only way these bonds could be redeemed would be if the Ministry of Finance doled out the cash itself. After all, the AMCs were designed to do little more than simply hold the loans, not actually rehabilitate them.

When the Chinese economy was growing at double-digit rates, the banks could stay ahead of the potential problem of NPLs. But with the economy effectively stalling at the same time banks are being asked to significantly increase the issuance of new loans, a major problem may be brewing. This means one of three things has to happen:

- The banks will have to write off these bonds, seeing a massive drop in their balance sheets.
- The Ministry of Finance will have to step in and recapitalize.
- The bonds will be rolled over, pushing the problem further out in the hopes that it either simply goes away or that the Chinese economy will have grown enough by that time to simply absorb the losses.

With the latter choice the most likely, and with the addition of some 5 trillion - 9 trillion yuan in new loans this year (with questionable performance on much of it), the Chinese are heading toward another future banking crisis. And the flight of foreign investors from Chinese banks certainly will not help this crisis.

In short, like many others, the Chinese are using short-term measures to deal with the current economic downturn. But these measures not only are building in renewed risks (like the compounding NPL problems), they also are reversing the small steps toward economic reform necessary for more stable and continued Chinese economic development. The government was able to boost domestic consumption in the first quarter of 2009, but this was primarily through coupons and incentives focused mainly on rural purchases of large appliances and automobiles. These are not sustainable efforts. Many Chinese economists have criticized the moves as building new dangers as rural consumers spend their meager savings on big-ticket items, leaving them with a car and refrigerator but no job or health insurance.

A Missed Opportunity

The surge in bank lending to Chinese companies, both for infrastructure projects and to cover old loans and payroll, also is not sustainable, particularly as bank profits fall, margins thin and the risk of a new surge in bad loans rises. And the strength of the Chinese economy remains undermined by allowing weak companies to be kept alive through loans and government incentives. The debate in Beijing is whether the financial crisis has offered China the opportunity to fundamentally make its economic system more profitable, efficient and able to adapt to changes in market forces, or whether the crisis is another moment when the government needs to do what it can to shore up the old system.

Beijing has chosen the latter path, which it deems less socially destabilizing, and thus greater government involvement in the economy will be expected. But the pent-up pressures on the Chinese economy, and on the Chinese leadership, are likely to be worse in the long run. And with the economy unlikely to return to double-digit growth anytime soon (if at all), the day of reckoning may come sooner rather than later.

Overcapacity in China's Steel Industry
Sept. 18, 2009

In Beijing's latest move to consolidate China's fragmented steel industry, the State Council agreed Aug. 26 to take further measures to curb the industry's overcapacity by restricting banks' loose lending, enforcing tighter environmental standards and prohibiting incremental capacity additions.

GLOBAL CRUDE STEEL PRODUCTION

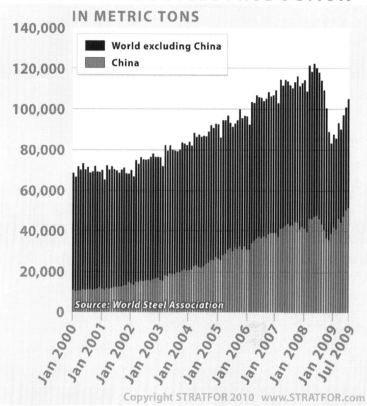

When China's crude steel production first outstripped domestic consumption in 2006, the excess capacity did not constitute an immediate threat because China was able to export the extra steel. But with the onset of the global financial crisis and a precipitous decline in global growth, the shortcomings of China's steel policies have been placed in sharp relief as demand for Chinese steel has only been buoyed by China's economic stimulus plan and government-funded infrastructure projects. The new measures are aimed at addressing the shortcomings and unintended consequences of the

National Development and Reform Commission's (NDRC) Steel Development Policy of 2005. However, since Beijing's latest efforts do nothing to address the need for comprehensive political reform, their ability to effectively consolidate China's steel industry will be greatly limited.

Steel and cement are pillars of industrial development. Roads, bridges, dams, reservoirs, machines, buildings and ships all require steel, cement or both. China, which has been industrializing rapidly over the past decade, now produces about half of the world's steel and cement.

Though China is the world's top producer of crude steel, with about 700 steel producers, the industry is incredibly fragmented. Whereas more developed countries' top five producers account for around 70 to 80 percent of their crude steel output, China's top five producers account for less than 30 percent of total output.

Much of this fragmentation is a legacy of Mao Zedong's Great Leap Forward. Emphasizing self-sufficiency and economic development, Mao encouraged every commune to produce its own steel. And while widely dispersing production may have made China less vulnerable to supply disruptions in times of war, encouraging the creation of tens of thousands of so-called "backyard blast furnaces" has come back to haunt the current central government as it attempts to consolidate the industry.

Unleashing China's full economic potential rests on Beijing's ability to effectively steer its growth- and employment-oriented economic model toward sustainable profitability. This means that unless China's industries consolidate and achieve economies of scale, they will never gain in efficiency what they lose in government support. Recognizing this, the NDRC in July 2005 approved China's Iron and Steel Industry Development Policy that sought to modernize, consolidate and recast the steel industry as a strategic sector. The policy called for the shuttering of inefficient, inland capacity by legislating minimum production requirements for mills, and for the scaling up of coastal production.

The new policy aimed to increase coastal production because China's value-added steel industry, which Beijing is trying to expand, currently depends on imported iron ore. Highly concentrated ore is needed to produce the higher value-added products, but while China's domestic ore averages an iron content of about 30 percent, the iron content in Australian and Brazilian ores is above 65 percent. There are concentrators in northern China, but it is still cheaper to import premium ore than to concentrate and transport domestic ore to the coastal regions. Importing ore also takes business away from those mines supplying inland mills the central government wants closed.

However, since it is the inland areas that really need new business and investment, this move has only exacerbated coastal-inland rivalries. Refusing to be sidelined, inland mines have continued to supply smaller mills — clandestinely or otherwise — in increasing amounts as the coastal demand for inland ore wanes, thereby undermining the NDRC's policy and allowing for inland mills' continued growth.

Additionally, as most of China's steel production is made by small, inefficient mills, their inefficient production's voracious appetite for raw materials had bid up input prices for all of China. To control these rising prices, Beijing has enacted an array of export quotas and taxes on the industry's vital inputs, such as coking coal, to keep domestic prices low. These measures, however, have not only ensured ample domestic supply of cheap coal and other inputs for smaller mills, but also muted a natural pricing mechanism that would otherwise dampen the industry's growth. For these reasons, China's steel industry remains both internally and geographically fragmented.

The steel policy also established minimum capacity requirements for mills with the aim of shuttering obsolete and inefficient production. However, much of this production capacity was located inland, where the provincial leaders' careers are based on metrics like production and employment. Understandably, those leaders are not keen on closing their mills and dealing with the fallout and attendant unrest. So to escape closure requirements, local and provincial leaders have attempted to protect their steel mills by adding capacity and increasing output – the exact opposite of the central government's intent. Thus the mills are producing even more excess steel and further entrenching their local mills' importance as drivers of growth, employment and tax receipts.

The central government also introduced differentiated electricity costs to price steel mills out of production, but the initiative was poorly prosecuted if not completely ignored. Ningxia province, for example, bypassed the higher energy costs altogether by simply taking the Qingtongxia steel mill off the national grid and provided electricity directly to the mill through a local utility.

Competition is usually healthy for any given industry, because the threat of losing market share to lower-cost producers motivates technological advancement and greater efficiency among participants. In China, however, intra-regional competition has had a deleterious effect, largely because China's steel industry does not lower costs through innovation.

Local officials know that the local steelmaker wants to grow his business, and the local steelmaker knows the official wants to report good employment figures. Naturally, this mutual interest leads to an agreement — subsidies in return for redundant employment. But while such a plan is rational on the local level, collectively it is detrimental to the industry and to China as a whole. Rather than spurring innovation, the competition forces local and regional authorities to increasingly subsidize their respective steel mills in their bids for social stability. While direct, indirect and structural subsidies keep the industry's local unemployment low, as the overall growth of the steel industry is only limited by provincial leaders' respect for environmental regulations, workers' rights or Beijing's authority, it is no wonder production capacity has mushroomed.

The subsidizing is also particularly harmful to privately owned steel mills. Unable to compete with the leaders' favored mills and without government recourse, private mills have been forced to downsize and lay off their workers. In July 2009, Jilin province reminded China of how unpleasant privatization can be when a proposed restructuring of the Tonghua Iron and Steel Works sparked riots that ended with a steel executive's death — ironically, somewhat reaffirming the importance of government intervention and control.

Reform in the steel sector is proving almost impossible for China because the industry has so much inertia. China must keep the industry stable and growing to maintain employment and adjust to changing demographic patterns, but since China imports 35 percent of its iron ore, it must also secure long-term iron ore contracts to minimize the risk of supply or price fluctuations that could stifle the industry's growth. But herein lies the problem: as stability allows the industry to grow, the bigger industry requires more imports, which ultimately requires more stability — a vicious circle whereby steelmakers' dependence on imports begets more and more dependence on imports. Even the Chinese central government knows that the steel industry cannot grow exponentially forever. The problem, however, is that no politician stands to gain from unilaterally initiating the reforms necessary to prevent the industry's eventual implosion. Without political reform, local and provincial authorities can only continue to serve their own self-interest at the expense of Beijing's national plans.

The Real Estate Market in China
Oct. 13, 2009

On Sept. 10, China Overseas Land and Investment, a Hong Kong-listed company and a subsidiary of state-owned China State Construction Engineering Corp., purchased a prime piece of real estate in the Putuo district in downtown Shanghai. The company paid 7.006 billion yuan ($1.026 billion) for the undeveloped property, which will amount to an average of 22,409.3 yuan ($3,283.9) per square meter of floor space (just in land costs) once the designed residential building is constructed.

The purchase created China's newest "land king," a term for the real estate developer who pays the highest price for a piece of real estate during a land auction. And 7.006 billion yuan was the highest price ever paid for a piece of Chinese real estate for any purpose — residential or commercial. The milestone is a result of an increasingly intense competition for land in major cities that began early in the year, when Beijing began distributing stimulus money to various industries — including the real estate sector — to sustain the economy. As a result, land prices have soared throughout China. And with increasing speculative investment in residential real estate, the market faces a surging bubble that jeopardizes the country's long-term economic development.

Since 1998, real estate investment in China has accounted for more than 10 percent of the country's gross domestic product (GDP), compared to only 3 percent to 5 percent in the United States. Such investment is also closely associated with many other industries, such as construction and finance, and it provides an abundance of jobs. Therefore, it is seen as a critical pillar of China's economy and enjoys favorable policies from the government and state-owned banks (more than 70 percent of real estate investment in China comes from bank loans). At the same time, real estate developers, local government officials and investors have escalated housing prices across the country by acquiring massive land holdings, limiting the supply and inflating prices, creating a real estate bubble that is not sustainable in the long run.

The bubble has grown mainly on the residential side of the market, where there is more demand and higher profits to be made. However, while fewer developers and investors have been chasing nonresidential projects, Beijing's 4 trillion yuan ($586 billion) stimulus package in early 2009 has generated more interest and activity in the commercial side. Indeed, there are signs that commercial real estate may also be headed for a bubble, and STRATFOR will be watching the situation closely.

REAL ESTATE INVESTMENT AND ANNUAL GROWTH RATE, 1986-2007

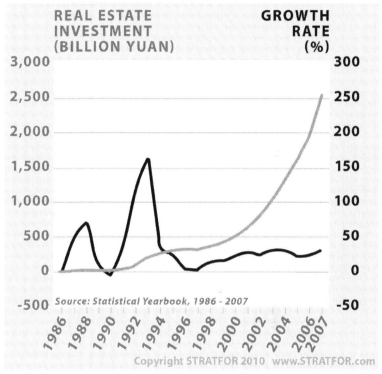

Source: Statistical Yearbook, 1986 - 2007

Origins of the Bubble

Since 1978, China's pace of urbanization has increased dramatically, with the number of middle-size and large cities (those having nonagricultural populations of more than 200,000) growing rapidly. Beginning in 1985, economic reforms implemented in urban areas to make China's planned economy more market-oriented added even more momentum to the real estate boom, with real estate investment increasing by 71 percent by 1987. The government's macroeconomic policy of monetary belt-tightening helped cool this overheated market, which was further tempered by the government's continuing to provide housing for state employees (fu li fen fang, or "welfare housing").

However, when the state significantly cut back on its welfare housing program in 1998, the Chinese perception of personal property changed, and this would have an important impact on the real estate sector. The government began this privatization process by making a private dwelling a "commodity" and granting the purchaser the right to own a newly built house for 70 years. (Likewise, the developer who buys the property on which residential or commercial buildings are to be constructed may own that property for 70 years.) Home ownership in China could now be a sound financial investment.

Thus, the residential real estate market would boom in almost every urban area in China — and particularly in the "first-tier" and "second-tier" cities (only Beijing, Shenzhen, Guangzhou and Shanghai are in the first tier, with more than 20 cities, and mostly provincial capitals or coastal ports are in the second tier). But rising land prices would eventually put housing prices out of reach for the general public. In Dongguan, a coastal second-tier city in Guangdong province, land prices averaged 4,957 yuan ($726.42) per square meter in 2007, a more than 500 percent increase from 2003, while personal disposable income increased 24 percent during the same period (from 20,526 yuan [$3,008] to 27,025 yuan [$3,960] per year).

A 2006 survey conducted by the National Development and Reform Commission showed that the average ratio between housing prices and income was approaching 12:1 in many large and middle-size cities in China (in Beijing it had reached 27:1). Twelve to one is significantly higher than the World Bank's suggested affordability ratio of 5:1 and the United Nations' 3:1. The problem was compounded by the fact that, of the more than 80 percent of Chinese who owned their own homes in urban areas (generally considered cities with populations of more than 20,000), 54.1 percent were making monthly mortgage payments that constituted 20 percent to 50 percent of their monthly incomes.

The Recovery Bubble

Following a temporary drop toward the end of 2007, land prices rose steadily, then began surging again with Beijing's stimulus package and a flood of easy credit in 2009. With much of this money flowing into the real estate sector, major beneficiaries included large state-owned enterprises (SOEs) involved in speculative real estate and housing investment, contributing to the inflating bubble. Among the 10 highest-priced land purchases in major cities in the first half of 2009, 60 percent went to SOEs.

Paradoxically, as the global financial crisis continues, China sees little choice but to loosen its monetary policy even further, fearing the opposite would curtail economic growth and result in massive unemployment, which could lead to social instability. Beijing knows that one of the country's underlying economic problems continues to be an overheated real estate market, but it also knows that the real long-term solution — limiting the flow of cash and credit — could have dire socio-economic ramifications. Meanwhile, real estate developers, government officials and investors continue to speculate on real estate, raising land and housing prices.

As housing prices continue to rise, a parallel trend is manifesting itself — rising vacancy rates in urban areas. A 2009 report by the Shanghai Yiju Real Estate Research Institute revealed that, by the end of 2008, the average vacancy rate for "commodity housing" (as opposed to welfare housing) in Beijing was 16.64 percent, and vacancies reached as high as 30 percent in some districts. Most of these vacant houses, however, are not unsold ones. They have been purchased by investors as speculative investments. While there are fewer and fewer ordinary people who can afford to buy houses, there is still excessive demand for investment housing — pressure that continues to drive up the prices.

This closed loop in the Chinese real estate market is facilitated by the country's political and bureaucratic system. In China, all land is initially owned by the state, and local governments have the sole authority to sell it. And income from property taxes and land sales are a primary source of revenue for local jurisdictions. According to estimates by the State Council's Development and Research Center, tax revenue from the land in some jurisdictions accounts for 40 percent of the local budget. Moreover, net income from land sales accounts for more than 60 percent of the local governments' extra-budgetary revenue. The soft budget and lack of accountability to the people reinforces the local governments' incentive to expand their real estate investments without much concern for cost or impact on public services.

Economic performance also is the prime prerequisite for bureau-cratic advancement, which gives local officials the incentive to gen-erate as much revenue as possible through land auctions. And this generally involves a level of collusion — and corruption — among government officials, real estate developers and investors.

One typical strategy is for a developer to buy a big chunk of urban land from the local government but leave the land undeveloped, or build on only a small portion of it, thereby keeping the housing sup-ply limited. Despite various state policies to lower land prices in order to make homes more affordable, local government officials and real estate developers control the land auctions. When a lower sale price is dictated from above, it is easy enough for the local sponsors to offi-cially deem the auction a failure. Even when the developer does build houses on the property, a speculative investor, working hand in hand with the developer and government officials, can bribe both parties to ensure that he can buy all the houses at a low volume price and keep them off the market, thereby maintaining a limited supply and high prices.

Another factor that enters the equation is a cultural one. The Chinese people generally prefer to buy new houses, as opposed to renting homes or buying secondary houses in which people have already lived. Indeed, in urban areas, marriage proposals often include a promise to buy a new commodity house. As a result, the secondary housing market remains very small in comparison (due also to fewer available bank loans for lived-in houses and the complicated process involved in transferring ownership).

All of these factors contribute to the burgeoning real estate bubble — and make it difficult to predict when that bubble will burst. With 70 percent of real estate investment in China coming from bank loans, a dramatic drop in land values could send shock waves throughout the economy. There are already signs of decline. In Shenzhen, one of China's first-tier cities, real estate prices have been dropping for the past two years (30 percent for housing), and many developers and speculators have suffered great losses. The threat looms in other large cities such as Beijing and Shanghai and may be emerging in many second-tier cities as well.

Given the current global economy and the economic balancing act it must maintain domestically, Beijing has few good choices. It must keep enough cash flowing to maintain economic growth and social stability in the short term while tightening credit to avoid a tsunami of bad loans and a market collapse over the long term. Certainly, Beijing does not want to face the kind of collapse in the housing market that Japan experienced in the 1990s, which triggered a financial crisis and more than a decade of economic malaise.

But in China's real estate, as in most sectors of this vast and complex land, implementing and enforcing prudent regulation has never been an easy task.

Revising Hukou as a Key to Economic Reform
Dec. 8, 2009

Emerging from the Central Economic Work Conference Dec. 5-6 in Beijing, chaired by Chinese President Hu Jintao, was the conclusion that modifying China's "hukou" system — which controls the residential movement of people within the country — is a key to genuine economic reform. According to China's Xinhua press, the conferees recommended revising the hukou system to allow eligible migrant workers to settle and work in urban areas and easing up on residential restrictions for small and medium-sized towns and cities to promote urbanization and domestic consumption.

Discussing hukou reform in China is not new, but the topic has taken on added importance during the global economic crisis. One of the main goals of China's stimulus program is to increase domestic consumption. The government has known for some time that its domestic consumption — approximately 40 percent of gross domestic product (GDP) — was lagging behind average global rates of 60-70 percent of GDP in wealthy countries and 50-60 percent in other Asian countries with high savings rates like China. But the economic crisis and the impact of changing consumption patterns in the United States has highlighted China's need to rebalance its economy and increase domestic consumption to a higher percentage of GDP, thereby dampening its reliance on export growth.

One important step in rebalancing China's economy is to increase urbanization and the higher levels of consumption that go along with it, for such products and services as food, shelter and transportation. In Hu's discussion of hukou reform at the economic conference, there was a noticeable change from past government statements on the issue. The focus now appears to be on shifting migration patterns to small and medium-sized towns and cities rather than the large coastal metropolises that are the biggest migrant destinations.

The hukou system, initiated under Mao Zedong in 1958, allowed the central government to control the population by limiting and controlling migration. The system was designed, in effect, to keep rural peasants tied to the land. After Deng Xiaoping's economic reforms in 1978, hukou restrictions were relaxed and China's population of migrants, also called the "floating population," is now believed to be as high as 200 million. After Deng's reforms, which opened China's economy to foreign trade and investment, particularly along the more accessible coast where trade infrastructure already existed, migrants began being lured to big coastal cities by the greater job availability and higher incomes. These migrant workers helped to further expand the coastal infrastructure, and the result was a widening economic gap between the developed coastal areas and the interior hinterlands.

Hukou reform has been discussed and carried out in China since the 1980s, and throughout this period local governments in large migrant-populated cities have added their own tweaks to the system. The provincial government in Guangdong, one of the country's most prosperous provinces, announced a plan Dec. 8 that rewards points to migrant workers in Guangdong for education, investment (e.g., buying a house) and length of stay in the province that would enable them to transfer their current hukou to a city in Guangdong. The plan also would allow the children of migrant workers to attend schools with their urban neighbors without having to pay exorbitant fees and would grant migrants workers access to social security, pensions and healthcare, which are generally not available to those without a hukou in a Guangdong.

The main problem, of course, is that the people most able to gain points are those who are educated, ambitious and have money. These are not the demographic characteristics of your typical Chinese migrant worker, who comes from a poor family, has a high school education at best and is expected to make a living as soon as possible.

Indeed, Guangdong's plan is similar to past hukou reforms in that it encourages permanent migration but only for a select few. Other reforms that have been implemented dismiss the hukou distinction between agricultural and non-agricultural households but do not change workers' residency status — they remain registered as residents of their birth places. This effectively limits where they can move and settle without transferring their hukou (which is no easy task). For any new reforms to be effective they must allow migrants to officially change their residency or provide a better balance of social services in rural and urban areas.

In any case, hukou reform in China, as necessary as it may be, will not be quick or uniform across the country. Beijing will start slowly and implement the reforms in piecemeal fashion, focusing on certain areas to ensure that the government can regain control if the experiment results in any challenge to central authority.

Carbon, Coal and Copenhagen
Dec. 16, 2009

On Dec. 17, Chinese Premier Wen Jiabao will arrive in Copenhagen for the U.N. Climate Change Conference that has been going on all week. China has taken the lead among developing nations that are arguing against an international treaty demanding binding carbon emissions reductions for developing states. China's position ultimately is not driven by ideology, but by its geopolitical situation: namely, its rapid economic growth and dependence on the consumption of carbon-intensive coal.

For months, it has been clear that the Copenhagen talks were unlikely to produce an international binding treaty — the most recent bit of bad news was the Dec. 16 resignation of Connie Hedegaard, the chief organizer of the U.N. conference. A massive split exists between developed and developing nations on the question of climate change policy, based on their divergent interests and different structural factors in their economies. Developed countries' economies tend to be driven by services and consumption, with technologically advanced and relatively energy-efficient industrial sectors that produce high-value added goods.

Developing states, meanwhile, are still undergoing industrialization. Their economies are driven by industry and exports and rely on industrial sectors that are less technologically savvy and more energy-intensive. Beijing took the lead in pressing the case for developing nations (despite its crucial financial differences from those poor nations that staged a walk-out in protest at Copenhagen on Dec. 14). Beijing argues that the developed countries historically have contributed the most carbon emissions, so the burden lies on them not only to dramatically cut their emissions but also to provide funds and technology to assist developing states. Without greater aid, says China, the developing world cannot be expected to make greater sacrifices.

When the Copenhagen summit began, these issues did not disappear. Major economies either had not determined their domestic policies and were not able to make promises (such as the United States), or were not willing to arrest their economic growth and did not intend to agree to binding cuts (such as China and India). In particular, the United States offered to cut emissions by around 17 percent from 2005 levels by 2020 — a move that was seen as too weak for a country that did not join the previous international climate change treaty (Kyoto) and came with no guarantees, since the domestic legislation it is based on has not received U.S. Senate approval. Meanwhile, China offered to reduce carbon intensity (carbon emissions calculated against gross domestic product) by 40-45 percent — essentially a do-nothing move, allowing carbon emissions to continue increasing but ostensibly at a slower rate — invoking the Kyoto protocol, which did not demand hard carbon emissions cuts from developing states.

Beneath China's claim of exemption from making hard emissions cuts lies a fundamental reality: China's hardwired dependence on coal for 70 percent of its primary energy demand. China is the world's largest coal producer and consumer (producing 42.5 percent and consuming 42.9 percent of the world's total in 2008). Moreover it holds roughly 14 percent of the world's coal reserves, which means coal — unlike oil and natural gas — can be mostly domestically sourced, which gives coal a strategic advantage as an energy source. Half of China's coal consumption is used for power generation, contributing about three-fourths of feedstock for power plants. About 36 percent of its total coal consumption goes toward manufacturing, with textiles and food processing consuming the most.

Coal is well-known for producing high carbon emissions — roughly double the emissions produced by a comparable amount of natural gas (unless advanced technologies like coal gasification are used). While Beijing has made a concerted effort to promote natural gas consumption in the energy mix and reduce coal dependency, China's economic fundamentals rest on coal consumption. The political influence of the coal industry, combined with regional dependencies on the industry, make it extremely difficult politically to restructure. China's overall energy consumption grew 7.2 percent from 2007 to 2008, even given the slowdown in the latter part of 2008.

With consistently high rates of growth, coal is for the foreseeable future the only energy source that can reliably meet China's rising demand, and China continues building new (and inefficient) coal-fired power plants apace. China contributes about 21 percent of global carbon emissions and 41 percent of global coal-produced carbon emissions; 82 percent of China's emissions come from burning coal. This strongly constrains Beijing's ability to compromise on its energy policy.

Maintaining strong economic growth is essential for China. With a population of 1.3 billion, including more than 700 million rural citizens, most living in poverty, China has both an enormous amount of labor to employ and enormous disparities in wealth. Beijing must manage the economy to continue to create new jobs and rising incomes — otherwise social stability, and potentially the regime itself, would be at risk. Rapid economic growth is fueled by coal, and the coal sector is labor-intensive. This means Beijing cannot afford politically or economically to slow its coal consumption through stringent restrictions on carbon emissions.

Therefore, Beijing is unwilling to embrace emissions cuts without major incentives, like access to high technology that could help transform its energy infrastructure, boost efficiency and reduce pollution, a major problem in China. China also wants access to new clean technology that its manufacturers can replicate and export more cheaply than China's competitors. The foundations exist for a bilateral agreement between China and the United States (even if tacit) for the United States to provide just such incentives — after all, China also must consider the possibility that climate change talks could collapse without China getting access to the high technology it needs.

While the United States took the occasion at Copenhagen to reject the idea of providing financial aid to China, one of the few countries flush with cash amid the global recession, the two have made progress toward deals in energy cooperation, giving China access to U.S. technology such as clean coal and U.S. businesses access to the Chinese market. But so far, the projects agreed upon are worth only a few billion dollars and are controversial in the United States because they use U.S. stimulus package money. A deeper agreement between the two sides has not yet materialized.

Hence the rift at Copenhagen. With China and the United States contributing the most to global carbon emissions and neither willing to make a greater sacrifice without first getting greater concessions and guarantees from the other — for instance, Washington wants a way to monitor and verify Beijing's efforts — it has become clear that other states would not be able to implement a forceful international treaty.

While there is a possibility for some important technocratic concessions to be made in the final days of Copenhagen, overall the heavy lifting on crafting an internationally binding treaty will remain to be done. Any progress will ultimately be held hostage to this American-Chinese dispute: the United States will not agree to a global climate treaty without China, and China cannot join unless there is some means of ending Chinese dependence on coal or reducing coal emissions through technology.

The Significance of China's Expanding Railway System
Dec. 17, 2009

China now has one of the biggest railway systems in the world, ranking only behind the United States in tons hauled per kilometer. The system connects the country across its vast distances, from Manchuria in the northeast, to the north, south and central regions, and now to the far western province of Xinjiang. In 2006, Tibet — the one exception — was brought into the loop with a line finally completed to the Tibetan capital Lhasa.

China's expansion of its railway system serves three critical strategic interests: it links up the poorer western regions with the more prosperous coastal areas; it provides jobs during the economic downturn; and it allows the Chinese military and security services the ability to better project power both within the country's borders and outside them if necessary. While China may have no problem building and paying for the expanded rail system, the matter of whether the system is run properly is another issue entirely.

Regional Imbalances

As with the overall Chinese economy, the railway system suffers from regional imbalances, primarily between the high consumption coastal industrial centers and the low consumption but resource-producing interior areas.

The vast majority of both passenger and freight traffic flows in two streams between the south near Guangzhou and an arc along the east coast between Shanghai and Beijing and Shenyang , while the interior regions have less traffic and lack quality service.

After shipping resources to the coastal consumption centers, trains often make the return trip to the interior with little cargo. Due to inadequate capacity and poor rail connections in some coal-producing regions (like Shaanxi), some high-energy-consuming southern provinces began in 2002 to import coal by ship from Australia rather than from domestic producers — Guangdong province gets more than half of its coal from outside China. Coal is by far the number one freight of China's rail system (about half of the country's total freight) and given that coal supplies about 70 percent of China's total energy consumption, the railways are vital to the entire economy.

'Go West'

During the 1990s, the government invested about $52 billion into modernizing the rail system. Since 2000, when the "Go West" development strategy was launched to improve infrastructure in

China's less wealthy western provinces, the total railway network has expanded from 20,000 to 30,000 kilometers, and plans call for 50,000 kilometers by 2020.

The expansion accelerated in 2009 with the onset of the global financial crisis. In November 2008, Beijing launched a massive government spending package to stimulate the sluggish economy. One component of the package was a fresh promise of 600 billion yuan ($88 billion) for rail expansion. Most notably, the new funds provided 358 billion yuan ($52 billion) for eight projects involving 4,600 kilometers of rail tracks in interior regions: building wholly new ones, doubling lines so as to separate passenger and freight, and upgrading the capacity of existing lines. Five of the eight projects are high-speed rail lines (part of a drive to build 42 new high-speed links by 2013).

Progress has been quick. In the first half of the year, construction began on the Chengdu-Lanzhou line (with the high-speed line to be completed by 2014-2015) and the second Xi'an-Ankang line. In November, construction commenced on the Lijiang-Xianggelila, Lanzhou-Urumqi (a second line for passengers only), and Xi'an-Baoji (another high-speed project) connections.

The foremost importance of these eight projects is their domestic economic impact. The 2009 projects were expected to create six million jobs and necessitate 20 million tons of steel and 130 million tons of cement — all during a time when construction would otherwise have ground to a halt as a result of the recession.

When coupled with all the supportive industries, these projects were estimated to add as much as 1.5 percent to growth of China's gross domestic product. While it is unclear whether this optimistic assessment has fulfilled expectations, the size and extent of the projects cannot be discounted. Moreover, by improving connectivity between regions and smoothing transportation across them, China is laying the groundwork for future growth in underdeveloped areas, long after the stimulus funds have been spent.

The new "Go West" rail plans are primarily meant to enhance transit across the country, bringing resources from the far west or the southwest to major consumption or processing centers, while benefiting the regions that host increasing commercial traffic. New railways will also enable better transit through the small southern province of Guizhou, a poor, difficult-to-access, mountainous region that lies between Yunnan and Sichuan and the coastal province of Guangxi, and between Lanzhou, Gansu province, and Urumqi, Xinjiang province. Gansu, in north central China, lies along the ancient Silk Road; Lanzhou serves as the rail hub linking the resource-rich far western Xinjiang, as well as connecting Kazakhstan and Central Asia, to the rest of China.

Other regions will serve as sources or destinations in themselves rather than as transit sites. Chengdu and the municipality of Chongqing both serve as rail hubs in the vibrant Sichuan basin region in China's southwest, which has a large population and economy and is also rich in natural resources. Improved rail connections here will link Sichuan's independent economic vibrancy with less prosperous neighbors, as well as make it easier for Sichuan to send workers and resources out of its borders. In addition, the Chinese government has targeted Kunming in southwestern Yunnan Province as a vital transport hub for tourism, mining and primary and secondary industries in South China. Kunming is the commercial point of contact for India, the Indian Ocean, as well as the Mekong region and broader Southeast Asia.

Meanwhile the government breathed new life into a number of rail projects that were waiting to break ground (such as the Chongqing-Guiyang and Kunming-Nanning connections), or projects that had been making only halting progress due to technical problems or complaints from citizens (such as the high-speed Shanghai-Nanjing link and the Wuhan-Guangzhou link, which were expedited and will be completed by the end of the year). Building is also scheduled to start soon on Lanzhou-Chongqing, Baoji-Chengdu, Sichuan-Qinghai and Sichuan-Tibet connections.

Security Considerations

While the primary reasons for the railway expansions are economic, there is an important military consequence. Rail is a crucial means of moving soldiers and heavy equipment and sustaining them efficiently — while air transport is faster, it is limited to fewer people and lighter gear, and is more difficult to sustain logistically.

Military mobility is critical for a country like China, which has vast borders to defend and buffer regions to control, such as Manchuria, Inner Mongolia, and especially conflict-prone Xinjiang and Tibet. In addition to the need to maintain internal security in its own provinces, China has in recent decades fought battles on its Manchurian, North Korean, Russian, Indian and Vietnamese borders — and the difficulty of logistics in these areas has not been lost on Chinese strategists as they conduct contingency planning.

The People's Liberation Army conducted a major military exercise in August called "Stride 2009," utilizing new high-speed trains that travel around 350 kilometers per hour. The exercise essentially involved swapping troops and equipment (heavy weapons, tanks, and infantry vehicles) from garrison to garrison along both the north-south (Shenyang-Lanzhou) and east-west (Jinan-Guangzhou) routes, highlighting the Chinese military planners' considered role for the expanded and upgraded rail infrastructure.

A Reform Stumbling Block

China has no problem building its rail system or paying for it — its massive cash reserves and surfeit of cheap labor guarantee that. But the Ministry of Finance (MOR), the agency tasked with managing 83 percent of the country's railroads, retains the command-economy mentality from China's past far more so than other ministries. As such, attempts to increase the efficiency of the Chinese rail system have met with decidedly little success. The MOR remains largely unchanged despite two decades of government initiatives designed to increase competition for passenger services in different areas, bring in foreign investors, adjust the price structure to shift away from old-fashioned low tariffs, break off and commercialize non-transport services, and privatize passenger lines as opposed to freight.

The railways are divided into 14 regional administrations, a system that causes difficulties managing transport across administrative divisions. In addition, all decision-making and resource allocation are both centralized and bureaucratic. As a result, the system responds slowly to outside changes.

Overall China's railway system is unprofitable but serves an essential economic and strategic purpose and will continue to be amply subsidized despite the inefficiencies.

The Dragon of Inflation
Feb. 11, 2010

The specter of runaway inflation in China is a topic of increasing debate, and countless Chinese leaders have in recent months stressed the need for controls to prevent general price increases. The Chinese economy is expected to grow at a rate of around 10 percent in 2010, and the banking system continues to support government stimulus policy with massive lending. While consumer prices in 2009 were negative overall, January 2010 statistics showed that consumer prices grew by 1.5 percent compared to the same month in 2009, underscoring inflation expectations.

However, for a developing economy, China has low inflation rates. The annual average change in its consumer price index (CPI) has rarely risen above 5 percent since the late 1990s, a rate that many developing states — to say nothing of one developing as rapidly as China — find enviable. In fact, the Chinese economy often shows deflationary tendencies. The concerns being voiced by China's leaders about inflation are therefore actually concerns over spiking prices in certain sectors, rather than any broad-based inflation more typical of economies at this stage of development. Price spikes in three key sectors — energy, real estate and especially food — could cause a great deal of social unrest, which Beijing hopes to avoid at all costs.

What is Inflation?

Inflation is the increase in the general level of prices across an economy. It is usually measured with the consumer price index (CPI), a basket of widely used goods and services. In general, it is distinct from price increases in any particular good or sector because it is more fundamental — it spans across a range of goods and sectors. While some inflation generally accompanies growth and employment, too much can be destabilizing. Excessive inflation results from economy-wide shocks in supply or demand, setting them abnormally off balance, and is frequently associated with panic buying, hoarding and shortages, as consumers will rush to buy things if they fear prices rising higher the longer they wait. Inflation can result from monetary and fiscal expansion, war or blockade, sharp demographic or labor shifts, drastic government policy shifts in a range of areas, and other large-scale phenomena.

Developing countries are often the most vulnerable to serious bouts of inflation. They are in the midst of erecting an entire industrial and social infrastructure, and so much activity — often where there was little in previous years — can create extraordinarily high and persistent demand for energy, raw materials and basic goods of which the supply cannot quickly be increased. Oftentimes supply chains need to be constructed from the ground up, and the establishment of these new processes where none existed before goes hand-in-hand with stronger price pressures — for example, think of how much it would cost to be the first person in town to install a backyard swimming pool. Additionally, consumers in developing countries usually have limited disposable income, spending most of what they earn on basics like food and energy. Demand for these items cannot be easily reduced, and supplies cannot be easily increased (though they can rapidly shrink). Everyone has to eat, and producing more food or energy requires long lead times. The results — particularly in a rapidly growing economy — are shocks in supply and demand that become apparent in greater price fluctuations. Rampant construction, intensive investment, growing private business and consumer demand — these are factors which, happening all at once in formerly undeveloped circumstances, tend to push the general level of prices up.

This is not the case in modern China. But before we can discuss the present, it is critical to understand how China got to where it is now.

Inflation in China

After China's initial economic opening in 1979, there were three major bouts of broad based inflation — in 1985, when average annual prices grew at more than 10 percent, in 1988-1989, when prices grew nearly 20 percent, and in 1993-1996, with price increases reaching nearly 25 percent. Each of these incidents was economically and socially disruptive, with dissatisfaction over high prices in 1989 contributing to the protests at Tiananmen Square. Imbalances of supply and demand naturally occurred as the Chinese economy transitioned from a Marxist command economy to a pseudo-free market economy. The worst bouts in 1988-1989 and 1993-1996 were caused by a variety of economic and financial factors, foremost of which were changes involving government price controls and state-owned enterprises (SOEs).

The 1980s, the period of initial liberalization, best illustrates this paradigm. Subsidies and price controls that had determined prices for decades were relaxed, and prices on a gradually widened range of goods and services were allowed to fluctuate more freely than before, as part of the process of allowing market forces to play a greater role in the allocation of resources. Since there were new opportunities for growth and profit, business and consumer demand were also increasing. In the countryside, the central government allowed rural businesses and markets to take shape, and also raised the prices it paid for procuring agricultural output, to boost farmers' incomes. The combination of higher incomes and price liberalization led to rising prices across the board, especially for food, where prices grew 77 percent in total between 1978 and 1986.

At the same time, changes were taking place in China's industrial sector. The SOEs were the dominant forces in China's industrial complex during the Maoist period, comprising 90 percent of gross domestic product (GDP) in 1978. With the market reforms, they were suddenly granted new freedoms to make investments, and they seized the moment by borrowing heavily from state-owned banks to undertake massive projects and expand in size and capacity. Supported by local and central government, they had no fear of bankruptcy, but did fear their competitors and thus borrowed money to grow as rapidly as possible and grab maximum market share — and yet their overall output fell, indicating serious inefficiencies. Subsidized loans, unblinking government support and a desire to grow as quickly as possible created a surge in demand that affected the entire economy.

Rising wages also contributed to inflation by stimulating demand and increasing input costs for producers. As the SOEs grew, they hired more and more employees, going from 74 million in 1978 to more than 100 million in 1990 — while that may not seem like a big increase for a country with China's population, it took place in the context of predominantly rural conditions and an isolated and defunct economy, magnifying its impact on society. With food prices high, urban workers demanded higher wages. Wages rose by an average of 15 percent per year during the mid-1980s, and they rose especially during peak inflation years (50 percent in 1985, 20 percent in 1988 and 35 percent in 1994), putting additional upward pressure on prices.

Underlying these changes were equally important changes in government monetary policy. The central government's adoption of loose monetary and credit policies designed to accommodate its own investments and budget deficits and the massive bank lending for local governments and SOEs amplified these inflationary trends.

61

Eventually, in the late 1980s, with food prices and wages both climbing and the system flush with cash, overall inflation skyrocketed, averaging nearly 19 percent in both 1988 and 1989. Consumers rushed grocery stores in the summer of 1988 fearing new government moves to raise prices. Ultimately domestic unrest broke out, culminating in the infamous June 4, 1989, crackdown on protesters at Tiananmen Square and the implementation of other tough security measures to maintain control.

Although a period of political tightening followed Tiananmen, in a few years economic liberalization resumed and the forces behind soaring inflation from 1993-1996 were essentially the same: food prices and wages were rising, and SOEs were gorging on subsidized credit as they made investments. The basic conditions of inadequate productive capacity and supply, combined with excessive demand and liquidity, continued to put pressure on existing resources and drove inflation.

Thus the first 20 years of reform were years in which whole-scale adjustments were taking place in the economy, and a modern industrial and manufacturing base was being built, in addition to an ongoing process of urbanization. After the tremendous price hikes in 1993-1994, the Communist Party was faced with the need to restructure, and the result was an overhaul of the SOEs that had been the source of so much credit-fueled spending. Retrenching and consolidating the sector took several years, with SOEs shedding over 30 million workers from 1996 to 2000 (and paring down more than 15 million since then) resulting in a current total of around 60 million workers. These reforms trimmed off some of the SOE demand that was an endemic cause of inflation in China's system.

Inflation Today

Since the inflationary mid-1990s, China's inflation landscape has been fundamentally different. With a massive and more fully developed productive capacity in place, China's economic system has maintained high production levels, flooding foreign and domestic markets with goods. Overcapacity and oversupply — made possible by the endless availability of subsidized loans — have been the dominant forces affecting prices. In contrast, consumer demand remains relatively low, as people for a variety of reasons prefer to save rather than spend. Steadily rising supply plus anemically growing demand pushes domestic prices on consumer goods down. Hence core inflation (calculated without energy and food prices) generally stays low.

In fact, sporadically from 1998 to 2003, and again in 2009, China fell into deflation — that is, negative change in the general level of prices. Growth and exports fell due to recessions abroad, and Chinese consumption dropped along with the prices of stockpiled goods for which there was little global demand. Even when inflation reached its most recent highs of 7-8 percent compared to the previous year, which lasted for a few months in 2008, the annual average inflation rate that year barely exceeded 5 percent — and that was for the first time since 1996. By contrast, from 2000-2009 Brazil averaged more than 15 percent inflation and Russia more than 12 percent. The inflation of 2008 was then cut short by a financial crisis that interrupted global trade, sending prices everywhere plummeting.

In 2009, overall inflation was -0.7 percent, revealing China's deflationary tendencies once again amid the latest global recession. Even in 2010, with overall economic growth expected to top 10 percent and massive amounts of liquidity in the system as part of government stimulus efforts, the central bank claims it expects inflation of 3 percent and no more than 4 percent. International demand remains constrained, keeping prices for China's imports down, and China is also looking for ways to wind down its stimulus measures. Domestic consumption has remained resilient, but mostly because of stimulus policies propping it up — it is not suddenly surging forward on its own accord. All of these factors apply downward pressure on prices.

While the Chinese government is not expecting a swelling of broad-based inflation comparable to the late 1980s or mid-1990s, it remains highly concerned that spiking prices in critical areas could stir up social unrest. Three sectors of particular concern are energy, real estate and especially food.

Real estate bubbles have been a constant in China for years, with the slowdown in 2009 being short-lived, and 2010 showing all the signs of a new bubble forming. Anywhere with limited land available for development, a large population, and an endless stream of subsidized credit will see property prices rise. Local governments derive an average of 40 percent of their tax revenues from land sales and therefore collude with property developers to drive prices up. The developers themselves want the land not only hoping to sell it later for a profit, but also as collateral to present to banks to get more loans.

There is no doubt a construction and real estate bubble taking shape (with serious implications for overall financial and economic stability), given the 3.2 trillion yuan or $530 billion invested in real estate in 2009 alone. But the impact on overall inflation is not presently a paramount concern. Housing prices in the CPI dropped by 3.6 percent in 2009 compared to 2008, reflecting the fall from recent highs in summer 2008 (though China's National Bureau of Statistics uses a variety of methods to underestimate the effect of housing prices on CPI).

The chief concern is the risk to social stability. The frantic pace of development frequently leads to peasants getting coerced from their homes, a major cause of protests. Moreover, housing prices have accelerated faster than incomes, putting pressure on families' pocketbooks. Beijing is attempting to limit social stresses by restricting forced evictions and restraining rising prices in the real estate sector through a variety of measures announced in January, but these central government policies will be difficult to enforce and will have at best mixed results on the local level. Beijing's best hope comes from the fact that prices on cheap housing and second-hand homes barely grew in 2009, constraining the impact of price increases on the poorest sectors of society.

Energy is another area where social stability is the primary focus. Maintaining China's booming industries requires energy and raw materials inputs, which have volatile prices and are certainly capable of driving inflation in other countries when prices soar. But the Communist Party uses price controls to ensure that prices of oil, refined oil products, natural gas, coal and electricity stay within socially acceptable ranges, so as to prevent fluctuations from wreaking havoc on the delicate balance of Chinese companies and households. State-owned energy companies are required to sell goods at low prices domestically, sometimes below the cost of production; in return, they receive subsidies from the government to make up for the lost profits. Such subsidies hide the true costs of many economic processes in China, transferring them to the government finances or banking system in some way. But one intentional outcome of these practices is that since the costs are not borne by the physical economy, they do not increase prices for all users downstream.

Of course, such price control policies create all kinds of distortions: during times of high input costs, energy producers will deliberately limit supply so they do not have to subsidize the domestic market from their own pockets — they will also seek to export their product as much as possible, and avoid reinvesting in capacity upgrades, since their goal is to make money and that is difficult to do when foreign oil is expensive and domestic prices are capped. Oil refiners resorted to such methods during the period of high international commodity prices in 2007 and 2008, and natural gas companies were accused of limiting supplies in winter 2009-2010 when cold weather increased demand for household heating. Artificially low domestic prices also encourage consumers to consume inefficiently, generating unnecessarily high demand. Normally, inflationary pressures would limit such demand growth, but to maintain social stability, the Chinese government has chosen to short-circuit market forces. As a result, energy shortages happen frequently in China.

Nevertheless, China's energy price controls have worked well enough to maintain internal order. Attempts to reform pricing mechanisms to allow higher prices are in the works, but always subject to reversal given the social risks. As long as bank loans are available for state energy companies, China can mask the costs of controlling energy prices.

Food is perhaps the sector most capable of sparking domestic unrest if prices spike. Food prices are inherently inflationary in

China, where too little arable land must feed too many people. Food price inflation generally runs well above overall CPI, such as the run from spring 2007 to fall 2008, when food prices rose well above 7 percent every month and reached a peak of 23 percent in February 2008. This is not a problem that can be solved easily, since food supply and demand are hard to change. Crop yields are unpredictable because of weather, and slow to adjust considering planting seasons. Meanwhile food demand has a stable basis, since population changes happen over generations, everyone eats, and there is no substitute for food.

The causes of food price inflation do not necessarily mark economy-wide changes but are often highly specific, contingent or localized. Farmers may create shortages of certain supplies that drive prices up — wheat farmers frequently turn to other crops during times of low wheat prices, inadvertently causing shortages later on. Pig farmers slaughtering their pigs (amid a disease outbreak) were the leading factor causing meat prices to rise by more than 40 percent (compared to the previous year) during spring 2008. The government may also buy domestic farm produce or restrict imports to control prices. But ultimately food prices are subject to factors beyond the control of short-term business or policy adjustments. Even during times of overall low inflation, food prices follow their own rules — for example, vegetable prices rose by 24 percent in November 2009 because of weather conditions. About 35 percent of expenditures by urban and rural households go to food, so price increases are sharply felt.

When China first emerged from its command economy, core inflation was a dangerous threat, and would remain so for decades. But over time China's economic structure became so heavily geared toward high production and low consumption that deflationary tendencies formed. Today when Chinese officials say they are concerned about inflation they are talking about price spikes in key economic sectors — energy, real estate and especially food. The risks posed by such spikes have the potential to spark social unrest that shakes the foundations of the central government's control, as they indeed have in the past, and could again in the future.

The Shaky Structure of an Economic 'Miracle'
April 26, 2010

At the root of the East Asian model of economic growth is the need to maintain employment for massive populations. East Asian states in general have high population densities and histories of labor-intensive agriculture. Governments that do not provide stable employment conditions inevitably end up with large and unhappy populations on their hands — frequently the cause of revolutions. In the modern context, East Asian governments have focused on harnessing the savings of the population and controlling the country's financial system to ensure credit is directed to expanding infrastructure and industrial capacity. Cheap credit enables businesses — especially export-oriented manufacturers — to maximize employment and output and seize greater international market share, bringing in more cash to perpetuate the cycle.

Following from the East Asian model of growth, China's economic "miracle" relies on the channeling of massive household and corporate savings into fixed capital investment to build the roads, factories, trains and buildings necessary to modernize and expand economic activity. But a serious defect of the East Asian model is that it discourages the development of household consumption as a third source of growth to complement exports and investment. Families are encouraged to save (which helps the government finance national policies) rather than spend (which would assist the local economy), depressing household consumption. Increasing government investment in recessionary periods means building more production capacity despite weak demand (domestically or abroad). This practice cannot be maintained indefinitely, and East Asian states have tended to undergo transitions (sometimes very rocky ones) during which policies are adjusted to stabilize or boost domestic consumption while allowing fixed investment to taper off. The result — if the restructuring is successful — is a more balanced economy sustained by consumption while varying degrees of exports and investment contribute to its growth.

Both Taiwan and South Korea have gone through this process. In Taiwan, rapid growth in exports, savings and investment between 1962 and 1985 was accompanied by the decreasing importance of consumption to the overall economy. Taiwan's exchange-rate depreciation in the late 1970s facilitated a rapid rise in exports, which outstripped domestic consumption as a share of gross domestic product (GDP). However, since Taiwan is a small island with limited room for heavy industry, capital formation never rose above 30 percent of GDP, meaning the economy never became so reliant on investment as to detract from consumption. After 1983, Taiwan implemented financial liberalization to allow for more efficient, market-oriented allocation of capital and to help make the transition into a high-tech economy. This transition facilitated a rise in private consumption from 47 percent of GDP in 1968 to 60 percent of GDP in 2008. Today, Taiwan maintains a balance of consumption (60 percent of GDP), exports (73 percent of GDP) and investment (21 percent of GDP).

Similarly, beginning in the 1970s, South Korea saw rapid growth in exports, savings and fixed investment, reaching the peak of fixed investment in the years leading up to and immediately following the Seoul Olympics of 1988. While geographically small, South Korea required large fixed investment to support the expansion of heavy industry by chaebol, or state-supported corporate conglomerates. Naturally, consumption fell as a portion of GDP until 1988, when it reached a low of 49 percent. After this period, currency appreciation (which increased domestic purchasing power) enabled consumption to remain stable, while the resulting drop in exports was offset by an increase in investment. Even after the 1997 Asian financial crisis, when consumption dropped to its lowest point amid domestic financial troubles and recession, South Korea was able to recover rapidly on the back of a policy-supported domestic consumption boom from 1998 to 2002. Today, Korea balances consumption (55 percent of GDP) with exports (53 percent of GDP) and investment (about 30 percent of GDP).

China, however, has not yet undergone this transition to consumer-led growth and remains heavily dependent on exports and investment. While consumption in Taiwan and Korea fell below half of GDP only once (and quickly recovered), in China consumption fell below half of GDP in 1990 and, especially since 2000, has continued to fall, hitting a low point of 35 percent of GDP in 2008. Of course, household consumption grew in absolute terms during this period as family incomes improved and consumer markets expanded. But as a portion of the overall economy, household consumption fell while savings, fixed investment and especially exports grew. In other words, unlike other East Asian states, China has not succeeded in shoring up the consumption share of its economy. A major danger of this economic structure is that it makes China extremely vulnerable to global slowdowns that affect trade. In fact, when exports plummeted during the 2009 global recession, a surge in investment from government stimulus accounted for more than 90 percent of growth while consumption contributed less than 10 percent.

A variety of historical factors account for the metamorphosis of the South Korean and Taiwanese economies, in contrast to China, beginning with the obvious fact that their development process began earlier. It is not a coincidence that in both South Korea and Taiwan, the shift from state-guided investment to consumption-driven economies occurred in tandem with democratization. More private control over wealth generated more popular demand for control over other things, like political representation and governance. Moreover, these states set out on the path of modernization sooner and were supported every step of the way by the United States, which provided them with security, capital investment and expertise and granted them access to the world's biggest consumer market. In China, the Communist Party remains resolutely opposed to popular-style governments that could challenge its regime and does not have the strategic option of opening its doors fully to the United States — though since its opening up in 1978 it has enjoyed the enormous advantage of exporting to the U.S. consumer market. Nevertheless, allowing greater domestic freedoms and more extensive foreign presence poses a threat to the Chinese regime's unity and stability. These factors have contributed to the government's reluctance to unleash the consumptive power of Chinese households.

Weak Consumption

Despite China's inherent handicaps, the trend of falling consumption as a share of China's economy was not inevitable. In the first decade of economic reforms, China experienced relatively balanced growth. Economic liberalization in 1979 unleashed 30 years of pent-up consumption as households, entrepreneurs and farmers gained the freedom to buy and sell. Consumption stayed at 50 percent of GDP throughout the 1980s, while exports and fixed investment expanded at a gradual rate averaging 25 percent and 18 percent per year respectively. However, by the late 1980s consumption growth became unstable, as rapid inflation and political unrest forced the government to re-centralize control, including control over economic policy in order to cool down the overheating economy.

Consumption has never contributed as much to the Chinese economy as it did in the 1980s, though it enjoyed a period of relative stability from 1994 to 2000. In 1992, then-leader Deng Xiaoping launched a growth strategy focused on promoting the coastal cities as manufacturing and export powerhouses. Initially, the booming export economy and investment led to a rapid rise in private employment in the export sector, stabilizing the decline in consumption, but this proved unsustainable. By the late 1990s, coastal cities and state-owned enterprises were flooded with subsidized capital, much of it misallocated by government-controlled banks, and the domestic banking system was at risk because of an increasing number of non-performing loans and an overheating real-estate sector. Blaming the inefficient management of state-owned enterprises (SOEs) for the economic problems, the government launched major reforms that caused rising unemployment and a breakdown of the "iron rice bowl" — the welfare system for the masses of state employees. After Premier Zhu Rongji initiated the process of downsizing the state sector in 1995, 48 million jobs were lost and the state sector contracted by 3 percent per year for the following decade. This downsizing, in addition to pro-export policies, resulted in China's consumption as a share of GDP falling more than it ever had. It was not that Chinese consumers were not earning more and spending more — rather, it was that their overall contribution to the economy was smaller relative to exports and investment.

In the last decade, the Chinese economy has been driven primarily by fixed investment (44 percent of GDP in 2008) and exports (32 percent of GDP) at the expense of domestic consumption (35 percent of GDP). Employment and wage growth have lagged behind rising costs for education, housing, health care and basic goods, leading to the rise in savings. And with few investment opportunities, most families deposit their savings in the state-run banking system, which converts the funds into government-planned investments. Meanwhile, consumers and small- and medium-sized businesses have trouble obtaining credit and must rely on their earnings for self-financing or on underground lending, thus perpetuating the high savings rate.

Limited capital for entrepreneurs and small and medium-sized enterprises has made China dependent on the export sector for employment. Over the last two decades, state-sector downsizing and a shrinking agricultural sector has put pressure on the Chinese government to create jobs. The relaxation of agricultural trade barriers leading up to China's World Trade Organization accession, in addition to greater job opportunities in the booming cities, caused rural jobs to fall as a proportion of China's labor force from 73 percent in 1990 to 61 percent in 2007. This created a contingent of at least 150 million migrant workers who move between rural and urban areas providing low-wage labor, which was soaked up — especially before the recent global recession — by export-oriented private and foreign enterprises. For most of the early 2000s, China's economy increasingly achieved growth through foreign consumer demand rather than its own.

Emerging from the global economic crisis, China's economy is in a period of flux, with exports diminishing in importance and government investment taking up the slack. There is much official rhetoric about economic "restructuring" to create sustainable household demand to drive growth in the future. Nevertheless, the economy at present retains the structure — and structural liabilities — of the patterns of development over the past two decades. The transition away from export dependency has only just begun, and stimulus policies targeting domestic-driven growth are necessarily temporary.

Regional Disparities

China's increasing economic dependency on exports and investment — and the accompanying decline of consumption — has contributed to regional disparities. Looking at China's provinces through the lens of economic structure, four major classes can be identified: those provinces that are the most heavily dependent on exports, those that are most heavily dependent on investment, those that show a relative balance and those with limited exports and investment.

The first category (orange on the accompanying map) consists of export-dependent regions, where exports generally take a greater share of regional GDP than consumption. These are the wealthy, cosmopolitan coastal provinces and municipalities, including Beijing, Tianjin, the Greater Shanghai region and Guangdong province. When Western countries speak of "China," they refer to these vibrant manufacturing hubs. Xinjiang, the autonomous region in the far northwest and the single non-coastal province in this category, is a newcomer to the category due to a recent push by Beijing to deepen economic links to Kazakhstan and Central Asia. But the wealth of these export centers is deceptive, and they are really China's most vulnerable regions. Not only are their economies extremely dependent upon international markets, but investment has surpassed what local consumption there is, making them uniquely vulnerable to factors well beyond their control.

Second (yellow on the map) come the investment-heavy regions, where fixed investment is vastly more important than consumption. Northeast China, previously known as Manchuria, the "Rust Belt" or old industrial heartland, lies in this category — a region kept alive by government subsidies and transfers. Sparsely populated regions such as Inner Mongolia in the north and Tibet in the west serve as geopolitical buffers that give China strategic depth and provide natural resources but otherwise have no economies to speak of. High fixed investment goes into the capital-intensive industries that exploit resources in these regions, including coal (China's number one source of energy by far). Beijing also needs to maintain sovereignty over these buffer regions for them to serve a strategic purpose effectively. This category also includes landlocked, poor, populous and resource-rich provinces that lie next to wealthier coastal areas, such as Shaanxi and Shanxi in the north and Anhui and Jiangxi in the south. These regions are — and probably always will be — dependent upon monies from Beijing to subsidize their social stability. It is not a coincidence that Mao Zedong's famous Long March began and ended in such regions (Jiangxi and Shaanxi, respectively).

Two neighboring provinces on the eastern coast, Jiangsu and Shandong, as well as Hebei in the north and Heilongjiang in the northeast, fall into their own category (white on the map). These four provinces present as close a semblance of "balanced" economic structure as China can provide. Exports are beneficial but not essential, and though investment is more important than consumption, the discrepancy between these sources of growth is not as warped as it is in the investment-dependent regions. Both these provinces are wealthy and have large populations, diversified natural resources and vibrant light manufacturing sectors, and benefit from foreign trade and investment. Many leading Chinese politicians come from this area, and if China has a region that could ever achieve the "success" of Taiwan or Korea it would be comprised of some combination of these provinces.

Finally, there are the interior provinces (green on the map) that cannot develop export industries and where the investment share of the economy is not outrageously high (though often more than half of GDP). These range from the heavily populated central provinces known for providing migrant labor to other provinces (Henan, Hubei, Hunan) to the sparsely populated western provinces (Gansu, Qinghai) as well as the poor, relatively isolated and self-contained Sichuan and Chongqing provinces in the southwest. These areas are exceedingly poor in absolute and relative terms, but they are not dependent on the outside world or subject to the most rapid or volatile forces of change.

Where Next?

Despite the massive amount of public funds spent in 2009 and 2010 to boost domestic consumption, no amount of incentives or subsidies will enable Beijing to turn domestic household consumption into the engine of China's growth in the near term. The past two decades of export-orientated growth have taken money out of the pockets of consumers to finance infrastructure and industrial capacity to the detriment of growth in consumer credit, wages and social services. The result is an economy with overcapacity, over-reliance on the outside world and anemic domestic consumption. A transition to a consumer-driven economy will take a long time and will come at the cost of rising unemployment for low-wage laborers from rural areas unable to find jobs in an economy that increasingly demands skilled labor. Rising unemployment in the export sector and falling government investment likely will create sociopolitical instability. Adding a sense of urgency to the dilemma, the Communist Party is preparing for a leadership transition in just two and a half years, and the outgoing administration must weigh the need for timely economic restructuring against the bleak realities of inertia in the system.

Spreading Labor Unrest
June 18, 2010

Recent labor unrest in China has spread to Japanese-owned Toyota Motor Corp. About 60 workers staged a brief strike June 15, the day before a national holiday, demanding a wage increase in affiliate Toyota Gosei Co.'s plant in the northeastern city of Tianjin. The company agreed to review the wage structure on June 17. On the same day, U.S. fast-food chain KFC signed the company's first collective labor contract in China, agreeing to raise workers' wages by 200 yuan (about $30) per month in Shenyang, Liaoning province. A growing number of labor strikes and creeping wage inflation are among the internal pressures confronting China as it tries to reshape its economy.

The Chinese government is responding to the recent increase in labor unrest by upgrading its mechanism for addressing labor disputes — the All China Federation of Trade Unions (ACFTU) — and gaining better control over emerging grassroots movements.

In China, all trade unions are controlled by the Communist Party-dominated ACFTU, which is deeply influenced by the government and does little to truly represent workers' interests. The purpose of the ACFTU so far has not been to advocate for more worker rights and benefits, but to keep tabs on workers and assist the central government in managing social problems arising from labor issues. In 2006, in the midst of a global economic boom that saw rising prices and more vocal cries from China's workers for higher wages, the ACFTU began to take a more active role in pressuring foreign enterprises to let their workers unionize. Most of these firms had hitherto avoided it, and Beijing saw the need both to use the unions as leverage against the companies and to gather more information about foreign firms through closer cooperation between unions and management. This process ground to a halt during the global financial crisis and recession. When wages froze, workers were laid off and the central government shifted its focus to mitigating the risks of unemployment.

In 2010, however, China has returned to blistering growth rates and rising prices, and so have workers' demands for higher wages. On the night of June 4, according to Xinhua news agency, the ACFTU issued an emergency notice calling for a strengthening of ACFTU authority and that of affiliated local trade unions. The notice urged trade unions to promote the establishment of unions in foreign-owned and private domestic enterprises, including companies owned by investors in Hong Kong, Macao and Taiwan. It also called for expanding union representation for migrant workers.

These ideas are not entirely new. Beijing has called several times for requiring a trade union presence in many private and foreign businesses, with the most notable move occurring in 2006, when Beijing called for at least 60 percent of foreign-owned enterprises operating in China to have trade unions by the end of the year. Beijing also has called for enhancing ACFTU's legitimacy by including migrant workers in its ranks. But the June 4 notice came on the heels of highly publicized strikes by migrant workers at foreign-owned manufacturing facilities demanding wage increases and a spate of suicides at a Foxconn plant in Shenzhen, Guangdong province.

In the recent strikes, the absence of trade unions or their use as intermediaries between management and labor has inspired employees to carry out spontaneous strikes on their own. These actions have been planned and executed outside the authority of the official trade unions, which has sidelined the ACFTU and could undermine Beijing's control.

Beijing has little objection to wage increases for Chinese workers, since part of its economic restructuring plan is to promote domestic consumption and since it is already encouraging local governments to increase minimum wages. But Beijing does not want unauthorized strikes by self-motivated (and often young) workers to spread beyond its control and become a nationwide movement that could eventually challenge its authority.

And it is becoming clear that Beijing's concerns are not unfounded. Workers' recent successes in getting wage increases and better working conditions have encouraged others to follow suit — even the

DEMOGRAPHICS OF CHINA IN 2010

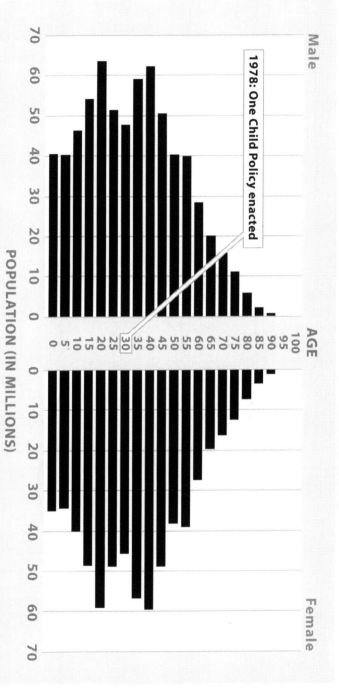

Male

Female

1978: One Child Policy enacted

AGE

100
95
90
85
80
75
70
65
60
55
50
45
40
35
30
25
20
15
10
5
0

POPULATION (IN MILLIONS)

70 60 50 40 30 20 10 0   0 10 20 30 40 50 60 70

ACFTU, whose June 4 notice reflects the federation's attempt to strengthen its power over foreign-owned businesses in China, nearly half of which have no trade unions, despite the ACFTU's attempt in 2006 to pressure foreign-owned businesses to let their workers unionize.

This will never be an easy task, however. Many foreign companies in China resist trade unions because they fear they will lead to excessive government control of business operations. The connections between businesses and local governments based on tax revenues can cause the latter to turn a blind eye to the absence of trade unions and be less willing to follow the dictates of the central government. Establishing trade unions in all foreign-owned and private domestic companies will be a tough sell, especially if trade unions are given more power. These pending policies will certainly factor into the calculations that anyone will make to determine the costs and benefits of investing in China.

Moreover, the June 4 ACFTU notice does not imply that the federation is trying to represent workers more effectively; it only suggests that the Communist Party is reasserting leadership of the ACFTU, and it even repeats a call for union leaders to be selected by the company rather than by the workers themselves. This means that the conditions driving workers to carry out spontaneous and unauthorized strikes will not go away.

On the surface, China's move to increase ACFTU control over workers as their demands grow is both necessary and desirable. Beijing not only wants to relieve social dissatisfaction and provide higher wages to workers to spur domestic consumption, it also wants foreign companies, which benefit from China's abundant cheap labor, to shoulder the burden of the wage increases first. And Beijing is happy to have a tool like the ACFTU with which to exert this pressure.

In the long run, however, these trends threaten to reduce China's attractiveness to foreign firms. Foreigners invest in China to take advantage of cheap labor. As labor costs rise, this advantage will erode, and the disadvantages of working in China (including heavy state influence and arbitrary political and regulatory practices) will become more obtrusive.

But there is an even deeper problem: China's demographics are shifting. Since the notorious "one child policy" was enacted in 1978, each subsequent generation has gotten smaller (with the brief exception of a small baby boom beginning in 1990). This means that, in the coming years, fewer people will be entering the Chinese workforce, which will contribute to labor shortages in some sectors (notably medium- and highly skilled manufacturing positions) and further increase labor costs. The combination of growing expectations for higher wages and a gradually shifting demographic that will diminish the labor supply will heavily influence foreign investors as they consider whether to put money into China over the coming decade.

CHAPTER 3: POLITICS

Understanding China's New Regime
June 20, 2002

In October, China will begin what may be the most important leadership transition since the founding of the People's Republic in 1949. Between meetings of the Communist Party Congress in October and the National People's Congress in March, nearly half of the Politburo is set to retire, and the nation's president, prime minister, party general secretary and NPC chairman all will step down. This will open the way for a new generation of leaders to guide China's economic and political future.

Much attention already has been paid to Vice President Hu Jintao, the enigmatic heir apparent expected to take over as president and possibly party chief from Jiang Zemin. Hu has revealed little about his true ideology and capabilities as China's soon-to-be paramount leader. As important as figuring out who Hu is will be understanding China's next prime minister, who will be tasked with directing the country's economic reform and opening program.

Individual personalities aside, the upcoming leaders — the so-called Fourth Generation — have several characteristics in common that will shape their domestic and foreign policies and China's economic direction. Their actions, however, will be constrained by the changing international system and — perhaps more important — by growing social and economic pressures at home.

Government in Transition

In late 2002, a massive generational shift in China's top leadership will begin. Starting with the 16th Congress of the Communist Party of China in October and continuing through the National People's Congress (NPC) session in March 2003, nearly half of the Politburo's 21 members (including five of seven members of the Standing Committee, the topmost government body) are scheduled to step down, having passed the mandatory retirement age of 70. President and Communist Party General Secretary Jiang Zemin, Prime Minister Zhu Rongji and NPC Chairman Li Peng all are expected to hand off power to successors.

The party has spent years preparing for the transition. Paramount leader Deng Xiaoping tapped current Vice President Hu Jintao as a future leader at the same time that Jiang was rising to power, in the wake of the 1989 Tiananmen Square incident. What Deng and other senior leaders wanted was a gradual and orderly transition of power between leaders and generations, avoiding the intra-party clashes and disruptions of previous leadership changes. This great experiment in generational turnover is about to begin.

The selection process for new leaders remains opaque — and even though the first changes are just a few months away, it is still too early to know who will take the reins of government. Yet most observers agree that some candidates apparently are being groomed for top jobs. Vice President Hu, who also is vice chairman of the Central Military Commission, is slated to take over at least one of Jiang's three positions: party general secretary, president or Central Military Commission chairman. Hu likely will emerge as China's next president and possibly even party general secretary, but Jiang appears intent on retaining his leadership of the Central Military Committee as this would allow him to retain power behind the scenes.

Jiang's protégé Zeng Qinghong, director of the Organization Department of the CPC Central Committee, also is considered a strong candidate for a future leadership position, on the basis of both Jiang's support and his own formidable abilities. He is vying with Hu for at least one of Jiang's titles and may take the post of general secretary. Vice Prime Minister Wen Jiabao looks set to replace Prime Minister Zhu Rongji, while Li Ruihuan, a current Standing Committee member, is the likely successor to NPC Chairman Li Peng.

Both Hu and Li Ruihuan offer some stability during the transition. Li, who likely will retain his position in the Politburo, is slightly older than most of the incoming Fourth Generation, and his continuation in the top circle fulfills the party core's desire to mingle old and new in the leadership lineup for continuity, guidance and rejuvenation. Ultimately, the goal of this transition is to keep the party perpetually at the core of Chinese politics and of China as a whole; therefore, those involved in the succession want to avoid allowing the process to fall into chaos.

Power will not be reallocated over night but gradually over a period of years — either peacefully or through factional infighting and power politics. While the current generation of leaders is serious about bringing younger cadre into the central leadership to invigorate the party and maintain its relevance in modern China, they are not yet prepared to relinquish ultimate power. This is the dilemma posed by the upcoming generational change, and one that ultimately may lead to tensions within the party.

Characteristics of the 'Fourth Generation'

The Fourth Generation of leaders are represented by figures like Vice President Hu Jintao, Vice Prime Ministers Wen Jiabao and Wu Bangguo and Politburo alternate Zeng Qinghong. Although a diverse group of individuals, most of these officials were born in the late 1930s and early 1940s, are well educated, hail mostly from China's east coast and appear committed to economic reforms — something not to be mistaken as "pro-Western."

Over the past few years, the Fourth Generation has begun to ascend across China at the local, provincial and, more recently, ministerial levels. The coming year will be the time that this generation finally asserts itself as the core of political power and steps into the top government roles in Beijing.

Like their immediate predecessors, these men — and a handful of women — are generally technocrats, having risen through both central and local bureaucracies in career tracks that made use of their specialized educations. Whereas the Third Generation leaders were predominantly engineers, the Fourth Generation includes a number of economists and a smattering of lawyers. This trend toward social science is likely to continue, possibly reshaping China's future political norms.

Power is still highly personalized in China, and personal relations remain the surest way to get ahead. During the more collegial administrations of Deng and Jiang, having ties to more than one senior leader has been the key to success. For an aspiring politician, having only a single sponsor actually may be viewed as a detriment rather than a strength. Protégés often have found their careers stifled when their mentors or sponsors fell afoul of other, more powerful factions. The Fourth Generation leaders have seen how internal party factions "solve" their problems, and they will be more attuned to the need to play multiple sides in their attempts to scale the ranks and — once in power — ensure they are not removed.

A binding characteristic of the incoming generation is their shared experience in the Cultural Revolution, which rocked China from 1966 to 1969. While some were members of the Red Guard and others were on the receiving end of its purges and rectification campaigns, most came out of the period with delayed educations and disrupted lives. The ideological and physical chaos of the Cultural Revolution left many of this generation less dogmatic and more pragmatic than their predecessors and perhaps even somewhat cynical about party ideals.

In a sense, these are political reformers. They do not seek to abandon China's system of leadership or their party, but rather to reform and revitalize the party from the inside, making it more relevant to the current social and economic situation. They are likely to build upon existing programs — ranging from the crackdown on corruption and nepotism among party functionaries to Jiang's calls for opening party ranks to private business executives and entrepreneurs. They view the party as a means of stabilizing and controlling China's vast population and strengthening the nation. The party, therefore, is viewed as a tool — not as a goal in and of itself — so changes in party structure, membership and operations are quite possible over time.

The Fourth Generation also is committed to China's economic reforms and restructuring. This is not due to a "pro-West" ideology, as some may believe. This is a generation of new nationalists whose goals are based less on revolutionary Communist zeal than on bringing China as a nation into a new era. The commitment to economic reforms, then, does not signal the abandonment of old political goals but a policy of moving forward and improving national strength and stability.

The Fourth Generation leaders have seen China rise from a low point during the 1960s to become a major economic power in East Asia — one now beginning to challenge Japan for regional dominance. In the past 18 months, China has gained entry into the World Trade Organization, been named host of the 2008 Summer Olympics and demonstrated an ability to stand up to the United States after a collision between a Chinese fighter jet and a U.S. surveillance aircraft. Yet in the past six months, the nation has gone from riding an international high to finding itself surrounded by U.S. forces in Central and Southeast Asia; seeing Russia, its tentative strategic partner, warming up to Europe and the United States; and recognizing that its political and economic influence is waning.

This decline in prestige, and concomitant loss of influence, will drive the new leaders to accelerate programs designed to strengthen China economically and militarily. This, however, must be carefully balanced with the inevitable social disruptions caused by the systemic overhaul of China's economy and society.

China's Future Direction

China's domestic situation, emerging needs and the regional and global environment will shape the Fourth Generation leaders as much as they will shape these issues. China's economy and security, both internal and external, are intimately linked. The Fourth Generation is taking power at a time of widespread change and potential instability: Social unrest, rampant corruption and widespread economic disparity are weakening the central government's authority and control.

The new leaders face an increasingly aware public, and their actions will be monitored closely both at home and broad. Social dissatisfaction and international strictures are making it ever more important to be seen as a "clean" politician, one with fresh ideas and charisma.

The importance of public opinion was evident in Beijing's initial choice of Jiang Zemin rather than Li Peng as party general secretary. A big factor in the decision was the image that Jiang, who was mayor of economically vibrant Shanghai, would create both within and beyond China. Though he was a loyal and ideologically consistent senior official, Li Peng was passed over mainly because he was viewed at home and abroad as a hard-line figure responsible for the Tiananmen crisis — someone who would only infuriate the populace if he were promoted.

Such ideas are likely even more important now, as economic reforms raise the internal and external pressure on Beijing. Widespread public dissatisfaction with the effects of economic reform; government corruption, nepotism and mismanagement; and the widening wealth gap between the regions require the central leaders to find replacements who will appease, quell or at least not further infuriate the masses.

Beijing has realized the damage that corrupt and unpopular leaders can do to the party's credibility. The government therefore has launched a highly publicized anti-corruption crackdown in recent years. By publicizing and punishing misconduct, mismanagement and graft among government officials, the central leadership is trying to reinforce its control over regional and local leaders while rebuilding trust among the general population.

As China's new leaders balance internal and external relations, their policies may grow more cautious. Afraid of rocking the boat and strongly influenced by older officials from behind the scenes, the new leaders promise little radical change — at least in the short run. Making changes too swiftly risks social upheaval, but ironically, acting too slowly runs the risk that the roots of problems will go unaddressed, leading to a bigger explosion later.

The solution to this precarious balancing act is already emerging. Beijing is cultivating a new nationalism — one designed to rally the masses around the central leadership while carefully controlling that nationalism to avoid irreparably damaging global economic ties.

The pace of economic reforms that China's new leaders will be able or willing to sustain will hinge heavily on social stability. Economic reforms are a road to prosperity and power, not an end in themselves. For Chinese leaders of any generation, maintaining the integrity of the state is always the core responsibility — and the Communist Party is the central organ of political, economic and social power.

Even if Beijing's new leaders are able to maintain the phenomenal growth rates of the past decade (though these are likely highly exaggerated), this could further weaken the centralized system. China's economic growth has not been spread equally but has remained concentrated in the coastal regions, particularly in the southeast.

This regional disparity is a long thread winding through Chinese history, and it often has led to the collapse of central authority. It also explains much of Beijing's recent focus on the western and central provinces. Chinese leaders will continue to find it imperative to expand foreign involvement in the oil and gas sectors and in infrastructure development of the west, in order to more evenly spread the benefits of the economic reform and opening program.

Agriculture, energy and high-tech are all sectors that Beijing views as vital. The government recognizes the need for foreign assistance in tapping its energy resources and building up its technology base, but it also wants to keep tight control over these industries.

These domestic pressures are compounded by an international system that had yet to reach equilibrium after the Cold War and was thrown into disarray by the Sept. 11 attacks on the United States. The geopolitical balance between Washington and Moscow that kept either from becoming a globally dominant force no longer exists. U.S. forces are in Central, South and Southeast Asia, Russia is sidling up to Washington and Japan is rapidly shifting the role and reach of its heretofore purely defensive Self Defense Forces. Complicating matters are Japan's ever more apparent financial troubles, which threaten to draw the rest of Asia — including China — into another economic crisis.

The encroaching U.S. military presence and Russia's apparent slide to the West will prompt the military to become more assertive in Chinese politics in coming years. Currently, only two career military officers have seats in the Politburo (an historic low); neither belongs to the Standing Committee, and both expected to retire. With Jiang likely to retain his position as head of the Central Military Commission, he will seek to maintain his influence over the new leaders by bringing more military figures into the government.

Despite changes in the police force and the creation of elite anti-riot squads in major cities, it ultimately will fall to the People's Liberation Army to quell any major internal unrest — just as it did over a decade ago in Beijing at Tiananmen.

The military, then, has a vested interest in tempering the pace of economic reform. However, military leaders also advocate continued economic growth, which now pays for much of their budget. Moreover, while the military elite may believe that future conflict is inevitable, they have a long way to go to bring their forces up to specs to compete with other modern armed forces.

As the Fourth Generation takes power in Beijing, China faces an unstable global environment. To mitigate the overwhelming international influence of the United States, these new leaders will continue to seek to expand China's ties with Europe and Asia while reaching out to the Middle East, Africa and even Latin America.

It will be domestic pressures, however, that ultimately drive the choices of the new regime.

Beijing's Tibetan Dilemma
March 17, 2008

Each March, there are demonstrations in Tibet commemorating a 1959 uprising against the Chinese occupation. This year, the normally small and easily contained demonstration progressed from marches to shouting, to rock-throwing, to burning things and attacking ethnic Chinese stores and businesses. The Han Chinese represent the economic elite in Tibet — as well as the political, military and security elite. The outburst was clearly focused on the economic dominance of the Chinese but wasn't confined to it.

What was extraordinary about the rioting was that it happened at all. The Chinese have confronted and contained Tibetan unrest with relative ease for years. Their normal approach would have been to seal off the area of unrest, arrest as many of the participants as possible and later release those deemed not to represent a particular threat. This time, the Chinese failed to contain events. Indeed, the protests turned into an international media spectacle, with China appearing to be simultaneously repressive and helpless — the worst of both worlds.

The reason the Chinese pulled their punches this time around is undoubtedly the upcoming Olympics in Beijing. China has tried to portray a dual image in the months leading up to the games. On the one hand, the government has tried to appear extremely vigilant on terrorism, hoping to allay tourist concerns. The Chinese, for example, went out of their way to showcase a foiled March 7 hijacking of a flight to Beijing from Urumqi in Xinjiang province. The Chinese claimed that the hijackers intended to crash the plane. At the same time, Beijing released new information on a January capture of a Xinjiang Islamist cell that allegedly was plotting attacks against the Olympics.

The Tibetan situation is another matter. The Dalai Lama, the exiled spiritual leader of Tibet in India, is extraordinarily respected and popular in the West. The question of Tibetan autonomy has been taken up by public figures in the West, and some companies have indicated they would not participate in sponsoring the Olympics because of the Tibetan issue. Tibet is not a shared concern, like terrorism, but rather an issue that puts China and the West at odds. Therefore, the Chinese didn't want to be seen as conducting another Tiananmen Square in Tibet. They were hoping that it would die down on its own, leaving them time later to deal with the instigators. Instead it got out of hand, in a way very visible to the international media.

Tibet matters to the Chinese geopolitically because it provides a buffer with India and allows Chinese military power to be anchored in the Himalayas. So long as that boundary is maintained, the Chinese are secure in the Southwest. Tibetan independence would shatter that security. Should an independent Tibet — obviously hostile to China after years of occupation — fall into an alliance with India, the regional balance would shift. There is, therefore, no way that the Chinese are going to give Tibet independence and they are unlikely to increase its autonomy. In fact, they have built a new rail line into Tibet that was intended to allow Han Chinese to move there more easily — an attempt to change Tibet's demographics and tie it even closer to China.

The Chinese are sensitive about their international image. They are even more concerned with their long-term geopolitical interests and with threats to those interests. The Chinese government has attempted to portray the uprising as a conspiracy undertaken by the Dalai Lama, rather than as a spontaneous rising. The Chinese have not mentioned this, but they undoubtedly remember the "color" revolutions in the former Soviet Union. During those uprisings, the Russian government accused the United States of fomenting unrest in countries such as Ukraine in order to weaken Russia geopolitically.

The Chinese government is not big on the concept of "spontaneous demonstrations" and undoubtedly is searching for explanations. Having identified the source of the trouble with the Dalai Lama, it is a short step to accusing India — or the United States — of having sparked the rising. Both have been official or unofficial allies of the Dalai Lama.

This is not the way the Chinese wanted the run-up to the Olympics to go. Their intention was to showcase the new China. But the international spotlight they have invited encourages everyone with a grievance — and there are plenty such in China — to step forward at a time when the government has to be unusually restrained in its response.

Undoubtedly the Tibetan situation is being watched carefully in Beijing. Xinjiang militants are one thing — Tibetan riots are another. But should this unrest move into China proper, the Olympics will have posed a problem that the Chinese government didn't anticipate when it came up with the idea.

China and the Enduring Uighurs
Aug. 6, 2008

On Aug. 4, four days before the start of the Beijing Olympics, two ethnic Uighurs drove a stolen dump truck into a group of some 70 Chinese border police in the town of Kashi in Xinjiang, killing at least 16 of the officers. The attackers carried knives and homemade explosive devices and had also written manifestos in which they expressed their commitment to jihad in Xinjiang. The incident occurred just days after a group calling itself the Turkistan Islamic Party (TIP) claimed responsibility for a series of recent attacks and security incidents in China and warned of further attacks targeting the Olympics.

Chinese authorities linked the Aug. 4 attack to transnational jihadists, suggesting the involvement of the East Turkistan Islamic Movement (ETIM), which Beijing has warned is the biggest terrorist threat to China and the Olympics. Despite the Chinese warnings and TIP claims and the intensified focus on the Uighurs because of the Aug. 4 attack, there is still much confusion over just who these Uighur or Turkistani militants are.

The Uighurs, a predominately Muslim Turkic ethnic group largely centered in China's northwestern Xinjiang Uighur Autonomous Region, have their own culture, language and written script distinct from their Han Chinese counterparts. Uighur ethnic nationalists and Islamist separatists have risen several times to challenge Chinese control over Xinjiang, but the Uighur independence movement remains fractured and frequently at odds with itself. However, recent evolutions within the Islamist militant Uighur movement, including growing links with transnational jihadist groups in Central and Southwest Asia, may represent a renewed threat to security in China.

Origins in Xinjiang

Uighur nationalism traces its origins back to a broader Turkistan, stretching through much of modern day Xinjiang (so-called "East Turkistan") and into Central Asia. East Turkistan was conquered by the Manchus in the mid-1700s and, after decades of struggle, the territory was annexed by China, which later renamed it Xinjiang, or "New Territories." A modern nation-state calling itself East Turkistan arose in Xinjiang in the chaotic transition from imperial China to Communist China, lasting for two brief periods from 1933 to 1934 and from 1944 to 1949. Since that time, "East Turkistan" has been, more or less, an integral part of the People's Republic of China.

The evolution of militant Uighur separatism — and particularly Islamist-based separatism — has been shaped over time by both domestic and foreign developments. In 1940, Hizbul Islam Li-Turkistan (Islamic Party of Turkistan or Turkistan Islamic Movement) emerged in Xinjiang, spearheading a series of unsuccessful uprisings from the

1940s through 1952, first against local warlords and later against the Communist Chinese.

In 1956, as the "Hundred Flowers" was blooming in China's eastern cities, and intellectuals were (very briefly) allowed to air their complaints and suggestions for China's political and social development, a new leadership emerged among the Uighur Islamist nationalists, changing the focus from "Turkistan" to the more specific "East Turkistan," or Xinjiang. Following another failed uprising, the Islamist Uighur movement faded away for several decades, with only minor sparks flaring during the chaos of the Cultural Revolution.

In 1979, as Deng Xiaoping was launching China's economic opening and reform, there was a coinciding period of Islamic and ethnic revival in Xinjiang, reflecting the relative openness of China at the time. During this time, one of the original founders of Hizbul Islam Li-Turkistan, Abdul Hakeem, was released from prison and set up underground religious schools. Among his pupils in the 1980s was Hasan Mahsum, who would go on to found ETIM.

The 1980s were a chaotic period in Xinjiang, with ethnic and religious revivalism, a growing student movement, and public opposition to China's nuclear testing at Lop Nor. Uighur student protests were more a reflection of the growing student activism in China as a whole (culminating in the 1989 Tiananmen Square incident) than a resurgence of Uighur separatism, but they coincided with a general movement in Xinjiang to promote literacy and to refocus on religious and ethnic heritage. Amid this revival, several Uighur separatist or Islamist militant movements emerged.

A critical moment occurred in April 1990, when an offshoot of the Uighur Islamist militant movement was discovered plotting an uprising in Xinjiang. The April 5 so-called "Baren Incident" (named for the city where militants and their supporters faced off against Chinese security forces) led Beijing to launch dragnet operations in the region, arresting known, suspected or potential troublemakers — a pattern that would be repeated through the "Strike Hard" campaigns of the 1990s. Many of the Uighurs caught up in these security campaigns, including Mahsum, began to share, refine and shape their ideology in prisons, taking on more radical tendencies and creating networks of relations that could be called upon later. From 1995 to 1997, the struggle in Xinjiang reached its peak, with increasingly frequent attacks by militants in Xinjiang and equally intensified security countermeasures by Beijing.

It was also at this time that China formed the Shanghai Cooperation Organization (SCO), enlisting Central Asian assistance in cracking down on Uighur militants, many of whom had fled China. In some ways this plan backfired, as it provided common cause between the Uighurs and Central Asian militants, and forced some Uighur Islamist militants further west, to Pakistan and Afghanistan, where they would link up with the Taliban, al Qaeda, and the Islamic Movement of Uzbekistan (IMU), among others.

Among those leaving China was Mahsum, who tried to rally support from the Uighur diaspora in Saudi Arabia, Pakistan and Turkey but was rebuffed. Mahsum and a small group of followers headed to Central Asia and ultimately Afghanistan, where he established ETIM as a direct successor to his former teacher's Hizbul Islam Li-Turkistan. By 1998, Kabul-based ETIM began recruiting and training Uighur militants while expanding ties with the emerging jihadist movement in the region, dropping the "East" from its name to reflect these deepening ties. Until the U.S. invasion of Afghanistan in 2001, ETIM focused on recruiting and training Uighur militants at a camp run by Mahsum and Abdul Haq, who is cited by TIP now as its spiritual leader.

With the U.S. attack on Afghanistan in October 2001, ETIM was routed and its remnants fled to Central Asia and Pakistan. In January 2002, Mahsum tried to distance ETIM from al Qaeda in an attempt to avoid having the Uighur movement come under U.S. guns. It did not work. In September 2002, the United States declared ETIM a terrorist organization at the behest of China. A year later, ETIM experienced what seemed to be its last gasps, with a joint U.S.-Pakistani operation in South Waziristan in October 2003 killing Hasan Mahsum.

A Movement Reborn?

Following Mahsum's death, a leaderless ETIM continued to interact with the Taliban and various Central Asian militants, particularly Uzbeks, and slowly reformed into a more coherent core in the Pakistan/Afghanistan frontier. In 2005, there were stirrings of this new Uighur Islamist militant group, the Turkistan Islamic Party (TIP), which established a robust presence on the Internet, posting histories of the Uighur/Turkistan people in western China and Central Asia and inspirational videos featuring Mahsum. In 2006, a new video surfaced calling for jihad in Xinjiang, and later that year there were reports that remnants of ETIM had begun re-forming and moving back into far western Xinjiang.

It was also around this time that Beijing began raising the specter of ETIM targeting the Olympics — a move seen at the time as primarily an excuse for stricter security controls. In early January 2007, Beijing raided a camp of suspected ETIM militants near the Xinjiang border with Tajikistan, and a year later raided another suspected camp in Urumchi, uncovering a plot to carry out attacks during the Olympics. This was followed in March by a reported attempt by Uighur militants to down a Chinese airliner with gasoline smuggled aboard in soda cans.

Publicly, the Uighur militant issue was quickly swept aside by the Tibetan uprising in March, leaving nearly unnoticed an anti-government protest in Hotan and a series of counterterrorism raids by Chinese security forces in late March and early April that reportedly found evidence of more specific plots to attack Beijing and Shanghai during the Olympics.

In the midst of this security campaign, TIP released a video, not disseminated widely until late June, in which spokesman Commander Seyfullah laid out a list of grievances against Beijing and cited Abdul Haq as calling on Uighur Islamist militants to begin strikes against China. The video also complained that the "U.S.-led Western countries listed the Turkistan Islamic Party as one of the international terrorist organizations," an apparent reference to the United States' 2002 listing of the ETIM on the terrorist exclusion list.

In addition to linking the TIP to the ETIM, the April video also revealed some elements of the movement's evolution since the death of Mahsum. Rather than the typical rhetoric of groups closely linked to the Wahhabi ideology of al Qaeda, TIP listed its grievances against Beijing in an almost lawyer-like fashion, following more closely the pattern of Hizb al-Tahrir (HT), a movement active in Central Asia advocating nonviolent struggle against corrupt regimes and promoting the return of Islamic rule. Although HT officially renounces violence as a tool of political change, it has provided an abundance of zealous and impatient idealists who are often recruited by more active militant organizations.

The blending of the HT ideologies with the underlying principles of Turkistan independence reflects the melding of the Uighur Islamist militancy with wider Central Asian Islamist movements. Fractures in HT, emerging in 2005 and expanding thereafter, may also have contributed to the evolution of TIP's ideology; breakaway elements of HT argued that the nonviolent methods espoused by HT were no longer effective.

What appears to be emerging is a Turkistan Islamist movement with links in Central Asia, stretching back to Afghanistan and Pakistan, blending Taliban training, transnational jihadist experiential learning, HT frameworks and recruiting, and Central Asian ties for support and shelter. This is a very different entity than China has faced in the past. If the TIP follows the examples set by the global jihadist movement, it will become an entity with a small core leadership based far from its primary field of operations guiding (ideologically but not necessarily operationally) a number of small grassroots militant cells.

The network will be diffuse, with cells operating relatively independently with minimal knowledge or communication among them and focused on localized goals based on their training, skills and commitment. This would make the TIP less of a strategic threat, since it would be unable to rally large numbers of fighters in a single or sustained operation, but it would also be more difficult to fight, since Beijing would be unable to use information from raiding one cell to find another.

This appears to be exactly what we are seeing now. The central TIP core uses the Internet and videos as psychological tools to trigger a reaction from Beijing and inspire militants without exposing itself to detection or capture. On July 25, TIP released a video claiming responsibility for a series of attacks in China, including bus bombings in Kunming, a bus fire in Shanghai and a tractor bombing in Wenzhou. While these claims were almost certainly exaggerated, the Aug. 4 attack in Xinjiang suddenly refocused attention on the TIP and its earlier threats.

Further complicating things for Beijing are the transnational linkages ETIM forged and TIP has maintained. The Turkistan movement includes not only China's Uighurs but also crosses into Uzbekistan, parts of Kazakhstan, Kyrgyzstan and Tajikistan and spreads back through Central Asia all the way to Turkey. These linkages may have been the focus of quiet security warnings beginning around March that Afghan, Middle Eastern and Central Asian migrants and tourists were spotted carrying out surveillance of schools, hotels and government buildings in Beijing and Shanghai — possibly part of an attack cycle.

The alleged activities seem to fit a pattern within the international jihadist movement of paying more attention to China. Islamists have considered China something less imperialistic, and thus less threatening, than the United States and European powers, but this began changing with the launch of the SCO, and the trend has been accelerating with China's expanded involvement in Africa and Central Asia and its continued support for Pakistan's government. China's rising profile among Islamists has coincided with the rebirth of the Uighur Islamist militant movement just as Beijing embarks on one of its most significant security events: the Summer Olympics.

Whatever name it may go by today — be it Hizbul Islam Li-Turkistan, the East Turkistan Islamic Movement or the Turkistan Islamic Party — the Uighur Islamist militant movement remains a security threat to Beijing. And in its current incarnation, drawing on internationalist resources and experiences and sporting a more diffuse structure, the Uighur militancy may well be getting a second wind.

Internal Divisions and the Chinese Stimulus Plan
Feb. 23, 2009

Due in large part to fears of dire consequences if nothing were done to tackle the economic crisis, China rushed through a 4 trillion yuan ($586 billion) economic stimulus package in November 2008. The plan cobbled together existing and new initiatives focused on massive infrastructure development projects (designed, among other things, to soak up surplus steel, cement and labor capacity), tax cuts, green energy programs, and rural development.

Ever since the package was passed in November, Beijing has recited the mantra of the need to shift China's economy from its heavy dependence on exports to one more driven by domestic consumption. But now that the sense of immediate crisis has passed, the stimulus policies are being rethought — and in an unusual development for China, they are being vigorously debated in the Chinese media.

Debating the Stimulus Package

In a country where media restrictions are tightening and private commentary on government officials and actions in blogs and online forums is being curtailed, it is quite remarkable that major Chinese newspaper editorials are taking the lead in questioning aspects of the stimulus package.

The question of stimulating rural consumption versus focusing the stimulus on the more economically active coastal regions has been the subject of particularly fierce debate. Some editorials have argued that encouraging rural consumption at a time of higher unemployment is building a bigger problem for the future. This argument maintains that rural laborers — particularly migrant workers — earn only a small amount of money, and that while having them spend their meager savings now might keep gross domestic product up in the short term, it will drain the laborers' reserves and create a bigger social problem down the road. Others argue that the migrant and rural populations are underdeveloped and incapable of sustained spending, and that pumping stimulus yuan into the countryside is a misallocation of money that could be better spent supporting the urban middle class, in theory creating jobs through increased middle-class consumption of services.

The lack of restrictions on these types of discussions suggests that the debate is occurring with government approval, in a reflection of debates within the Communist Party of China (CPC) and the government itself. Despite debate in the Chinese press, Beijing continues to present a unified public face on the handling of the economic crisis, regardless of internal factional debates. Maintaining Party control remains the primary goal of Party officials; even if they disagree over policies, they recognize the importance of showing that the Party remains in charge.

But, as the dueling editorial pages reveal, the Party is not unified in its assessment of the economic crisis or the recovery program. The show of unity masks a power struggle raging between competing interests within the Party. In many ways, this is not a new struggle; there are always officials jockeying for power for themselves and for their protégés. But the depth of the economic crisis in China and the rising fears of social unrest — not only from the migrant laborers, but also from militants or separatists in Tibet and Xinjiang and from "hostile forces" like the Falun Gong, pro-Democracy advocates and foreign intelligence services — have added urgency to long-standing debates over economic and social policies.

In China, decision-making falls to the president and the premier, currently Hu Jintao and Wen Jiabao respectively. They do not wield the power of past leaders like Mao Zedong or Deng Xiaoping, however, and instead are much more reliant on balancing competing interests than on dictating policy.

Party and Government Factions

Hu and Wen face numerous factions among the Chinese elite. Many officials are considered parts of several different factional affiliations based on age, background, education or family heritage. Boiled down, the struggle over the stimulus plan pits two competing views of the core of the Chinese economy. One sees economic strength and social stability centered on China's massive rural population, while another sees China's strength and future in the coastal urban areas, in manufacturing and global trade.

Two key figures in the Standing Committee of the Politburo (the center of political power in China), Vice President Xi Jinping and Vice Premier Li Keqiang, highlight this struggle. These two are considered the core of the fifth-generation leadership, and have been tapped to succeed Hu and Wen as China's next leaders. They also represent radically different backgrounds.

Li is a protege of Hu and rose from the China Youth League, where Hu has built a strong support base. Li represents a newer generation of Chinese leaders, educated in economics and trained in less-developed provinces. (Li held key positions in Henan and Liaoning provinces.) Xi, on the other hand, is a "princeling." The son of a former vice premier, he trained as an engineer and served primarily in the coastal export-oriented areas, including Hebei, Fujian and Zhejiang provinces and Shanghai.

In a way, Li and Xi represent different proposals for China's economic recovery and future. Li is a stronger supporter of the recentralization of economic control sought by Hu, a weakening of the regional economic power bases, and a focus on consolidating Chinese industry in a centrally planned manner while spending government money on rural development and urbanization of China's interior. Xi represents the view followed by former President Jiang Zemin and descended from the policies of Deng. Under that view, economic activity and growth should be encouraged and largely freed from central direction, and if the coastal provinces grow first and faster, that is just fine; eventually the money, technology and employment will move inland.

Inland vs. the Coast

In many ways, these two views reflect long-standing economic arguments in China — namely, the constant struggle to balance the coastal trade-based economy and the interior agriculture-dominated economy. The former is smaller but wealthier, with stronger ties abroad — and therefore more political power to lobby for preferential treatment. The latter is much larger, but more isolated from the international community — and in Chinese history, frequently the source of instability and revolt in times of stress. These tensions have contributed to the decline of dynasties in centuries past, opening the space for foreign interference in Chinese internal politics. China's leaders are well aware of the constant stresses between rural and coastal China, but maintaining a balance has been an ongoing struggle.

Throughout Chinese history, there is a repeating pattern of dynastic rise and decline. Dynasties start strong and powerful, usually through conquest. They then consolidate power and exert strong control from the center. But due to the sheer size of China's territory and population, maintaining central control requires the steady expansion of a bureaucracy that spreads from the center through the various administrative divisions down to the local villages. Over time, the bureaucracy itself begins to usurp power, as its serves as the collector of taxes, distributor of government funds and local arbiter of policy and rights. And as the bureaucracy grows stronger, the center weakens.

Regional differences in population, tax base and economic models start to fragment the bureaucracy, leading to economic (and at times military) fiefdoms. This triggers a strong response from the center as it tries to regain control. Following a period of instability, which often involves foreign interference and/or intervention, a new center is formed, once again exerting strong centralized authority.

This cycle played out in the mid-1600s, as the Ming Dynasty fell into decline and the Manchus (who took on the moniker Qing) swept in to create a new centralized authority. It played out again as the Qing Dynasty declined in the latter half of the 1800s and ultimately was replaced — after an extended period of instability — by the CPC in 1949, ushering in another period of strong centralized control. Once again, a more powerful regional bureaucracy is testing that centralized control.

The economic reforms initiated by Deng Xiaoping at the end of the 1970s led to a three-decade decline of central authority, as economic decision-making and power devolved to the regional and local leadership and the export-oriented coastal provinces became the center of economic activity and power in China. Attempts by the central government to regain some authority over the direction of coastal authorities were repeatedly ignored (or worse), but so long as there was growth in China and relative social stability, this was tolerated.

With Hu's rise to power, however, there was a new push from the center to rein in the worst of excesses by the coastal leaders and business interests and refocus attention on China's rural population, which was growing increasingly disenfranchised due to the widening urban-rural economic gap. In 2007 and early 2008, Hu finally gained traction with his economic policies. The Chinese government subsequently sought to slow an overheating economy while focusing on the consolidation of industry and the establishment of "superministries" at the center to coordinate economic activity. It also intended to put inland rural interests on par with — if not above — coastal urban interests. When the superministries were formed in 2008, however, it became apparent that Hu was not omnipotent. Resistance to his plans was abundantly evident, illustrating the power of the entrenched bureaucratic interests.

Economic Crisis and the Stimulus Plan

The economic program of recentralization and the attempt to slow the overheating economy came to a screeching halt in July 2008, as skyrocketing commodity prices fueled inflation and strained government budgets. The first victim was China's yuan policy. The steady, relatively predictable appreciation of the yuan came to a stop. Its value stagnated, and there is now pressure for a slight depreciation to encourage exports. But as Beijing began shaping its economic stimulus package, it became clear that the program would be a mix of policies, representing differing factions seeking to secure their own interests in the recovery plan.

The emerging program, then, revealed conflicting interests and policies. Money and incentives were offered to feed the low-skill export industry (located primarily in the southeastern coastal provinces) as well as to encourage a shift in production from the coast to the interior. A drive was initiated to reduce redundancies, particularly in heavy industries, and at the same time funding was increased to keep those often-bloated industrial sectors afloat. Overall, the stimulus represents a collection of competing initiatives, reflecting the differences among the factions. Entrenched princelings simply want to keep money moving and employment levels up in anticipation of a resurgence in global consumption and the revitalization of the export-based economic growth path. Meanwhile, the rural faction seeks to accelerate economic restructuring, reduce dependence on the export-oriented coastal provinces, and move economic activity and attention to the vastly underdeveloped interior.

Higher unemployment among the rural labor force is "proving" each faction's case. To the princelings, it shows the importance of the export sector in maintaining social stability and economic growth. To the rural faction, it emphasizes the dangers of overreliance on a thin coastal strip of cheap, low-skill labor and a widening wealth gap.

Fighting it Out in the Media

With conflicting paths now running in tandem, competing Party officials are seeking traction and support for their programs without showing division within the core Party apparatus by turning to a traditional method: the media and editorials. During the Cultural

Revolution, which itself was a violent debate about the fundamental economic policies of the People's Republic of China, the Party core appeared united, despite major divisions. The debate played out not in the halls of the National People's Congress or in press statements, but instead in big-character posters plastered around Beijing and other cities, promoting competing policies and criticizing others.

In modern China, big posters are a thing of the past, replaced by newspaper editorials. While the Party center appears united in this time of economic crisis, the divisions are seen more acutely in the competing editorials published in state and local newspapers and on influential blogs and Web discussion forums. It is here that the depth of competition and debate so well hidden among the members of the Politburo can be seen, and it is here that it becomes clear the Chinese are no more united in their policy approach than the leaders of more democratic countries, where policy debates are more public.

The current political crisis has certainly not reached the levels of the Cultural Revolution, and China no longer has a Mao — or even a Deng — to serve as a single pole around which to wage factional struggles. The current leadership is much more attuned to the need to cooperate and compromise — and even Mao's methods would often include opportunities for "wayward" officials to come around and cooperate with Mao's plans. But a recognition of the need to cooperate, and an agreement that the first priority is maintenance of the Party as the sole core of Chinese power (followed closely by the need to maintain social stability to ensure the primary goal), doesn't guarantee that things can't get out of control.

The sudden halt to various economic initiatives in July 2008 showed just how critical the emerging crisis was. If commodity prices had not started slacking off a month later, the political crisis in Beijing might have gotten much more intense. Despite competition, the various factions want the Party to remain in power as the sole authority, but their disagreements on how to do this become much clearer during a crisis. Currently, it is the question of China's migrant labor force and the potential for social unrest that is both keeping the Party center united and causing the most confrontation over the best-path policies to be pursued. If the economic stimulus package fails to do its job, or if external factors leave China lagging and social problems rising, the internal party fighting could once again grow intense.

At present, there is a sense among China's leaders that this crisis is manageable. If their attitude once again shifts to abject fear, the question may be less about how to compromise on economic strategy than how to stop a competing faction from bringing ruin to Party and country through ill-thought-out policies. Compromise is acceptable when it means the survival of the Party, but if one faction views the actions of another as fundamentally detrimental to the authority and strength of the Party, then a more active and decisive struggle becomes the ideal choice. After all, it is better to remove a gangrenous limb than to allow the infection to spread and kill the whole organism.

That crisis is not now upon China's leaders, but things nearly reached that level last summer. There were numerous rumors from Beijing that Wen, who is responsible for China's economic policies, was going to be sacked — an extreme move given his popularity with the common Chinese. This was staved off or delayed by the fortuitous timing of the rest of the global economic contraction, which brought commodity prices down. For now, China's leaders will continue issuing competing and occasionally contradictory policies, and just as vigorously debating them through the nation's editorials. The government is struggling with resolving the current economic crisis, as well as with the fundamental question of just what a new Chinese economy will look like. And that question goes deeper than money: It goes to the very role of the CPC in China's system.

China's Core Power Struggle
Sept. 16, 2009

History repeats itself, the oft-repeated maxim goes. And in fact, patterns and cycles do exist that show strong underlying similarities over the long term, even where short-term details vary widely. These cycles often reflect geographic constraints on nations, constraints that shape the options available for governance no matter what faction or force is in power.

In China, one of the defining trends has been a cycle of centralization and decentralization of power. A strong centralized political power has trended toward an expanding bureaucracy that ultimately supplants central power. This pattern, which arises to a large extent from China's geography, has left the central leadership weakened and often unable to withstand major stresses. Tracing this cycle over the years, it becomes apparent that today's China is part and parcel of this ongoing pattern.

Geography, Ethnicity and the Central-Local Dynamic

China's population is concentrated in the east and south of the country. This area is roughly bounded by a line stretching from the North Korean border west to Beijing, southwest to the city of Chengdu in Sichuan province and then southeast to the Vietnamese border. It is here that the average annual rainfall and system of major rivers (the Yellow, Yangtze, and to a lesser degree the Pearl) allow for the majority of Chinese agriculture, and thus Chinese population. Within this area, the largest single ethnic group is the Han Chinese, though numerous smaller ethic groups are scattered throughout border areas or isolated in mountains and valleys. Even the Han themselves are divided by strong regional, nearly mutually incomprehensible dialects; these include Mandarin in the north and Cantonese in the south, along with a range of regional dialects in between.

Unifying and controlling China means first and foremost unifying the Han and controlling the means of agricultural production and

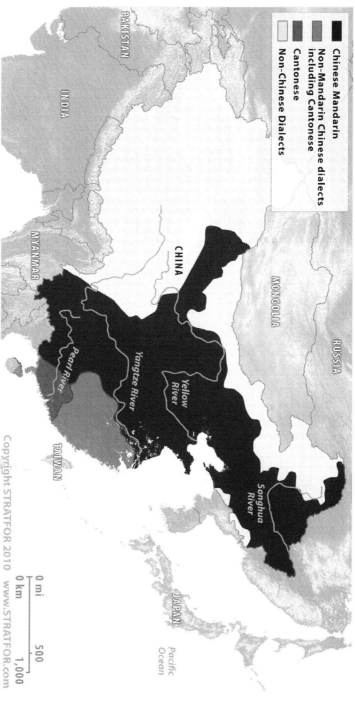

CHINESE DIALECTS

Chinese Mandarin
Non-Mandarin Chinese dialects including Cantonese
Cantonese
Non-Chinese Dialects

CHINA

Songhua River

Yellow River

Yangtze River

Pearl River

PAKISTAN

INDIA

MYANMAR

MONGOLIA

RUSSIA

TAIWAN

JAPAN

Pacific Ocean

0 mi   500
0 km   1,000

Copyright STRATFOR 2010   www.STRATFOR.com

distribution. This has played out as the establishment of a very strong, centralized regime at the beginning of any given dynasty. This unifying power maintains tight control to avoid allowing any challenge from local ethnic minorities or regional rivals. But the geographic core of China is not entirely secure: The sedentary Chinese agricultural society is surrounded to the west and north by vast plains and plateaus easily traversed by enemies — and at the other end of these plains and plateaus were skilled nomadic horsemen. Securing the Chinese core also meant securing the routes of approach — in other words, conquering or at least subduing the buffer states of Tibet, Xinjiang and Mongolia. And this required the expansion of Chinese territory.

Controlling the vast and varied empire, the pathways of taxation and food distribution required more than just a strong centralized regime: It led to the establishment of a large and powerful bureaucracy supported by the wealth of the society designed to take central edicts and implement them down to the regional and local levels. Over time, the bureaucracy itself became more powerful as the central regime grew isolated in the capital, shielded from the day-to-day reality by bureaucratic layers.

So long as China remained insular, this cycle was not a major problem. The center retained nominal control, the bureaucracy controlled the flow of goods and money internally, and the local elite could enjoy the overall protection of the center while coming to accommodation with bureaucrats. Although there were occasional struggles, the system largely held. But things changed when China became more engaged internationally.

China's vast territory meant that, for the most part, it had nearly all the natural resources it needed. When China sought to move beyond subsistence to economic growth, however, it required trade. Much of this trade traditionally was carried out along the old Silk Road routes; the importance of these routes can be seen in the various historical maps of Chinese dynasties. Even when Chinese borders have receded back to the core, they often still included nominal control over the long, thin paths through Xinjiang on to Central Asia. Power and wealth grew along the trade routes, and the central government had to be vigilant to avoid losing control. The isolated nature of the land trade routes, however, also meant the center had to rely on local authorities to provide security and collect taxes and fees. This created a dual-reliance structure, where the central government was reliant on the local authorities, but the local authorities had to be careful not to overstep their bounds or find themselves countered administratively or militarily by the center.

Things grew much more complex when industrialization shifted the balance, and coastal trade became the key route for the accumulation of national wealth. China had many troubles with the Silk Road route, but it did manage to reinforce control through expansion of territory. The more powerful navies of Europe (and eventually Japan and the United States) dominated coastal trade, however. The Europeans outgunned the Chinese army and navy, and thus outsiders set the terms for Chinese economic interaction with the outside world. To increase national security and strength, the center needed to take advantage of the new trading paradigm. But trading ports were concentrated in the southeast, both for geographic reasons and to try to insulate the central government from foreign encroachment.

This isolation of the central government meant several layers of bureaucracy lay between the center and the foreign trading partners, which left responsibility for dealing with foreigners to the bureaucracy and local governments. Through this control of trade, the southeastern local governments and elite eventually obtained more and more power. But they did not use this power to rise against the center, as they still relied on the center to provide other services, like national security. The center, meanwhile, relied on the local elite for money to redistribute to the poorer but more populous interior.

The trade patterns created an economic imbalance, a regional competition for wealth that the center was responsible for managing but unable to fully control. Too much central pressure on the wealthy trading regions along the coast could disrupt the flow of money desperately needed to quell social unrest in the interior and to strengthen national defense against more industrialized nations. The center found itself stuck between the rising dissatisfaction of a poor but heavily populated interior being left behind economically and an increasingly autonomous and self-serving coast that was the only source of revenue needed to appease the interior.

The center became a hostage to geography and trade patterns. Its only options were to cut trade and plunge China into poverty — though at least unified poverty — or to accept the decentralization of power and hope that things could be kept under control until the country could develop the industrial capacity to counter its overdependence on trade and rectify its geographic economic disparities. The power of the wealthy elite usually meant the center chose the latter option, but this left the central government weakened and susceptible to shock. As throughout Chinese history, in the late 19th and early 20th century, the devolution of power and strong disparity of resources and wealth signaled the beginning of the end of a dynasty. External forces could now overwhelm the fragile system, sending the country into political chaos until a new strong central leadership could re-emerge, unify and consolidate power — and begin the cycle all over again as the center began relying on spreading bureaucracy to manage the diverse and dispersed population.

The Central-Local Dynamic in the PRC

This cycle thus has repeated itself in the modern era. The collapse of the Qing Dynasty in the early 20th century reflected the steady degradation of central power and control as the coastal provinces became more connected to the needs of the merchants and their foreign trading partners than to the interests of the inland peasants. The Nationalist government that briefly held power (though it never exerted full control over China) was closely tied to the business elite along the coast. Mao tried to rally these same elites to foment his revolution, but failing that, moved to the interior. There, he raised an army of peasants, exploited the clear sense of socio-economic imbalance, and emerged victorious to found the People's Republic of China (PRC) in 1949.

Like the beginnings of dynasties in the past, Communist China began with tight centralized control, this time focusing on the interests of the peasantry, the redistribution of wealth, and the reclamation of the buffer territories in the west. Attention was also turned toward Taiwan in the east, but any military attempts to finally quell the Nationalist forces that fled to the island were sidelined by the outbreak of the Korean War. The balance of power after the U.S. intervention left mainland China without any real opportunity to seize Taiwan thereafter. Beijing recognized the need to maintain power over the large nation, but wanted to avoid the pitfalls of a large-scale bureaucracy. Instead, it focused on the commune system in a bid to exercise administrative control without (at least in theory) an overly powerful bureaucracy.

Once again, it became clear that China could be fairly secure and isolated from global interactions (in this case the early moves of the Cold War) only so long as it was willing to remain poor. But many among China's elite were not willing to be poor, and even Mao recognized the need to increase the standard of living and spur production to keep China from falling too far behind the rest of the world. The Great Leap Forward (GLF) represented an attempt to kick-start economic growth without weakening central authority or exposing China to the influences and intervention of the outside, but it failed miserably.

The GLF also revealed one of the characteristics of Communist-era Chinese government statistics that continues to today: namely, that official numbers are unreliable. This is largely because local authorities are responsible to those above them (not those below them, as there are no popular elections), and their future is based on whether they meet expectations. Quotas and targets are set from above, and when they are not reached — or prove unreachable — the local officials simply report that the targets have been achieved and exceeded. At each successive layer up the reporting chain, an additional level of overachievement is added into the numbers to impress the immediate superior. And this results in numbers that not only bear little resemblance to reality, but also leaves the central authorities

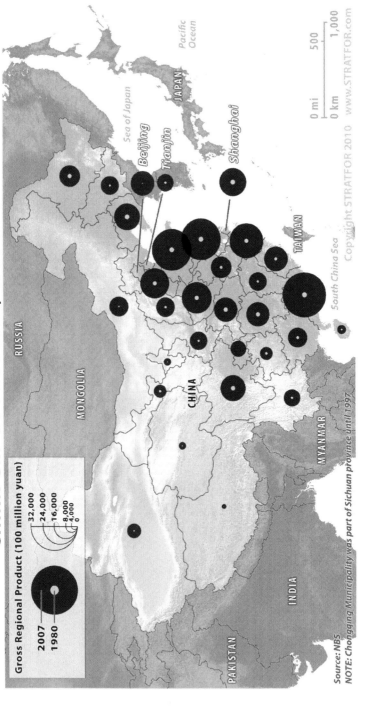

CHINA GRP BY PROVINCE, 1980 AND 2007

Gross Regional Product (100 million yuan)

32,000
24,000
16,000
8,000
4,000
0

2007
1980

Source: NBS

NOTE: Chongqing Municipality was part of Sichuan province until 1997.

Copyright STRATFOR 2010   www.STRATFOR.com

0 mi   500   1,000
0 km

Pacific
Ocean

Sea of Japan

JAPAN

Beijing
Tianjin

Shanghai

TAIWAN

South China Sea

RUSSIA

MONGOLIA

CHINA

MYANMAR

INDIA

PAKISTAN

making decisions based on wildly inaccurate information and expectations. The GLF ultimately failed to bring China roaring into the upper echelons of the modern world. Instead, it brought famine and nearly internal collapse.

In the face of growing economic decentralization and political competition, Mao launched the Great Proletarian Cultural Revolution, or simply the Cultural Revolution, which, beginning in 1966, harnessed students and peasants to target anything deemed even remotely bourgeois or elite by radical ideology.

The subsequent chaos, and the death of Mao, paved the way for Deng Xiaoping's massive reversal of China's economic policies. The Economic Opening and Reform program, beginning with a few select localities in 1978, threw economic initiatives down to the provincial and local governments. It made economic growth a top priority for political advancement. The idea was that though some would get rich more quickly than others, the rising tide would eventually lift all boats. By some measures, this was accurate, and both urban and rural per capita gross regional product did rise. But rather than rising across the board, the cities began rapidly outpacing the countryside, leaving the peasants behind.

Once again, China was creating a polar system, with economic activity and growth largely concentrated along the east and southeast coast, and the interior left lagging far behind. Under former President Jiang Zemin and current President Hu Jintao, different efforts were mounted to address this imbalance. Jiang's attempt at reallocation of resources by fiat — the so-called "Go West" policy — saw little progress, due both to institutional resistance and geographic realities. (While a factory may be able to make cheaper Christmas ornaments in far inland China, the higher transportation costs eliminate that advantage.)

In a more successful bid to reassert central economic control and not lose the means of authority and power in China, the central government under Jiang set its sights on the People's Liberation Army (PLA). The PLA, which had been funding much of its own budget via a massive and sometimes only semiofficial business empire, saw most of its enterprises divested under government orders. Instead, it received a much larger budget from the state. This was a critical program, for if the PLA had continued to be largely economically independent from the state or party, it is unclear where its loyalties would have lain in times of stress.

Hu has sought to regain some control over the economic devolution of power, targeting key industries like steel, coal and oil (with limited success thus far). Hu has also pursued the "Harmonious Society" initiative, which aims to address the socio-economic disparities that the continued decentralization of economic control has exacerbated. This program has been met with plenty of lip service, but little action when it comes to the wealthier regions sacrificing their industry or revenues with less fortunate regions.

The Decentralization Cycle and its Impact Today

Reclaiming centralized economic control is not easy, despite central recognition of the critical need to address the widening disparities across economic regions and the attendant social instability such disparities can stir. The devolution of power, which allowed rapid growth since the economic opening three decades ago, has become an entrenched element of Chinese administration. And as always in Chinese history, the interests of the local officials do not always coincide with central interests. At the same time, the center is unwilling or unable to take too strong a stand against the regional leaders. Beijing fears such action could undermine China's economy and links to foreign investments and trade, trigger stronger local resistance or unrest, and start to pull down central government officials, who have links through the webs of power down to the regional and local levels. The pattern of bureaucracy accumulating more power at the expense of the center thus continues.

Significantly, the current decentralization primarily relates to economic power, not political power. The Communist Party of China (CPC) has been the unchallenged central authority since the founding of the PRC in 1949. The structure of government and political affairs ensures this. Party and government functions are often highly intertwined, to the point of overlapping roles (Hu is both president of China and general secretary of the CPC; he also serves as chairman of both the government's Central Military Commission and the Party's Central Military Commission — in reality, the same commission with two different entities to which it must report). This means that while the local leadership may resist economic dictates from the center if they are not conducive to local interests, at the same time, they are not challenging the central authority of the Party. In fact, they are all members of the same party, or on occasion members of one of the smaller "democratic" parties that are themselves in existence only so long as they support fully the central rule of the CPC.

This Party-state system in the form of two-tier leadership reaches from the top echelons all the way down to the local governments (and even into the state-owned enterprises). Beginning at the provincial level, the party-government dual administrative system is arranged hierarchically. A Party chief at each level holds policymaking authority, while his administrative counterpart (governors, mayors and the like) is responsible for implementing the policy and coordinating the local budgets. In this manner, the Party secretary is often more influential and important than the governor or mayor he serves beside. A good example is Bo Xilai, Party secretary in Chongqing, a city being used as a testing ground for new economic and social policies. One rarely hears of Bo's counterpart, Chongqing Mayor Wang Hongju. In part this is because Bo himself is somewhat of a celebrity, but it is more so because it is the Party secretary who is guiding policy, not the mayor.

In practice, government and Party officials at each level (from province down through the township in most regions) are appointed by the level one step higher. Such institutional arrangements mean local government and Party officials are only responsible to the officials directly above them in the hierarchy, and not to the people they govern. Local governments are rewarded for their economic growth, and thus encouraged to develop their local economies, but this development is rarely designed with any broader national efficiencies or needs in mind. In short, local governments are unintentionally induced to pursue overinvestment and duplication of industry on a national level, because their policies are focused on local growth and personal self-interest.

The lack of an effective accountability and supervision system in the political structure further exacerbates this situation. Local officials frequently hold near-absolute power within their jurisdiction, and the drive for economic growth and the personal power relationships spawn rampant corruption and nepotism. Distrust of the Party at the local level due to corruption and lack of accountability threatens to weaken support for the Party in general, a major concern for the central leadership.

Further complicating matters, personal relationship networks (guanxi) are often as important as Party and government dictates and regulations in determining policy promotion and application. These close webs of relationships serve by default as a check to any major political reforms, or even to initiatives to clean up corruption or try to regain centralized control. Just as the lower-level officials rely on their performance reports and the good graces of those above them, so too do the higher officials increase their own relative power and influence if those in their network below them are seen to perform well, particularly in regard to economic growth or quelling dissent.

These chains are not only vertical: Horizontal relations are built to protect against possible factional fighting or purges. This further complicates any bids at institutional reform, or even cracking down on local corruption (a frequent trigger for localized social instability). This is because investigations easily can move through the networks of relationships and come back to strike at the initial instigators of the investigation, or at least their close allies.

These interlinking networks of guanxi also insulate local officials from stronger action by Beijing to implement more centralized economic controls. Shutting down a steel mill in one city to rectify inefficiencies across the whole sector may make sense from a macroeconomic viewpoint. But the personal links from the local steel mill manager through his local party officers up through the provinces

116

and into the national level means there are many potential individuals along the way with an interest in not undermining the specific local economic interest, even if the local interest does not mesh with a national initiative.

Central government macroeconomic policy pronouncements often fall on deaf ears at the provincial or local levels (even within major state-owned enterprises, like the oil companies). It is one thing to call for a consolidation of the steel industry to make it more profitable; it is quite another for a local official to agree to close the steel plant in his jurisdiction and lose the profits and kickbacks as well as have to deal with the newly unemployed workers. With population movement between provinces — and even between cities within a province — still highly restrained by the household registration system, it is not easy to shift populations to follow jobs. Instead, jobs must be created and maintained for populations.

And this is a major dilemma for Beijing. To manage China, the center must shift a fair amount of administrative and fiscal responsibility to the regional and local level. But this leaves the local leadership more closely tied to its own local interests than to those in other provinces. And at times, this means a local government is more attuned to the interests of a foreign investor or market than to other Chinese provinces, or even the central government. And when things devolve to this level, it often represents the chaotic end of a dynasty.

China's Shaky Statistics
Sept. 21, 2009

The Beijing Municipal Development and Reform Commission announced on Sept. 2 that the gross domestic product (GDP) per capita in Beijing in 2008 was $9,075 and is likely to reach $10,000 by the end of 2009. The 2008 GDP figure is a 12.5 percent increase over the previous year. It also means that the standard of living in Beijing

— if not the rest of China — has reached "above the middle level," according to commission officials (presumably comparing Beijing to other comparably sized cities in the world). But the news did little to enthuse the Chinese people, who are inherently suspicious of official statistics and aware of the frequent discrepancy between government numbers and the reality of their lives.

Indeed, unreliable statistics are nothing new in China, where the methodology of collecting, interpreting and presenting numerical data remains a mystery, not only to the outside world but also within China itself. There are many reasons for this. China is a vast country with a huge population that is difficult to measure simply because of its size and distribution. China also has traditionally used its own statistical tools and techniques in order to avoid apples-to-apples comparisons using international norms and to appear more developed than it may actually be.

Even more important, China's bureaucratic structure, extending from Beijing down to the lowest township level, gives the politicized local governing body too much influence over the local statistical office. This creates an environment in which officials are less interested in "reality" than in climbing the bureaucratic ladder. Motivated by the need to impress their superiors, Chinese bureaucrats at most levels have the incentive to falsify or exaggerate their reporting of statistics, thus giving the central government an unclear picture of the actual situation on the ground.

And when official statistics are unreliable, it is difficult for the central government to gain a sufficient macro view to make accurate socio-economic forecasts — and thus sound policy decisions. This handicap has certainly been evident during the global financial crisis, during which Beijing has had a particularly tough time determining the country's true economic condition and direction. The central government has had such difficulty that it has begun taking steps toward comprehensive statistical reform. This has been attempted before, however, and it is no easy task.

DISCUSSION AND SUSPICIONS OF STATISTICAL DISCREPANCY IN 2009

STATISTICAL ITEMS	TIME	DISCUSSIONS/SUSPICIOUS
Urban Registered Unemployment Rate	1/19/09	China Academy of Social Science estimates it to be 9.4 percent for 2008, while the Ministry of Human Resources and Social Security says it is 4.2 percent.
Purchasing Managers' Index (PMI)	4/6/09	China Federation of Logistics and Purchasing (CFLP) estimates the March PMI to be 52.4, while international agency CLSA Asia-Pacific Markets suggested only 44.8.
Urban Residents' Average Gross Salary	4/10/09	National Bureau of Statistics (NBS) announced the figure in 2008 increased 17.2 percent from 2007, which sharply contradicts public perception.
GDP Growth Rate	5/14/09	The International Energy Agency questioned China's first quarter 2009 growth rate, saying the increased growth rate isn't consistent with falling oil demand.
Industrial Output	6/17/09	National Bureau of Statistics (NBS) estimated May industrial growth to be 8.9 percent, while some scholars suspected it would be only 5 percent. Moreover, the industrial growth figure is inconsistent with declining electricity consumption.
Average Salary of Urban Employees	7/30/09	NBS estimated the average salary of urban employees for the first half of the year to be 14,638 yuan ($2,145), a 12.9 percent increase from the same period of 2008. However, many Internet users joked that their wages were raised by the government and they were unaware of it.
GDP Account	8/4/09	The total value of the GDP account of China's 31 provinces and municipalities is 10 percent higher than the national account by NBS.

Sources: State and Semi-State Agencies, and STRATFOR

A History of 'Reform'

Before the 1960s, official statistics in China, reliable or not, were considered a state secret. During the so-called "Great Leap Forward," beginning in 1958, nearly all figures were highly distorted, as regional officials competed to produce exaggerated information to meet the central government's unreachable goals and to secure their paths through the ranks of government. Economic growth in a given locale was often rewarded by promoting the bearers of good news. This misinformation contributed to the great Chinese famine that lasted from 1959 to 1961 and killed tens of millions of people. Beginning in 1978, to accompany the dramatic socio-economic reforms of Deng Xiaoping's "Opening Up," efforts were made to modernize statistical measurement and standardize the system in China. Despite these efforts, skepticism over statistical reliability would become only more pronounced.

China's entry into the World Trade Organization (WTO) in 2001, while not contingent on its meeting WTO statistical standards, did require China's methods to be compatible with those of its trading partners. In October 2002, Chinese Premier Zhu Rongji made an inspection visit to China's National Bureau of Statistics (NBS) and called for the creation of a "scientific, reliable and efficient modernized statistical system." Since then, the NBS has adopted certain methods that comply with international standards set by the U.N., but given the dependence of local NBS offices on corresponding local governments (more about this later), little progress has been made so far in improving statistical credibility.

When Ma Jiantang took over as head of the NBS in September 2008, just as the global financial crisis intensified, calls increased for China to revamp its statistical processes. The world economic situation created great uncertainty and challenges for the central government, which found it increasingly difficult to gain a big-picture view of the impact of the crisis on China. State-controlled media began to editorialize about the need for such reform, and under growing pressure from the WTO, U.N., International Energy Agency and other international entities, Beijing began to intensify its efforts.

In June 2009, the country's top legislative body (the National People's Congress) revised the 1983 Statistics Law to prevent the falsification of official data and to impose severe penalties on officials who "intervene in government statistical work and manipulate or fabricate data." Smaller improvements are also under way or apparently in the offing. The NBS promises, among other things, to improve the calculation of average urban income by including employees of private enterprises, who were previously excluded from the accounting process (employees of state-owned enterprises typically earn more money).

Processes and Power

China's official statistics are processed by two different and parallel systems: the "integrated statistical system" and the "government department statistical system." The integrated statistical system consists of bureaus at each level, from the NBS in Beijing down to offices in the townships. Although the local bureaus have the authority to validate the numbers, they are heavily influenced by the corresponding local government offices, which have the authority to promote the employees of the bureaus and fund their operations. The other system, called the government department statistical system, consists of statistical departments set up by the ministries of the central government. For example, the Ministry of Finance provides statistics on financial matters; the General Administration of Customs provides statistics on imports and exports; the Ministry of Commerce provides statistics on foreign investment; and the Ministry of Justice provides statistics on legal matters.

Problems arise mainly due to the makeup of the integrated statistical system. Under China's political structure, every government official in the country is appointed rather than elected (except at the county and village level and in some cities). As a result, most government officials as well as public employees are responsible only to their superiors, who determine their promotions and career paths. And the government continues to consider high economic performance the primary prerequisite for official advancement.

Statistical Myths

Criticism of Chinese statistical methods has long been concentrated on economic data, such as the GDP or consumer price index, which the government uses to make macro-economic policies and promote China's image at home and abroad. In February 2009, a debate began regarding the reported decline of electricity consumption along with the reported growth of the GDP. Observers argued that with an expansion of both the service and industrial sectors, electricity consumption must also be increasing. In April, this debate was followed by further suspicion of China's average urban income as reported by the NBS, which claimed the figure in 2008 was 29,229 yuan, an increase of 17.2 percent from 2007. The public suspected the reported figure was significantly inflated (many Internet users joked in their chat rooms that their wages were raised by the government and their employers were unaware of it).

Moreover, figures showing that industrial output grew in May were not consistent with electricity consumption, which declined, and the NBS later attributed the inconsistency to industrial use of energy-saving technologies. Nevertheless, the inconsistency piqued public skepticism, which was further heightened on Aug. 4 when 31 provincial and municipal governments provided their GDP estimates. The estimates added up to 15.38 trillion yuan for the first half of 2009, which is almost 10 percent higher than the 13.99 trillion yuan reported by the NBS.

The debate has also focused on employment data, amid sharply increased social unrest since 2008. Traditionally, local governments conceal social problems such as unemployment and ethnic strife from the central government. It has been reported that local statistical officials help companies "structure" their lay-offs in order for the unemployment numbers to appear lower, thereby rendering the national unemployment rate meaningless. For example, since the onset of the global financial crisis, Chinese workers in some parts of the country have been encouraged to resign by being given higher severance packages than those who are involuntarily laid off, yet those who are laid off are the only workers counted in the unemployment numbers. Unaware of the magnitude of unemployment at the local level, Beijing can be caught by surprise when simmering social instability breaks into a boil. And it is strategically important for the central government to give the people the impression that it is successfully dealing with the localized crisis at hand, lest the social instability widen.

Then there is the matter of statistical standards inconsistency. China's GDP, for example, is measured by comparing one quarter of the year to the same quarter of the previous year (year over year). European countries, Japan and the United States use both year over year and quarter on quarter (comparing one quarter with the preceding quarter), but most countries use quarter-on-quarter comparisons for international purposes. The NBS has announced it will begin using quarter-on-quarter instead of year-over-year figures to report GDP in 2010.

The NBS also accounts for inflation in a manner contrary to international practice. Most countries use either current prices (measuring GDP at prices of the current reporting period) or constant prices (measuring GDP at prices of a base period). The NBS, on the other hand, employs a "comparable-price" method, comparing the prices of new products to those of products from a benchmark year. To employ this method, Chinese companies are given price manuals that cover only certain products. As a result, they have ample opportunity to exaggerate business performance by understating actual inflation.

Similar inconsistencies are seen in other statistical areas. For example, investments in fixed assets, such as real estate, are counted as having been made when the funds are disbursed, rather than when the money is actually spent (meaning many unsold houses are actually counted as investment). Retail sales are counted when a factory ships products to a retailer, not when the retailer sells products to a consumer. Also, unsold products that the retailer returns to the factory, which in turn ships the products to other retailers, are also counted in the sales figures, as are items procured by the government.

By now, the NBS is acutely aware of the urgent need for comprehensive statistical reform, but the NBS can only do so much. The central government is trying to balance a number of urgent statistical needs: It must have better numbers to assess the state of the economy and society so that it can make accurate forecasts and more effective policies; it must manipulate those numbers at the top in order to achieve political goals, internally and externally; and it must do all that without scaring off foreign investment, which is vital in maintaining the "Chinese economic miracle."

Of course, not on the list is the need to address the institutional and structural reasons that the statistical process is inherently flawed in China. It is one thing for the National People's Congress to give national laws governing statistics more teeth; it is quite another to overhaul China's political structure to make officials more accountable. And since true political reform is not on the central government's agenda, "Chinese numbers" will continue to be an issue in assessing and dealing with China.

Leadership Transition and Economic Challenges
March 9, 2010

China's National People's Congress (NPC) remains in session. As usual, the meeting has provided Beijing an opportunity to highlight the past year's successes and lay out the problems that lie ahead. On the surface at least, China has shown remarkable resilience in the face of global economic crisis. It has posted enviable gross domestic product (GDP) growth rates while keeping factories running (if at a loss) and workers employed. But the economic crisis has exposed the inefficiencies of China's export-dependent economic model, and the government has had to pump money into a major investment stimulus package to make up for the net drain the export sector currently is exacting on the economy.

For years, China's leaders have recognized the risks of the current economic model. They have debated policy ideas to shift from the current model to one that is more sustainable in the long run and incorporates a more geographically equitable growth and a hefty rise in domestic consumption. While there is general agreement on the need for change, top leaders disagree on the timing and method of transition. This has stirred internal debates, which can lead to factionalization as varying interests align to promote their preferred policy prescription. Entrenched interests in urban areas and the export industry — along with constant fears of triggering major social upheaval — have left the government year after year making only slight changes around the margins. Often, Beijing has taken one step forward only to take two back when social instability and/or institutional resistance emerge.

And this debate becomes even more significant now, as China deals simultaneously with the aftermath of the global economic slowdown and preparations for a leadership transition in 2012.

The Hu Agenda

Chinese President Hu Jintao came into office eight years ago with the ambitious goal of closing a widening wealth gap by equalizing economic growth between the rural interior and coastal cities. Hu inherited the results of Deng Xiaoping's opening and reform, which focused on the rapid development of the coastal areas, which were better geographically positioned for international trade. The vast interior took second billing, being kept in line with the promise that in time the rising tide of economic wealth would float all ships. Eventually it did, somewhat. But while the interior saw significant improvements over the early Mao period, the growth and rise in living standards and disposable income in the urban coastal areas far outstripped rural growth. Some coastal urban areas are now approaching Western standards of living, while much of the interior remains mired in Third World conditions. And the faster the coast grows, the more dependent China becomes on the money from that growth to facilitate employment and subsidize the rural population.

Hu's predecessor, Jiang Zemin, also recognized these problems. To address them, he promoted a "Go West" economic policy designed to shift investment further inland. But Jiang faced the same entrenched interests that have opposed Hu's efforts at significant change. While Jiang was able to begin reform of the bloated state-owned enterprises, he softened his Westward economic drive. Amid cyclical global economic downturns, China fell back on the subsidized export model to keep employment levels up and keep money flowing in. Concern over social instability held radical reform in check, and the closer Jiang got to the end of his term in power, the less likely he was to make significant changes that could undermine social cohesion. No Chinese leader wants to preside over a major economic policy that fails out of fear of being the Chinese Mikhail Gorbachev.

For those like Hu who have argued that rapid reform is worth the risk of potential short-term social dislocation, the global downturn was seen as validating their policies — and as confirming that the risks to China of not changing far outweigh the risks of changing now. The export industry's drag on GDP has forced Beijing to enact a massive investment and loan program. By some accounts, fixed investments in 2009 accounted for more than 90 percent of GDP. Those arguing for faster reform have noted that the pace of investment growth is unsustainable in the long run, and that the flood of money into the system has created new inflationary pressures.

Much of this investment came in the form of bank loans that need to be serviced and repaid. But as the government tries to cool the economy, the risk of companies defaulting on their loans looms. Cooling the economy also threatens to burst China's real estate bubble. This not only compounds problems in related industry sectors, it could also trigger massive social discord in the urban areas, where housing has taken the place of the stock market as the investment of choice.

Beijing's Ongoing Dilemma

Chinese leaders face the constant dilemma of needing to allow the economy to maintain its three-decade long export-oriented growth pattern even though this builds in long-term weaknesses, but shifting the economy is not something that can be done without its own consequences. Social pressures are convincing the government of the need to raise the minimum wage to keep up with economic pressures. At the same time, misallocation of labor and new job formation incentives in the interior are causing shortages of labor in some sectors in major coastal export zones. If coastal factories increase wages to attract labor or appease workers, they run the risk of going under due to the already razor-thin margins. But if they don't, the labor fueling these industries at best may riot and at worst might simply move back home, leaving exporters with little option but to close shop.

Looming demographic changes around the globe also impact the Chinese situation, and the government can no longer rely on an ever-increasing export market to drive the Chinese economy. Some international companies operating in China already are beginning to consider relocating manufacturing operations to places with cheaper labor or back to their home countries to save on transportation costs Chinese wages are no longer mitigating.

With its export markets unlikely to recover to pre-crisis levels any time soon, competition and protectionism are on the rise. The United States is growing bolder in its restrictions on Chinese exports, and China may no longer avoid having the U.S. government label it a currency manipulator. While this may be an extreme measure in 2010, the pressures for such a scenario are rising.

Amid its domestic and global challenges, Chinese leaders are engaged in economic policy debates. It appears that internal criticism is being directed against Hu as social tensions over issues like rising housing prices and inflation grow. In some ways, this is not unusual. National presidents often bear the brunt of dissatisfaction with economic downturns no matter whether their policies were to blame. In China, however, criticism against economic policy falls on the premier, who is responsible for setting the country's economic direction. The focus on Hu reflects both the depth of the current crisis and the underlying political tensions over economic policy in a time of both global economic unpredictability and preparations for the end of Hu's presidency in 2012.

To bridge the gulf between the urban coast and the rural interior, Hu and his supporters have pursued a multiphase plan. First, they sought to rein in some of the most independent of the coastal areas — Shanghai in particular, which served as a center of power and influence not only in promoting the continuation of unfettered coastal growth but also of Hu's predecessor, Jiang. Second, a plan was put in motion to consolidate redundancies in China's economy and to shift light- and low-skilled industry inland by increasing wages in the key coastal export manufacturing areas, reducing their cost competitiveness. And Beijing added an urbanization drive in traditionally rural and inland areas. Together, this represented a joint attempt to bring the jobs to the interior rather than continue the pattern of migrant workers moving to the coast.

The core of the Hu policies was an overall attempt to re-centralize economic control. This would allow the central government to begin weeding out redundancies left over from Mao's era of provincial self-sufficiency, which the Deng and Jiang eras of uncoordinated and locally-directed economic growth often driven by corruption and nepotism exacerbated. In short, Hu planned to centralize the economy to consolidate industry, redistribute wealth and urbanize the interior to create a more balanced economy that emphasized domestic consumption over exports. However, Hu's push, under the epithet "harmonious society," has been anything but smooth and its successes have been limited at best.

Hu Meets Resistance

Institutional and local government resistance to re-centralization has hounded the policy from its inception, and resistance has grown with the economic crisis. Money is now pouring into the economy via massive government-mandated bank lending to stimulate growth through investments as exports wane. Consequently, housing prices and inflation fears now plague the government — two issues that could lead to increased social tensions and are already leading to louder questioning of Hu's policies. With just two years to go in his administration, Hu already is looking to his legacy, weighing the risks and rewards between promoting long-term economic sustainability or short-term economic survival. The next two years will witness seemingly incongruent policy pronouncements as the two opposing directions and their proponents battle over China's economic and political landscape.

Hu's rise to the presidency was all but assured long before he took office. From a somewhat simplified perspective, the PRC has had only four leaders: Mao Zedong, Deng Xiaoping, Jiang Zemin and Hu Jintao. When Mao died, his appointed successor, Hua Guofeng (who was settled upon after several other candidates fell out of favor), lasted only a short time. Amid the political chaos of the post-Cultural Revolution era, Deng rose to the top. Both Mao and Deng were strong leaders who, although contending with rivals, could rule almost single-handedly when the need arose.

To avoid the confusion of the post-Mao transition, Deng created a long-term succession plan. He ultimately settled on Shanghai Mayor Jiang Zemin as his successor. But in an effort to preserve his vision and legacy, Deng also chose Jiang's successor, Hu Jintao. Barring some terrible breach of office, Hu was more or less guaranteed the presidency a decade before he took office, and there was little Jiang could do to alter this outcome. Jiang, however, made sure that he left his mark by lining up Hu's successor, Xi Jinping. Despite Jiang's support, Xi has not risen through the ranks in the same manner as Hu did, raising speculation of internal disagreements on the succession plan.

Vice President Xi is considered one of the "princelings," leaders whose parents were part of the revolutionary-era governments under Mao and Deng who mainly have cut their teeth through business ventures concentrated in the coastal regions. Hu, on the other hand, is considered among the "tuanpai" or "tuanxi," leaders who come primarily from the ranks of the Communist Youth League and interior provinces. While these "groups" are not in and of themselves cohesive factions, and China's political networks are complex, Hu's and Xi's backgrounds reflect their differing policy approaches. As such, the question of the next Chinese leader is shaped by opposing economic plans.

On one hand are those like Hu who support a more rapid and immediate refocusing on rural and interior economic growth, even at the cost of reduced coastal and urban power. On the other hand, those like Jiang and his protege Xi have an interest in maintaining the status quo of regionalized semi-independence in economic matters and continued strong coastal growth. They are proceeding on the assumption that a strong coastal-led economy will both provide more immediate rewards for themselves and strengthen China's international position and its national defense.

It is important not to overstress the differences. Each has the same ultimate goal, namely, maintaining the CPC as the central authority and building a strong China; it is just their paths to these ends that differ. But the economic policy differences are now becoming key questions of Party survival and Chinese stability and strength. Factional struggles that in normal circumstances can be largely controlled, or at least would not get out of hand, are now shaping up in an environment where China's three-decade economic growth spurt may be reaching its climax. Meanwhile, social pressures are rising amid uncertainties and instabilities in Chinese economic structures.

Beijing has emerged from the economic crisis bolder and more self-confident than ever. But this is driven more by a recognition of weakness than a false assessment of strength. China's leadership is in crisis mode, and at this time of economic instability and uncertainty, the leadership must also manage a transition that is bringing competing economic policies into stark contrast. And this is the sort of pressure that can cause the gloves to come off and throw expectations of unity and smooth transitions out the window.

Everything may pass smoothly; two years is a long time, after all. But if there is one thing certain about the upcoming change of presidents, it is that nothing is certain.

Looking to 2012: China's Next Generation of Leaders
Sept. 14, 2010

In 2012, the Communist Party of China's (CPC) leaders will retire and a new generation — the so-called fifth generation — will take the helm. The transition will affect the CPC's most powerful decision-making organs, determining the makeup of the 18th CPC Central Committee, the Political Bureau (Politburo) of the Central Committee, and most important, the nine-member Politburo Standing Committee that is the core of political power in China.

While there is considerable uncertainty over the handoff, given China's lack of clear, institutionalized procedures for succession and the immense challenges facing the regime, there is little reason to anticipate a succession crisis. But the sweeping personnel change comes at a critical juncture in China's modern history, with the economic model that has enabled decades of rapid growth having become unsustainable, social unrest rising, and international resistance to China's policies increasing. At the same time, the characteristics of the fifth generation leaders suggest a cautious and balanced civilian leadership paired with an increasingly influential and nationalist military. This will lead to frictions over policy even as both groups remain firmly committed to perpetuating the regime.

The Chinese leadership that emerges from 2012 will likely be unwilling or unable to decisively carry out deep structural reforms, obsessively focused on maintaining internal stability, and more aggressive in pursuing the core strategic interests it sees as essential to this stability.

Just as China's civilian leadership will change, China's military will see a sweeping change in leadership in 2012. The military's influence over China's politics and policies has grown over the past decade, as the country has striven to professionalize and modernize its forces and expand its capabilities in response to deepening international involvement and challenges to its internal stability. The fifth generation military leaders are the first to have come out of the military modernization process, and to have had their careers shaped by the priorities of a China that has become a global economic power. They will take office at a time when the military's budget, stature and influence over politics is growing, and when it has come to see its role as extending beyond that of a guarantor of national security to becoming a guide for the country as it moves forward and up the ranks of international power.

Civilian Leadership

Power transitions in the People's Republic of China have always been fraught with uncertainty because the state does not have clear and fixed institutional procedures for the transfer of power between leaders and generations. The state's founding leader, Mao Zedong, did not establish a formal process before he died, giving rise to a power struggle. Mao's eventual successor, Deng Xiaoping, was also a strong leader whose personal power could override rules and institutions. But Deng's retirement also failed to set a firm succession precedent. He saw two of his chosen successors lose out amid factional struggles, and Deng maintained extensive influence well after formally retiring and passing power to Jiang Zemin and naming Jiang's successor, current President Hu Jintao.

Even though China does not have any fixed rules on power transfers, a series of precedents and informal rules have been observed. Recent years have seen a move toward the solidification of these rules. Deng set a pattern in motion that smoothed the 2002 presidential transition from Jiang to Hu despite behind-the-scenes factional tensions. As mentioned, Deng had also appointed Hu to be Jiang's successor. This lent Hu some of Deng's great authority, thus establishing an air of inevitability and deterring potential power grabs. This leap-frog pattern was reinforced when Jiang put Vice President Xi Jinping in line to succeed Hu in 2012. The coming transfer will test whether the trend toward stable power transitions can hold.

Characteristics of the Fifth Generation

While all countries experience leadership changes that can be described as generational in one sense or another, modern Chinese history has been so eventful as to have created generations that, as a group, share distinct characteristics and are markedly different from their forbearers in their historical, educational and career experiences. Deng created the concept of the "generational" framework by dubbing himself the core second-generation leader after Mao, and events and patterns in leadership promotion and retirement reinforced the framework. The most defining factor of a Chinese leadership generation is its historical background. The first generation defined itself by the formation of the Communist Party and the Long March of exile in the 1930s, the second generation in the war against the Japanese (World War II), and the third during civil war and the founding of the state in 1949. The fourth generation came of age during the Great Leap Forward in the late 1950s, Mao's first attempt to transform the entire Chinese economy.

The fifth generation is the first group of leaders that cannot — or can only barely — remember a time before the foundation of the People's Republic. These leaders' formative experiences were shaped during the Cultural Revolution (1967-77), a period of deep social and political upheaval in which the Mao government empowered hard-liners to purge their political opponents in the bureaucracy and Communist Party. Schools and universities were closed in 1966 and youths were sent down to rural areas to do manual labor, including many fifth-generation leaders such as likely future President Xi Jinping. Some young people were able to return to college after 1970, where they could only study Marxism-Leninism and CPC ideology, while others sought formal education when schools were reopened after the Cultural Revolution. Very few trained abroad, so they did not become attuned to foreign attitudes and perceptions in their formative days (whereas the previous generation had sent some young leaders to study in the Soviet Union). Characteristically, given the fuller educational opportunities that arose in the late 1970s, the upcoming leaders have backgrounds in a wide range of studies. Many were trained as lawyers, economists and social scientists, as opposed to the engineers and natural scientists who have dominated the previous generations of leadership.

In 2012, only Vice President Xi Jinping and Vice Premier Li Keqiang will remain on the Politburo Standing Committee, the core decision-making body in China. Seven new members will join, assuming the number of total members remains at nine, which has been the case since 2002. All seven will hail from the broader Politburo and were born after October 1944, in accordance with an unwritten rule established under Deng requiring Chinese leaders to retire at age 70 (it was lowered to 68 in 1997). The retiring leaders will make every effort to strike a deal preventing the balance of power within the Politburo and the Politburo Standing Committee from tipping against them and their faction.

At present, China's leaders divide roughly into two factions broadly defined as the populists and the elitists.

The populists are associated with Hu Jintao and the China Communist Youth League (CCYL) and are more accurately referred to as the "league faction" (in Chinese, the "tuanpai"). In the 1980s Hu led the league, which comprises his political base. The CCYL is a massive organization that prepares future members of the CPC. It is structured with a central leadership and provincial and local branches based in the country's schools, workplaces, and social organizations. In keeping with the CCYL's rigid hierarchy and doctrinal training, the policies of Hu's "CCYL clique" focus on centralizing and consolidating power, maintaining social stability, and seeking to redistribute wealth to alleviate income disparities, regional differences, and social ills. The clique has grown increasingly powerful under Hu's patronage.

He has promoted people from CCYL backgrounds, some of whom he worked with during his term as a high-level leader in the group in the early 1980s, and has increased the number of CCYL-affiliated leaders in China's provincial governments. Several top candidates for the Politburo Standing Committee in 2012 are part of this group, including Li Keqiang and Li Yuanchao, followed by Liu Yandong, Zhang Baoshun, Yuan Chunqing, Liu Qibao and Wang Yang.

The elitists are leaders associated with former President Jiang Zemin and his Shanghai clique. Their policies aim to maintain China's rapid economic growth, with the coastal provinces unabashedly leading the way. They also promote economic restructuring to improve China's international competitiveness and reduce inefficiencies, even at the risk of painful changes for some regions or sectors of society. The infamous "princelings" — or the sons, grandsons and relatives of the CPC's founding fathers and previous leaders who have risen up the ranks of China's system through these familial connections — are often associated with the elitists. The princelings are criticized for benefiting from nepotism, and some have suffered from low support in internal party elections. Still, they have name recognition from their proud Communist family histories, the finest educations and career experiences and access to personal networks set up by their fathers. The Shanghai clique and princelings are joined by economic reformists of various stripes who come from different backgrounds, mostly in the state apparatus such as the central or provincial bureaucracy and ministries, who often are technocrats and specialists. Prominent members of this faction eligible for the 2012 Politburo Standing Committee include Wang Qishan, Zhang Dejiang, Bo Xilai, Yu Zhengsheng and Zhang Gaoli.

The struggle between the populist and elitist factions is a subset of the deeper struggle in Chinese history between centralist and regionalist impulses. Because of China's vast and diverse geography, China historically has required a strong central government, usually located on the North China Plain, to maintain political unity. But this cyclical unity tends to break down over time as different regions pursue their own interests and form relationships with the outside world that become more vital to them than unity with the rest of China. The tension between centralist and regionalist tendencies has given rise to the ancient struggle between the north (Beijing) and the south (Shanghai), the difficulties that successive Chinese regimes have had in subordinating the far south (i.e. Guangdong and the Pearl River Delta), and modern Beijing's anxiety over the perceived threat of separatism from Taiwan, Xinjiang and Tibet. In this context, the struggle between the two dominant political factions appears as the 21st century political manifestation of the irresolvable struggle between the political center in Beijing and the other regions, whose economic vibrancy leads them to pursue their own ends. While Hu Jintao and his allies emphasize central control and redistributing regional wealth to create a more unified China, the followers of Jiang tend to emphasize the need to let China's most competitive regions grow and prosper, often in cooperation with international partners, without being restrained by the center or weighed down by the less dynamic regions.

Factional Balance

The politicians almost certain to join the Politburo Standing Committee in 2012 appear to represent a balance between factional tendencies. The top two, Xi Jinping and Li Keqiang, are the youngest members of the current Politburo Standing Committee and are all but certain to become president and premier, respectively. Xi is a princeling — son of Xi Zhongxun, an early Communist revolutionary and deputy prime minister — and his leadership in Fujian, Zhejiang and Shanghai exemplifies the ability of coastal manufacturing provinces to enhance an official's career. But Xi is also popular with the public, widely admired for his hardships as a rural worker during the Cultural Revolution. He is the best example of bridging both major factions — promoting economic reforms but seen as having the people's best interests at heart. Li was trained as an economist under a prestigious teacher at Beijing University, received a law degree, and is a former top secretary of the CCYL and stalwart of Hu's faction. Economics is his specialty, not in itself but as a means

136

PROSPECTIVE 2012 CORE LEADERSHIP

TOP CANDIDATES FOR THE COMMUNIST PARTY'S POLITBURO STANDING COMMITTEE

XI JINPING

CURRENT TITLE: Vice President

BORN: 1953

REGIONAL AFFILI-ATION: Shaanxi, Fujian, Zhejiang, Shanghai

EDUCATION: Tsinghua U

FACTION: Princeling and Jiang Zemin/Shanghai clique

LI KEQIANG

CURRENT TITLE: Vice Premier

BORN: 1955

REGIONAL AFFILI-ATION: Anhui, Henan, Liaoning

EDUCATION: Peking U

FACTION: Hu Jintao and CCYL clique

LI YUANCHAO

CURRENT TITLE: Director, CPC Organization Dept.

BORN: 1950

REGIONAL AFFILI-ATION: Jiangsu, Shanghai

EDUCATION: Fudan U and Peking U, Central Party School

FACTION: Hu Jintao and CCYL clique

WANG YANG

CURRENT TITLE: Member, CPC Politburo, and Party-Secretary of Guangdong Province

BORN: 1955

REGIONAL AFFILI-ATION: Anhui, Chongqing, Guangdong

EDUCATION: Central Party School

FACTION: Hu Jintao and CCYL

LIU YUNSHAN

CURRENT TITLE: Director, CPC Propaganda Department

BORN: 1947

REGIONAL AFFILI-ATION: Shanxi, Inner Mongolia

EDUCATION: Central Party School

FACTION: Jiang Zemin/Shanghai clique

WANG QISHAN

CURRENT TITLE: Vice Premier

BORN: 1948

REGIONAL AFFILI-ATION: Shanxi, Hainan, Guangdong, Beijing, Shaanxi

EDUCATION: Northwestern U

FACTION: Princeling and Jiang Zemin/Shanghai clique

ZHANG DEJIANG

CURRENT TITLE: Vice Premier

BORN: 1946

REGIONAL AFFILI-ATION: Liaoning, Jilin, Zhejiang, Guangdong

EDUCATION: Yanbian U and Kim Il Sung Comprehensive U, North Korea

FACTION: Jiang Zemin/Shanghai clique

BO XILAI

CURRENT TITLE: Party Secretary of Chongqing municipality

BORN: 1949

REGIONAL AFFILI-ATION: Shanxi, Liaoning, Chongqing

EDUCATION: Peking U

FACTION: Princeling

ZHANG GAOLI**

CURRENT TITLE: Party Secretary of Tianjin municipality

BORN: 1946

REGIONAL AFFILI-ATION: Fujian, Guangdong, Shandong, Tianjin

EDUCATION: Xiamen U

FACTION: Jiang Zemin/Shanghai clique

LING JIHUA**

CURRENT TITLE: Director, CPC General Office

BORN: 1956

REGIONAL AFFILI-ATION: Shanxi, Beijing

EDUCATION: China Youth U and Hunan U

FACTION: Hu Jintao and CCYL clique

CCYL = China Communist Youth League

CPC = Communist Party of China

*Princeling = Descendant or relative of former high-ranking Communist Party leader

**Position in Politburo Standing Committee less certain

The Politburo Standing Committee increased from seven members to nine in 2002. In 2012, it will likely retain nine members, though a reversion to seven is possible.

to social harmony. For example, he is famous for promoting further revitalization of northeastern China's industrial rust belt of factories that have fallen into disrepair. Li also has held leadership positions in provinces like Henan, an agricultural province, and Liaoning, a heavy-industrial province, affording him a view of starkly different aspects of the national economy.

After Xi and Li, the most likely contenders for seats on the Politburo Standing Committee are Li Yuanchao, director of the CPC's powerful organization department (CCYL clique), Wang Yang (CCYL), member of the CPC's Politburo, Liu Yunshan (CCYL), director of the CPC's propaganda department, and Vice Premier Wang Qishan (princeling/Jiang's Shanghai clique). The next most likely candidates include Vice Premier Zhang Dejiang (Jiang's Shanghai clique), Chongqing Party Secretary Bo Xilai (princeling), Tianjin Party Secretary Zhang Gaoli (Jiang's Shanghai clique) and CPC General Office Director Ling Jihua (secretary to Hu Jintao, CCYL clique). It is impossible to predict exactly who will be appointed to the Politburo Standing Committee. The lineup is the result of intense negotiation between the current committee members, with the retiring members (everyone except Xi Jinping and Li Keqiang) wielding the most influence. Currently, of the nine Politburo Standing Committee members, as many as six are Jiang Zemin proteges, and they will push for their followers to prevent Hu from taking control of the committee.

It accordingly seems possible that the 2012 Politburo Standing Committee balance will lean slightly in favor of Jiang's Shanghai clique and the princelings, given that Xi Jinping will hold the top seat, but that by numbers the factions will be evenly balanced. Like his predecessors, Xi will have to spend his early years as president attempting to consolidate power so he can put his followers in positions of influence and begin to shape the succeeding generation of leaders for the benefit of himself and his circle. An even balance, if it is reached, may not persist through the entire 10 years of the Xi and Li administration: the CCYL clique looks extremely well-situated for the 2017 reshuffle, at which point many of Jiang's proteges will be too old to sit on the Politburo Standing Committee while a number of rising stars in the CCYL currently serving as provincial chiefs will be well-placed for promotion.

There is a remote possibility that the number of seats on the Politburo Standing Committee could be cut from nine to seven, the number of posts before 2002. This would likely result in a stricter enforcement of age limits in determining which leaders to promote, perhaps setting the cutoff age at 66 or 67 (instead of 68). Stricter age criteria could eliminate three contenders from Jiang's Shanghai clique (Zhang Gaoli, Zhang Dejiang, and Shanghai Party Secretary Yu Zhengsheng) and one from Hu's clique (Politburo member Liu Yandong). This would leave Bo Xilai (a highly popular princeling with unorthodox policies, but like Xi Jinping known to straddle the factional divide) and CPC General Office Director Ling Jihua (secretary to Hu Jintao, CCYL clique) as the most likely final additions to the Politburo Standing Committee. The overall balance in this scenario of slightly younger age requirements would then lean in favor of Hu's clique.

Collective Rule

The factions are not so antagonistic that an intense power struggle is likely to rip them apart. Instead, they can be expected to exercise power by forging compromises. Leaders are chosen by their superiors through a process of careful negotiation to prevent an imbalance of one faction over another that could lead to purges or counter-purges. That balance looks as if it will roughly be maintained in the configuration of leaders in 2012. In terms of policymaking, powerful leaders will continue to debate deep policy disagreements behind closed doors. Through a process of intense negotiation, they will try to arrive at a party line and maintain it uniformly in public. Stark disagreements and fierce debates will echo through the statements of minor officials and academics, and in public discussions, newspaper editorials, and other venues, however. In extreme situations, these policy battles could lead to the ousting of officials who end up on the wrong side. But the highest party leaders will not contradict each other openly on matters of great significance unless a dire breakdown has occurred, as happened with fallen Shanghai Party Secretary Chen Liangyu.

That the fifth generation leadership appears in agreement on the state's broadest economic and political goals, even if they differ on the means of achieving those goals, will be conducive to maintaining the factional balance. First, there is general agreement on the need to continue with China's internationally oriented economic and structural reforms. These leaders spent the prime of their lives in the midst of China's rapid economic transformation from a poor and isolated pariah state into an international industrial and commercial giant, and were the first to experience the benefits of this transformation. They also know that the CPC's legitimacy has come to rest, in great part, on its ability to deliver greater economic opportunity and prosperity to the country — and that the greatest risk to the regime would likely come in the form of a shrinking or dislocated economy that causes massive unemployment. Therefore, for the most part they remain dedicated to continuing with market-oriented reform. They will do so gradually and carefully, however, and will not seek to intensify reformist efforts to the point of dramatically increasing the risk of social disruption. Needless to say, while the elitists can be energetic in their pursuit of economic liberalization, the populists tend to be more suspicious and more willing to re-centralize controls to avoid undesirable political side effects, even at the expense of long-term risks to the economy.

More fundamentally, all fifth generation leaders are committed to maintaining CPC rule. The chaos of the Cultural Revolution impressed upon the fifth generation a sense of the extreme dangers of China's having allowed an autocratic ruler to dominate the decision-making process and intra-party struggle to run rampant. Subsequent events have reinforced the fear of internal divisions: the protest and military crackdown at Tiananmen Square in 1989, the threat of alternative movements exemplified by the Falun Gong protest in 1999, the general rise in social unrest throughout the economic boom of the 1990s and 2000s. More recent challenges have reinforced this, such as natural disasters like the Sichuan earthquake in 2008, ethnic violence and riots in Tibet in 2008 and Xinjiang in 2009, and the pressures of economic volatility since the global economic crisis of 2008. These events have underscored the need to maintain unity and stability in the Party ranks and in Chinese society, by force when necessary. So while the fifth generation is likely to agree on the need to continue with economic reform and perhaps even limited political reform, it will do so only insofar as it can without destabilizing socio-political order. It will delay, soften, undermine, or reverse reform to ensure stability. Once again, the difference between the factions lies in judging how best to preserve and bolster the regime.

Regionalism

Beyond the apparent balance of forces in the central party and government organs, there remains the tug-of-war between the central government in Beijing and the 33 provincial governments (not to mention Taiwan) — a reflection of the timeless struggle in China between center and periphery. If China is to be struck by deep destabilization under the watch of the fifth generation leaders (which is by no means impossible, especially given the economic troubles facing them), the odds are this would occur along regional lines. Stark differences have emerged, as China's coastal manufacturing provinces have surged ahead while provinces in the interior, west and northeast have lagged. The CPC's solution to this problem generally has been to redistribute wealth from the booming coast to the interior in hopes that subsidizing the less developed regions eventually will nurture economic development. In some instances, such as in Shaanxi or Sichuan provinces, urbanization and development have indeed accelerated in recent years. But overall, the interior remains weak and dependent on subsidies from Beijing.

The problem for China's leadership is that the coastal provinces' export-led model of growth that has worked well over the past three decades has begun to peak, and China's annual double-digit growth rates are expected to slow due to weakening external demand, rising labor and material costs and other factors. The result will be louder demands from poor provinces and tighter fists in rich provinces — exposing and deepening competition, and in some cases leading to animosity between the regions.

More so than any previous generation, the fifth generation has extensive cross-regional career experience. This is because climbing to the top of Party and government has increasingly required that many of these leaders first serve in central organizations in Beijing and then do a stint (or more) as governor or Party secretary of one of the provinces (the more far-flung, the better), before returning to a higher central Party or government position in Beijing. Hu Jintao followed such a path, as have many of the aforementioned candidates for the Politburo Standing Committee. Moreover, it has become increasingly common to put officials in charge of a region other than the one from which they originally hailed to reduce regionalism and regional biases. This practice has precedent in China's imperial history, when it was used to prevent the rise of mini-fiefdoms and the devolution of power. More of the likely members of the 2012 Politburo Standing Committee than ever before have experience as provincial chiefs. This means that when these leaders take over top national positions, they theoretically will have a better grasp of the realities facing the provinces they rule, and will be less likely to be beholden to a single regional constituency or support base. This could somewhat mitigate the central government's difficulty in dealing with profound divergences of interest between the central and provincial governments.

But regional differences are grounded in fundamental, geographical and ethnic realities, and have become increasingly aggravated by the disproportionate benefits of China's economic success. Temporary changes of position across the country have not prevented China's leaders from forming lasting bonds with certain provinces to the neglect of others; and many politicians still have experience exclusively with the regional level of government, and none with the central. The patron-client system, by which Chinese officials give their loyalty to superiors in exchange for political perks or monetary rewards, remains ineradicable. Massive personal networks extend across party and government bureaus, from the center to the regions. Few central leaders remain impervious to the pull of these regional networks, and none can remain in power long if his or her regional power base or bases have been cut. The tension between the center and provinces will remain one of the greatest sources of stress on the central leadership as it negotiates national policy.

As with any novice political leadership, the fifth generation leaders will take office with little experience of what it means to be fully in charge of a nation. Provincial leadership experience has provided good preparation, but the individual members have yet to show signs of particularly strong national leadership capabilities. The public sees only a few of the upcoming members of the Politburo Standing Committee as successfully having taken charge during events of major importance (for instance, Xi Jinping's response to Tropical Storm Bilis, Wang Qishan's handling of the SARS epidemic and the Beijing Olympics); only one has military experience (Xi, and it is slight); and only a few of the others have shown independence or forcefulness in their leadership style (namely Wang Qishan and Bo Xilai). Because current Politburo Standing Committee members or previous leaders (like former President Jiang Zemin) will choose the future committee members after painstaking negotiations, this might preserve the balance of power between the cliques. It might also result in a "compromise" leadership — effectively one that would strive for a middle-of-the-road approach, even at the cost of achieving mediocre results. A collective leadership of these members, precariously balanced, runs the risk of falling into divisions when resolute and sustained effort is necessary, as is likely given the economic, social and foreign policy challenges that it will likely face during its tenure.

This by no means is to say the fifth generation is destined to be weak. Chinese leaders have a time-tested strategy of remaining reserved for as long as possible and not revealing their full strength until necessary. And China's centralist political system generally entails quick implementation once the top leadership has made up its mind on a policy. Still, judging by available criteria, the fifth generation leaders are likely to be reactive, like the current administration.

Where they are proactive, it will be on decisions pertaining to domestic security and social stability.

Military Leadership

The Rise of the People's Liberation Army

After Deng's economic reforms, the Chinese military began to use its influence to get into industry and business. Over time, this evolved into a major role for the military on the local and provincial level. Military commands supplemented their government budget allocations with the proceeds from their business empires. Ultimately, the central government and Party leadership became concerned that the situation could degenerate into regional warlordism of the sort that has prevailed at various times in Chinese history — with military-political-business alliances developing more loyalty to their interests and foreign partners than to Beijing. Thus when Jiang launched full-scale reforms of the military in the 1990s, he called for restructuring and modernization (including cutting China's bloated ground forces and boosting the other branches of service) and simultaneously ordered the military to stop dabbling in business. Though the commanders only begrudgingly complied at first, the military-controlled businesses eventually were liquidated and their assets sold (either at a bargain price to family members and cronies or at an inflated price to local governments). To replace this loss of revenue and redesign the military, the central government began increasing budgetary allocations focusing on acquiring new equipment, higher technology, and training and organization to promote professionalism. The modernization drive eventually gave the military a new sense of purpose and power and brought a greater role to the PLA Navy (PLAN), the PLA Air Force (PLAAF), and the Second Artillery Corps (the strategic missile corps).

The military's influence appears highly likely to continue rising in the coming years for the following reasons:

- Maintaining internal stability in China has resulted in several high-profile cases in which the armed forces played a critical role. Natural disasters such as massive flooding (1998, 2010) and earthquakes (especially in Sichuan in 2008) have required the military to provide relief and assistance, giving rise to more attention on military planning and thereby improving the military's propaganda efforts and public image and prestige. Because China is prone to natural disasters and its environmental difficulties have worsened as its massive population and economy have put greater pressure on the landscape, the military is expected to continue playing a greater role in disaster relief, including by offering to help abroad. At the same time, the rising frequency of social unrest, including riots and ethnic violence in regions like Xinjiang and Tibet, has led to military involvement in such matters. As the trend of rising social unrest looks to continue in the coming years, so the military will be called upon to restore order, especially through the elite People's Armed Police, which falls under the joint control of the Central Military Commission and State Council.

- As China's economy has become the second largest in the world, its international dependencies have increased. China depends on stable and secure supply lines to maintain imports of energy, raw materials, and components and exports of components and finished goods. Most of these commodities and merchandise are traded over sea, often through choke-points such as the straits of Hormuz and Malacca, making them vulnerable to interference from piracy, terrorism, conflicts between foreign states, or interdiction by navies hostile to China (i.e., the United States, India or Japan). Therefore it needs the PLAN to expand its capabilities and reach so as to secure these vital supplies — otherwise the economy would be exposed to potential shocks that could translate into social and political disturbances. This policy has also led the PLA to take a more active role in U.N. peacekeeping efforts and other international operations, expand integrated training and ties with foreign militaries, and build a hospital ship to begin military-led diplomacy.

- Competition with foreign states is intensifying as China has become more powerful economically and internationally conspicuous. In addition to building capabilities to assert its sovereignty over Taiwan, China has become more aggressive in defending its sovereignty and territorial claims in its neighboring seas — especially in the South China Sea, which Beijing elevated in 2010 to a "core" national interest (along with sovereignty over Taiwan and Tibet) and also in the East China Sea. This assertiveness has led to rising tension with neighbors that have competing claims on potentially resource-rich territory in the seas, including Vietnam, the Philippines, Indonesia, Malaysia, Brunei and Japan. Moreover, Beijing's newfound assertiveness has collided with U.S. moves to bulk up its alliances and partnerships in the region, which Beijing sees as a strategy aimed at constraining China's rise.

- China's military modernization remains a primary national policy focus. Military modernization includes acquiring and developing advanced weaponry, improving information technology and communications, heightening capabilities on sea and in the air, and developing capabilities in new theaters such as cyberwarfare and outer space. It also entails improving Chinese forces' mobility, rapid reaction, special operations forces and ability to conduct combined operations between different military services.

- The PLA has become more vocal, making statements and issuing editorials in forums like the PLA Daily and, for the most part, receiving positive public responses. In many cases, military officers have voiced a nationalistic point of view shared by large portions of the public (though one prominent military officer, Liu Yazhou, a princeling and commissar at National Defense University, has used his standing to call for China to pursue Western-style democratic political reforms). Military officials can strike a more nationalist pose where politicians would have trouble due to consideration for foreign relations and the concern that nationalism is becoming an insuppressible force of its own.

Of course, a more influential military does not mean one that believes it is all-powerful. China will still try to avoid direct confrontation with the United States and its allies and maintain relations internationally given its national economic strategy and the fact that its military has not yet attained the same degree of sophistication and capability as its chief competitors. But the military's growing influence is likely to encourage a more assertive China, especially in the face of heightened internal and external threats.

The Central Military Commission

The Central Military Commission (CMC) is the state's most powerful military body, comprising the top ten military chiefs, and chaired by the country's civilian leader. This means the CMC has unfettered access to the top Chinese leader, and can influence him through a more direct channel than through its small representation on the Politburo Standing Committee. Thus the CMC is not only the core decision-making body of the Chinese military, it is also the chief conduit through which the military can influence the civilian leadership.

Promotions for China's top military leaders are based on the officer's age, his current official position — for instance, whether he sits on the CMC or in the CPC Central Committee — and his personal connections. Officers born after 1944 will be too old for promotion since they will be 68 in 2012, past the de facto cutoff age after which an officer is no longer eligible for promotion to the CMC. Those officers meeting the age requirement and holding positions on the CMC, the CPC Central Committee, or a command position in one of China's military services or its seven regional military commands

PROSPECTIVE 2012 MILITARY LEADERSHIP

TOP CANDIDATES FOR THE CENTRAL MILITARY COMMISSION

CMC = Central Military Commission
PLA = People's Liberation Army
The Central Military Commission consisted of seven seats at its formation in 1982, and has expanded to its current level of 11 seats.

XI JINPING
CURRENT TITLE: Vice President
BORN: 1953
REGIONAL AFFILIATION: Shaanxi, Fujian, Zhejiang, Shanghai

XU QILIANG
CURRENT TITLE: Commander, PLA Air Force; CMC member
RANK: General, 2007
BORN: 1950
SERVICE: Air Force
REGIONAL AFFILIATION: Shandong; Shenyang Military Region

CHANG WANQUAN
CURRENT TITLE: Director, PLA General Armaments Department; CMC member
RANK: General, 2007
BORN: 1949
SERVICE: Army
REGIONAL AFFILIATION: Henan; Lanzhou, Beijing and Shenyang Military Regions

WU SHENGLI
CURRENT TITLE: PLA Navy Commander; CMC member
RANK: General, 2007
BORN: 1945
SERVICE: Navy
REGIONAL AFFILIATION: Hebei; Guangzhou Military Region; East Sea Fleet, South Sea Fleet

ZHANG HAIYANG
CURRENT TITLE: PLA Political Commissar, Chengdu Military Region.
RANK: General, 2009
BORN: 1949
SERVICE: Second Artillery Corps
REGIONAL AFFILIATION: Hunan; Beijing and Chengdu Military Regions

ZHANG QINSHENG
CURRENT TITLE: Deputy Chief of General Staff
RANK: General, 2010
BORN: 1948
SERVICE: Army
REGIONAL AFFILIATION: Shanxi; Guangzhou Military Region

MA XIAOTIAN
CURRENT TITLE: Deputy Chief of the General Staff
RANK: General, 2009
BORN: 1949
SERVICE: Air Force
REGIONAL AFFILIATION: Henan; Guangzhou, Lanzhou and Nanjing Military Regions

SUN JIANGUO
CURRENT TITLE: Deputy Chief of the General Staff
RANK: Lieutenant General, 2006
BORN: 1952
SERVICE: Navy
REGIONAL AFFILIATION: Hebei

FANG FENGHUI
CURRENT TITLE: Commander, Beijing Military Region
RANK: General, 2010
BORN: 1951
SERVICE: Army
REGIONAL AFFILIATION: Shaanxi; Guangzhou and Beijing Military Regions

WEI FENGHE
CURRENT TITLE: Chief of Staff, Second Artillery Corps
RANK: Lieutenant General, 2008
BORN: 1954
SERVICE: Second Artillery Corps
REGIONAL AFFILIATION: Shandong

ZHANG YOUXIA
CURRENT TITLE: Commander, Shenyang Military Region
RANK: Lieutenant General, 2007
BORN: 1950
SERVICE: Army
REGIONAL AFFILIATION: Beijing, Shaanxi; Beijing and Shenyang Military Regions

(or the parallel posts for political commissars) may be eligible for promotion.

China's paramount leader serves simultaneously as the president of the state, the general-secretary of the Party, and the chairman of the military commission, as Hu does. The top leader does not always hold all three positions, however: Jiang held onto his chair on the CMC for two years after his term as president ended in 2002. Since Hu did not become CMC chairman until 2004, it is not unlikely that he will maintain his chair until 2014, two years after he gives up his presidency and leadership of the party. But this is a reasonable assumption, not a settled fact, and some doubt Hu's strength in resolving such questions in his favor.

Interestingly, Hu has not yet appointed Vice President Xi Jinping to be his successor on the CMC, sparking rumors over the past year about whether Hu is reluctant to give Xi the vice chairmanship or whether Xi's position could be at risk. But Hu will almost certainly dub Xi his successor as chairman of the CMC soon, probably in October. Given the possibility that Hu could retain his CMC chairmanship till 2014, Xi's influence over the military could remain subordinate to Hu's until then, raising uncertainties about how Hu and Xi will interact with each other and with the military during this time. Otherwise, Xi will be expected to take over the top military post along with the top Party and state posts in 2012.

Old and New Trends

Of the leading military figures, there are several observable trends. Regional favoritism in recruitment and promotion remains a powerful force, and regions that have had the greatest representation on the CMC in the past will retain their prominent place: Shandong, Hebei, Henan, Shaanxi and Liaoning provinces, respectively, appear likely to remain the top regions represented by the new leadership, according to research by Cheng Li, a prominent Chinese scholar. These provinces are core to the CPC's support base. There is considerably less representation in the upper officer corps from Shanghai, Guangdong,

Sichuan, or the western regions, all of which are known for regionalism and are more likely to stand at variance with Beijing. (This is not to say that other provinces, Sichuan for instance, do not produce a large number of soldiers.)

One group of leaders, the princelings, are likely to take a much greater role in the CMC in 2012 than in the current CMC, in great part because these are the children or relatives of Communist Party revolutionary heroes and elites and were born during the 1940s-50s. Examples include the current naval commander and CMC member Wu Shengli, political commissar of the Second Artillery Corps Zhang Haiyang, and two deputy chiefs of the general staff, Ma Xiaotian and Zhang Qinsheng. In politics, the princelings are not necessarily a coherent faction with agreed-upon policy leanings. Though princeling loyalties are reinforced by familial ties and inherited from fathers, grandfathers and other relatives, they share similar elite backgrounds, their careers have benefited from these privileges, and they are viewed and treated as a single group by everyone else. In the military, the princelings are more likely to form a unified group capable of a coherent viewpoint, since the military is more rigidly hierarchical and personal ties are based on staunch loyalty. The strong princeling presence could constitute an interest group within the military leadership capable of pressing more forcefully for its interests than it would otherwise be able to do.

A marked difference in the upcoming CMC is the rising role of the PLAN, PLAAF and Second Artillery Corps, as against the traditionally dominant army. This development was made possible by the enlargement of the CMC in 2004, elevating the commanders of each of these non-army services to the CMC, and it is expected to hold in 2012. The army will remain the most influential service across the entire fifth generation military leadership, with the navy, air force, and missile corps following close behind. But crucially, in the 2012 CMC the army's representation could decline relative to the other branches of service, since of the three members of the current CMC eligible to stay only one comes from the army (General Armaments Department Director Chang Wangquan) and many of the next-highest candidates also hail from other services. After all, missile capabilities and sea and air power are increasingly important as China focuses on the ability to secure its international supply chains and prevent greater foreign powers (namely the United States) from approaching too closely areas of strategic concern. The greater standing of the PLAN, PLAAF, and Second Artillery Corps is already showing signs of solidifying, since officers from these services used not to be guaranteed representation on the CMC but now appear to have a permanent place.

There is also a slight possibility that the two individuals chosen to be the CMC vice chairmen could both come from a background in military operations. Typically the two vice chairmen — the most powerful military leaders — are divided between one officer centered on military operations and another centered on political affairs. This ensures a civilian check on military leadership, with the political commissar supervising the military in normal times, and the military commander having ultimate authority during times of war. However, given the candidates available for the position, the precedent could be broken and the positions filled with officers who both come from a military operational background. Such a configuration in the CMC could result in higher emphasis on the capability and effectiveness of military rather than political solutions to problems and a CMC prone to bridle under CPC orders. But having two military affairs specialists in the vice chairmen seats is a slim possibility, and personnel are available from political offices to fill one of the vice chairmanships, thus preserving the traditional balance and CPC guidance over military affairs.

Civilian Leadership Maintained

The rising current of military power in the Chinese system could manifest in any number of ways. Sources tell STRATFOR that military officers who retire sooner than civilian leaders may start to take up civilian positions in the ministries or elsewhere in the state bureaucracy. Nevertheless, the overall arc of recent Chinese history has reinforced the model of civilian leadership over the military. The Communist Party retains control of the CMC, the central and provincial bureaucracies, the state-owned corporations and banks, mass organizations, and most of the media. Moreover, there does not appear to be a single military strongman who could lead a significant challenge to civilian leadership. So while the military's sway is undoubtedly rising, and the upcoming civilian leadership could get caught in stalemate over policy, the military is not in a position to seize power. Rather, it is maneuvering to gain more influence within the system, adding another element of intrigue to the already tense bargaining structure that defines elite politics in China. But despite possible military-civilian frictions, the PLA will seek to preserve the regime, and to manage or suppress internal or external forces that could jeopardize that goal.

CHAPTER 4: SECURITY

Space and Sea-Lane Control in Chinese Strategy
Jan. 24, 2007

Aviation Week & Space Technology magazine, citing U.S. intelligence sources, has reported that China has successfully tested an anti-satellite (ASAT) system. According to the report, which U.S. officials later confirmed, a missile was launched, and then intercepted and destroyed a Feng Yun 1C weather satellite, also belonging to China, on Jan. 11. The weather satellite was launched into polar orbit in 1999. The precise means of destruction is not clear, but it appears to have been a kinetic strike (meaning physical intercept, not laser) that broke the satellite into many pieces. The U.S. government wants to reveal as much information as possible about this event in order to show its concern — and to show the Chinese how closely the Americans are monitoring their actions.

The Jan. 17 magazine report was not the first U.S. intelligence leak about Chinese ASAT capabilities. In August 2006, the usual sources reported China had directed lasers against U.S. satellites. It has become clear that China is in the process of acquiring the technology needed to destroy or blind satellites in at least low-Earth orbit, which is where intelligence-gathering satellites tend to operate.

Two things about this are noteworthy. The first is that China is moving toward a space warfare capability. The second is that it is not

153

the Chinese who are announcing these moves (they maintained official silence until Jan. 23, when they confirmed the ASAT test), but Washington that is aggressively publicizing Chinese actions. These leaks are not accidental: The Bush administration wants it known that China is doing these things, and the Chinese are quite content with that. China is not hiding its efforts, and U.S. officials are using them to create a sense of urgency within the United States about Chinese military capabilities (something that, in budgetary debates in Washington, ultimately benefits the U.S. Air Force).

China has multiple space projects under way, but the one it is currently showcasing — and on which the United States is focusing — involves space-denial capabilities. That makes sense, given China's geopolitical position. It does not face a significant land threat: With natural barriers like the Himalayas or the Siberian wastes on its borders, foreign aggression into Chinese territory is unlikely. However, China's ability to project force is equally limited by these barriers. The Chinese have interests in Central Asia, where they might find power projection an enticing consideration, but this inevitably would bring them into conflict with the Russians. China and Russia have an interest in containing the only superpower, the United States, and fighting among themselves would play directly into American hands. Therefore, China will project its power subtly in Central Asia; it will not project overt military force there. Its army is better utilized in guaranteeing China's internal cohesiveness and security than in engaging in warfare.

Geopolitics and Naval Power

Its major geopolitical problem is, instead, maritime power. China — which published a defense white paper shortly before the ASAT test — has become a great trading nation, with the bulk of its trade moving by sea. And not only does it export an enormous quantity of goods, but it also increasingly imports raw materials. The sea-lanes on which it depends are all controlled by the U.S. Navy, right up to China's brown water. Additionally, Beijing retains an interest in

Taiwan, which it claims as a part of China. But whatever threats China makes against Taiwan ring hollow: The Chinese navy is incapable of forcing its way across the Taiwan Strait, incapable of landing a multidivisional force on Taiwan and, even if it were capable of that, it could not sustain that force over time. That is because the U.S. Navy — using airpower, missiles, submarines and surface vessels — could readily cut the lines of supply and communication between China and Taiwan.

The threat to China is the U.S. Navy. If the United States wanted to break China, its means of doing so would be naval interdiction. This would not have to be a close-in interdiction. The Chinese import oil from around the world and ship their goods around the world. U.S. forces could choose to stand off, far out of the range of Chinese missiles — or reconnaissance platforms that would locate U.S. ships — and interdict the flow of supplies there, at a chokepoint such as the Strait of Malacca. This strategy would have far-reaching implications, of course: the Malacca Strait is essential not only to China, but also to the United States and the rest of the world. But the point is that the U.S. Navy could interdict China's movement of goods far more readily than China could interdict American movement of goods.

For China, freedom of the seas has become a fundamental national interest. Right now, China's access to the sea-lanes depends on U.S. acquiescence. The United States has shown no interest whatsoever in cutting off that access — quite the contrary. But China, like any great power, does not want its national security held hostage to the goodwill of another power — particularly not one it regards as unpredictable and as having interests quite different from its own. To put it simply, the United States currently dominates the world's oceans. This is a source of enormous power, and the United States will not give up that domination voluntarily. China, for its part, cannot live with that state of affairs indefinitely. China may not be able to control the sea itself, but it cannot live forever with U.S. control. Therefore, it requires a sea-lane-denial strategy.

Quite naturally, China has placed increased emphasis on naval development. But the construction of a traditional navy — consisting of aircraft carriers, nuclear attack submarines and blue-water surface systems, which are capable of operating over great distances — is not only enormously expensive, but also will take decades to construct. It is not just a matter of shipbuilding. It is also a matter of training and maturing a generation of naval officers, developing viable naval tactics and doctrine, and leapfrogging generations of technology — all while trying to surpass a United States that already has done all of these things. Pursuing a conventional naval strategy will not provide a strategic solution for China within a reasonable timeframe. The United States behaves in unexpected ways, from the Chinese point of view, and the Chinese will need a solution within five years — or certainly within a decade.

They cannot launch a competitive, traditional navy in that period of time. However, the U.S. Navy has a general dependency on — and, therefore, a vulnerability related to — space-based systems. Within the U.S. military, this is not unique to the Navy, but given that the Navy operates at vast distances and has sea-lane-control missions — as well as the mission of launching aircraft and missiles against land-based targets — it has a particular dependency on space. The service relies on space-based systems for intelligence-gathering, communications, navigation and tactical reconnaissance. This is true not only for naval platforms, but also for everything from cruise missile guidance to general situational awareness.

Take out the space-based systems and the efficiency of the Navy plummets dramatically. Imagine an American carrier strike group moving into interdiction position in the Taiwan Strait without satellite reconnaissance, targeting information for anti-ship missiles, satellite communications for coordination and so on. Certainly, shipboard systems could substitute, but not without creating substantial vulnerabilities — particularly if Chinese engineers could develop effective jamming systems against them.

If the Chinese were able to combine kinetic ASAT systems for low-Earth orbit, high-energy systems for communications and other systems in geostationary orbit and tools for effectively denying the electromagnetic spectrum to the United States, they would have moved a long way toward challenging U.S. dominance of space and limiting the Navy's ability to deny sea-lanes to Chinese ships. From the Chinese point of view, the denial of space to the United States would undermine American denial of the seas to China.

Conjecture and Core Interests

There has been some discussion — fueled by Chinese leaks — that the real purpose of the Chinese ASAT launch was to prompt the Americans to think about an anti-ASAT treaty. This is not a persuasive argument because such a treaty would freeze in place the current status quo, and that status quo is not in the Chinese national interest.

For one thing, a treaty banning ASAT systems would leave the Chinese without an effective means of limiting American naval power. It would mean China would have to spend a fortune on a traditional navy and wait at least a generation to have it in place. It would mean ceding the oceans to the United States for a very long time, if not permanently. Second, the United States and Russia already have ASAT systems, and the Chinese undoubtedly assume the Americans have moved aggressively, if secretly, to improve those systems. Treaty or no, the United States and Russia already have the technology for taking out Chinese satellites. China is not going to assume either will actually dismantle systems — or forget how to build them fast — merely because of a treaty. The only losers in the event of an anti-ASAT treaty would be the countries that do not have them, particularly China.

The idea that what China really wants is an anti-ASAT treaty is certainly one the Chinese should cultivate. This would buy them time while Americans argue over Chinese intentions, it would make the Chinese look benign and, with some luck, it could undermine U.S. political will in the area of the military utilization of space. Cultivating perceptions that an anti-ASAT treaty is the goal is the perfect diplomatic counterpart to Chinese technological development. But the notion itself does not stand up to scrutiny.

The issue for the United States is not so much denying space to China as ensuring the survivability of its own systems. The United States likely has the ability to neutralize the space-based systems of other countries. The strategic issue, however, is whether it has sufficient robustness and redundancy to survive an attack in space. In other words, do U.S. systems have the ability to maneuver to evade attacks, to shield themselves against lasers, to continue their missions while under attack? Moreover, since satellites will be damaged and lost, does the United States have sufficient reserve satellites to replace those destroyed and launchers to put them in place quickly?

For Washington, the idea of an ASAT treaty is not the issue; the United States would love anything that blocks space capabilities for other nations. Rather, it is about building its own space strategy around the recognition that China and others are working toward denying space to the United States.

All of this is, of course, fiendishly expensive, but it is still a lot cheaper than building new naval fleets. The real problem, however, is not just money, but current military dogma. The U.S. military is now enthralled by the doctrine of asymmetric warfare, in which nonstate actors are more important than states. Forever faithful to the assumption that all wars in the future will look like the one currently being fought, the strategic urgency and intellectual bandwidth needed to prepare for space warfare does not currently exist within the U.S. military. Indeed, an independent U.S. Space Command no longer exists — having been merged into Strategic Command, which itself is seen as an anachronism.

For the United States, one of the greatest prices of the Iraq war is not simply the ongoing conflict, but also the fact that it makes it impossible for the U.S. military to allocate resources for emerging threats. That always happens in war, but it is particularly troubling in this case because of the intractable nature of the Iraq conflict and the palpable challenge being posed by China in space. This is not a challenge that many — certainly not those at the highest levels of military leadership — have time to think about while concerned about the future of a few city blocks in Baghdad; but U.S. leaders might, in 10 years, look back on 2007 and wonder what their predecessors were thinking about.

Peacekeeping and the Responsible Stakeholder
Aug. 28, 2007

A Chinese national, Maj. Gen. Zhao Jingmin, was appointed to head a U.N. mission for the first time Aug. 27. Zhao will lead the U.N. peacekeeping mission in Western Sahara.

The appointment marks a big step for China, which only began sending observers and police personnel overseas a few years ago. China is frustrated, however, that its attempts to answer U.S. calls for it to play the role of a "responsible stakeholder" via participation in international peacekeeping operations have led anti-China factions in the U.S. Congress to express concerns about Beijing's expansionist ambitions in Africa.

China hopes to use the participation to gain experience, clean up its image, strengthen its internationalist credentials and prove that China — not Japan — is the responsible international player in Asia. China first dipped its toe into U.N. peacekeeping missions in 2000, but sent only a handful of police and observers. Three years later, China contributed troops; it now has more than 1,500 troops deployed under U.N. auspices in five countries: Liberia, Sudan, Lebanon, the Democratic Republic of the Congo and East Timor.

As it expands its foreign investments, Beijing has found it must expand its overseas activities beyond economic and political engagement to include a security component. This is especially the case in regions where political involvement does not always guarantee the safety of Chinese investment interests, as in Ethiopia, where an attack by 200 militants left nine Chinese workers dead and an energy exploration facility damaged. Energy security sits high on the Chinese leadership's list of priorities, explaining Beijing's current spending spree across the world's top energy/resource producers. And for the fruit of any overseas energy asset acquisition to be reaped, security is a must.

Beijing continues to use its political leverage to this end, engaging in both checkbook diplomacy and more innovative economic packages (such as the China Development Bank's recent purchase of a stake in Barclays) to secure its investment interests overseas. But more than just political leverage is needed.

The struggle to secure its interests has become especially urgent as other countries have started following China in using money to strike up political friendships in energy-rich states. Japanese Prime Minister Shinzo Abe's ruling Liberal Democratic Party announced in June that Japan's Africa budget will be tripled over the next five years. Sensing the competition in aid monies, Beijing is keen to expand its assistance in areas where Tokyo has less flexibility — namely, overseas troop deployment, which the pacifist Japanese Constitution constrains. Japan is the second-largest cash contributor to the U.N. peacekeeping budget, providing 17 percent of the fund, while China is the seventh-largest, giving 3 percent. In terms of troop contributions, however, China surpasses Japan by far: China is the 13th-largest contributor of troops, while Japan does not even place in top 15.

Operating as part of a U.N. mission lends China's expansion into international security operations a more nonthreatening cast.

China already has security personnel stationed abroad to protect its interests in countries such as Sudan, but these forces are privately contracted. By contrast, sending state-funded security personnel overseas inevitably will spark U.S. criticism. Operating as part of a U.N. mission, however, lends China's expansion into international security operations a more peace-orientated, nonthreatening cast: it gives the impression that China is spending its security budget overseas not just for itself, but for the world.

An enhanced global stakeholder reputation will help Beijing defuse the negative international public relations China has been receiving on its other economic issues, such as substandard Chinese exports, trade imbalances with the United States and European Union, or the yuan appreciation issue. It also will help Beijing counter foreign criticism of its human rights track record. Beijing's financial support to the Sudanese government, for example, was mentioned during German Chancellor Angela Merkel's visit to China to lobby Beijing on the subject of climate change.

Ultimately, China hopes that its peacekeeping participation will enhance its credentials as a peaceful alternative to the United States as a global police force. And with Japan busy extracting itself from its pacifist constitutional chains, Beijing will be the only Asian alternative to the United States.

The Challenges of a 'Defensive' Nuclear Arsenal
June 2, 2008

U.S. Secretary of Defense Robert Gates, speaking at a regional security conference in Singapore on June 1, dismissed China's claims that its intercontinental ballistic missile (ICBM) arsenal is for defensive purposes only. While this sort of political banter is not normally of much interest to STRATFOR — Beijing and Washington have long been at odds over defense-related issues — in this case, it is emblematic of the nuclear dynamic between the two countries.

In one sense, of course, Gates is correct: An ICBM is inherently an offensive weapon. China is indeed moving to modernize its arsenal with more capable solid-propellant missiles that can deliver more warheads more accurately to the continental United States.

But at the same time, China does not have anything close to the strategic force structure to pretend to a meaningful first-strike capability — the ability to attempt to conduct a debilitating surprise attack against U.S. nuclear forces. As it moves to modernize its arsenal, Beijing still has much ground to cover to ensure the survivability of its own second-strike or retaliatory capability. China's work on its strategic deterrent, in other words, can hardly be termed provocative.

Ultimately, neither Beijing nor Washington is interested in any sort of escalating arms race; both have far more pressing problems, and neither has the resources right now to devote to an accelerated nuclear weapons acquisitions program (and, of course, the United States is well ahead of China in both qualitative and quantitative terms). However, each is forced to consider not just the other's near-term intent, where the two can see eye-to-eye, but also long-term capabilities and the potential for the emergence of a strategic threat to national interests. Beijing especially is left hedging its bets while attempting to mold perceptions of its military prowess as both defensive and representative of a world-class military power (positions which are not exactly compatible).

While this diplomatic justification for a nuclear arsenal is of little more concern, strategically speaking, than a spat between two defense officials in Singapore, Beijing is edging its way into a very difficult corner.

China is continuing to modernize its intercontinental-range arsenal in order to ensure its nuclear deterrent's long-term survivability and credibility (and not just with the United States, but also with China's nuclear-armed neighbors Russia, Pakistan and India). Beyond the deployment of a small ballistic missile submarine fleet, however, much of China's modernization has been one-for-one replacement of existing systems — essentially sustaining the arsenal rather than growing it. (Of course, Washington is not required to view it that way, and part of the problem with nuclear arsenals the world over is the lack of outward transparency.)

But the United States has its own "defensive" ploy: ballistic missile defense (BMD). The Pentagon's deployment of both sea- and land-based BMD systems from California and Alaska to Japan will only continue. While all of this is ostensibly directed at North Korea's extremely limited Taepodong arsenal, it will also affect China's limited deterrent (China has as few as a couple of dozen missiles capable of targeting the U.S. eastern seaboard).

As more capable and more robust BMD systems are fielded by the United States (and thus by the Japanese Self Defense Force), they will begin to erode Chinese ICBMs' ability to penetrate this nascent missile shield. Beijing will soon find itself forced either to expand its forces more meaningfully — both quantitatively and qualitatively — or to accept the slow marginalization of the currency of its deterrent in Washington. The former could easily be interpreted as a prelude to an arms race — one China knows it is all too likely to lose.

But this boxing in of the Chinese nuclear arsenal is only a side benefit of U.S. efforts in BMD, which will also begin to erode the survivability of Beijing's space-based assets.

China's New Need for a Maritime Focus
March 30, 2009

The Chinese People's Liberation Army Navy (PLAN) will mark its 60th anniversary April 23 with a fleet review off Qingdao, the headquarters of the PLAN's North Sea Fleet. The highlights of the review will be the destroyers Haikou (171) and Wuhan (169), both of which are scheduled to return to China from deployment off the Somali coast sometime in late March. The Somali anti-piracy operation represents another step in an expanding role for the PLAN that is driven in part by China's changing economy. This new role places Beijing on a maritime collision course with its neighbors, including Japan and India, and ultimately with the United States.

Limiters on China's Naval Development

China historically has been a land power, with its core centered along the Yellow and Yangtze rivers and protected by a combination of natural features, such as mountains and deserts, and acquired buffer zones like Tibet, Xinjiang, Inner Mongolia and Manchuria. As such, China has developed over time as an enclosed continental power surrounded by potential enemies, defending interminable land borders and harassed along the coast by regional rivals.

For much of its history, China was largely able to rely on its own natural resources to support its population. What it couldn't get or produce at home was brought in primarily by land. Chinese international trade focused on the land routes into Central Asia and beyond, following the great Silk Road. This further focused Chinese military power on preserving these land routes, and it reduced the funding — and the need — for a heavy focus on maritime power.

From the ninth through the 14th century, Chinese maritime trade stayed primarily within the confines of the South China Sea, with some excursions into the Indian Ocean. While this period saw the establishment of Chinese trading settlements in Southeast Asia, the Chinese state did not pursue a major colonizing effort or seek to establish a true empire through these trading ports. The Chinese landmass provided ample space and resources. As kingdoms in China rose and fell, the intervening dynasties and competing states were focused firmly on the shifting land borders and terrestrial threats.

During the Yuan Dynasty in the 13th century, when China was part of the Mongol Empire, Kublai Khan attempted to use sea power to extend the empire's reach to Japan and Southeast Asia. This brief two-decade effort was abandoned, however, due to military failures and raw economics; the security and extension of the western land-based trade routes allowed the Yuan Dynasty to carry out whatever trade it wished all the way to Europe. While Chinese states had been trading along the Silk Road routes for centuries, with varying degrees of security and control, under the Mongol empire the routes were once again secured and expanded.

With the decline and collapse of the Yuan empire in the latter half of the 14th century, the Han Chinese Ming replaced the Mongol Yuan leadership. In the early 15th century, several factors coincided to trigger a rapid (but brief) expansion of Chinese maritime trade and power.

The fracturing of the Mongol Empire and the military activities of Tamerlane in Central and Southwest Asia at the end of the 14th century undermined the security of the Silk Road trade routes once again. In China, meanwhile, the Ming consolidated and expanded power along the southern periphery and began launching attacks to the north to keep the Mongols at bay; Tamerlane's planned invasion of China collapsed with his death in 1405. With the Ming at the height of their power in the first quarter of the 15th century and the land routes to the west disrupted, China embarked upon a series of major maritime expeditions over three decades, seeking new trade and demonstrating the power of the Chinese empire.

From 1405 to 1433, the Ming court eunuch Zheng He, a Muslim, led a massive Chinese fleet complete with "treasure ships," support ships and a substantial military escort on a series of seven voyages through Southeast Asia, the Indian Ocean, the Middle East and Africa. Zheng and his treasure fleets carried out trade in goods and technology, demanded (sometimes with military force) recognition of the centrality of the Chinese emperor, established or enhanced Chinese trading ports throughout the region and brought gifts and luxuries back to the Ming court.

While there are conflicting historical claims as to how far Zheng's fleets sailed, and the recorded size of some of his ships has been questioned, it is generally agreed that the flotilla was one of the pre-eminent displays of naval power of that time. Yet just as quickly as China launched its foray into naval exploration and power, it ended it, destroying the treasure fleets (and many records of their activities) after three expeditionary decades.

Three factors contributed to this. First was court politics, an ongoing factional conflict between inner-court eunuchs and Confucian scholars (the latter backed in part by Chinese merchants who were losing out because of the state-run trading expeditions). Then there was the argument that expenditures on the treasure fleet were emptying the Chinese treasury with little to show in return. This view held that the trips were not profitable, that they were merely the frivolities of a wealthy and powerful Chinese elite and that money spent on sending expeditions abroad was not available for coastal defense against the ravages of Japanese pirates. Finally, there was the fact that land expeditions into Mongolia had done little to reduce the threat from the north, and China needed to shift military resources from an expeditionary navy to the army to secure the nation.

China's Traditional Imperatives

It is this latter point, the constant threat to China's long land borders, that has always won out over the development of an expeditionary navy — particularly when there is no real economic benefit from or need for state-sponsored maritime activity. China's geopolitical imperatives have developed in relation to its geography, demography and economy. These traditional imperatives are to maintain internal unity in the Han Chinese regions, maintain control of the buffer regions, and protect the coast from foreign encroachment.

China's defense priorities have always been directed mainly toward land-based concerns, from control of the population and security of the buffer zones to protection of land-based trade routes and defense against regional threats. Given the cost and scale of China's land-based defense priorities, protecting the coasts was often done administratively (limiting trade and foreign concessions), or by relying on the size of China's population as a deterrent to invasion. China rarely threw substantial funding and development into a navy, and when it did, it was almost always used for coastal defense.

This pattern has held true since the Ming scuttled their vast treasure fleets, and China's military priorities have continued to focus on the army over the navy — until recently. China's opening and reform at the end of the 1970s ultimately led to a significant shift in the country's economy, with consumption of raw materials outstripping domestic production and creating an increasing needing to source materials from far overseas.

Economic Shift and a Change in Focus

Oil, an economic driver and facilitator, provides a clear example of the new stresses facing China. At the beginning of the economic opening, Chinese domestic oil production exceeded consumption,

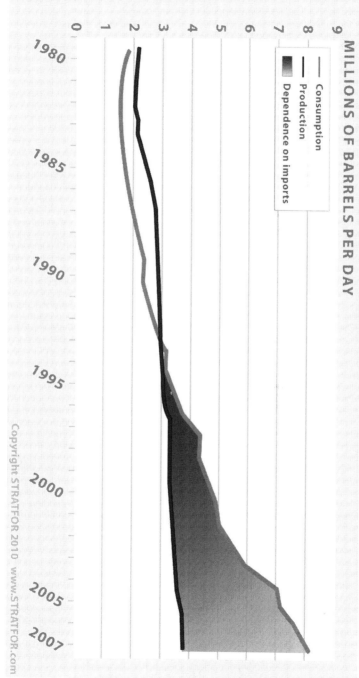

CHINESE CRUDE OIL CONSUMPTION AND PRODUCTION

MILLIONS OF BARRELS PER DAY

Consumption
Production
Dependence on imports

and the trend continued for more than a decade. But in 1993, Chinese consumption began to outstrip production as the economy started to take off. In 2003, China became the world's second-largest oil consumer, surpassing Japan. In 2005, Chinese oil consumption rose to twice the rate of domestic production, and by 2008, China passed Japan as the world's second-largest oil importer.

While oil is one of the most obvious resource issues for China, it is not the only one. From 1987 to the present, Chinese production of iron ore from domestic mines more than quadrupled, growing from about 160 million metric tons to over 800 million metric tons. But far more significant to the explosive growth in China's steel industry has been the importation of iron ore. During the same period, Chinese imports of iron ore surged from 11 million metric tons to more than 440 million metric tons. The disparity between domestic growth and imports means that, while 6 percent of China's raw iron ore was imported in 1987, this figure had doubled by 1993 and continued rising to reach a peak of around 40 percent in 2004 and 2005. Though it has since declined to about 35 percent, China's dependence on imported iron ore remains significant.

Other minerals pose problems as well. While domestic production of bauxite grew from 3.2 million metric tons in 1987 to 30 million metric tons in 2007, imports surged from a mere 323,000 metric tons to more than 30 million metric tons over the same period, causing imports to shift from 9 percent of consumption to about half. Perhaps most troubling for China is the inadequacy of its domestic copper-mining industry. Production of the metal increased from 350,000 metric tons in 1987 to 946,000 metric tons in 2007. Imports, meanwhile, shot up from 116,000 metric tons in 1987 to more than 3 million metric tons in 2007. This disparity has caused China's reliance on copper imports to increase from 25 percent in 1987 to a whopping 76 percent in 2007.

With China growing ever more dependent on foreign commodities and markets, its supply lines were becoming increasingly vulnerable, and the Chinese navy had little capability or even doctrinal guidance to protect China's interests far beyond its shores. By the

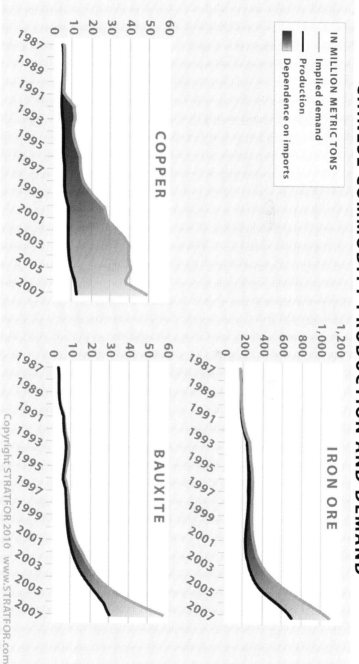

CHINESE COMMODITY PRODUCTION AND DEMAND

IN MILLION METRIC TONS

- Implied demand
- Production
- Dependence on imports

COPPER

IRON ORE

BAUXITE

mid-1990s, China was facing a stark reality regarding its supply-line vulnerability if it wanted to maintain its economic growth. Options were limited:

- Accept the vulnerability (particularly if the cost of developing and deploying naval protection exceeds the potential risk and cost of a disruption of trade) or ally with a naval power to protect China's interests.
- Reduce vulnerability by diversifying trade routes and patterns, including pushing into Central Asia and Southeast Asia.
- Devise a counterweight to defend Chinese trade routes and supply lines — i.e., develop a more robust navy.

China's economic shift and rising economic power meant that the risk of inaction finally outweighed the cost of ensuring maritime security. With the collapse of the Soviet Union, China began tapping into Central Asian energy resources, but this was only a stopgap measure. It was time for the Chinese navy to reassert itself not only as a defender of the coast, but also as a force that could travel the world's oceans and protect China's emerging maritime interests.

China's Plan for a Blue-Water Fleet
March 31, 2009

In 1999, as the Chinese People's Liberation Army Navy (PLAN) marked its 50th anniversary, Chinese naval officials already were planning to expand the range and role of the navy, with a clear eye toward moving beyond a traditional coastal defense capability (the so-called "green-water" navy) to a true "blue-water," or oceangoing, navy. But they knew the change would be neither quick nor easy. It would require not only new ships, but also new logistics systems, new training and new communications protocol — in essence, an entirely new navy.

Beyond the obvious budget constraints, other hurdles loomed, including debate over the pros and cons of a carrier fleet, domestic security concerns that would shift budgets and attention back to dry land and the age-old Chinese concern over the strategic logic of an expeditionary navy.

Clearly, developing an entirely new navy would not happen overnight. Moving from a coastal fleet to an expeditionary fleet would take at least a generation, and the PLAN needed a way to maintain its coastal mission while expanding its operational reach long before such a transition could be completed. (Chinese analysts have begun looking into building a coast guard, patterned after that of the United States, that would take on the coastal role while the navy focused on blue-water force projection.) To accomplish this transition, the PLAN embarked upon four steps that are not necessarily sequential; action on one does not depend on the completion of another, nor do all the steps need to be accomplished in full. Taken together, however, these overlapping steps create a path for China to protect its interests while moving toward its objective of deploying a robust blue-water navy:

- Secure China's claimed exclusive economic zone (EEZ), which includes most of the South China Sea, in order to create a maritime buffer similar to the terrestrial buffers of Xinjiang and Tibet.

- "Extend" the Chinese shoreline via port agreements and island development to create a string of logistical hubs that would enable coastal vessels to operate farther from the mainland.

- Develop and deploy asymmetrical countermeasures to deal with the technological gap between China and the world's dominant naval power, the United States.

- Begin building the ships, logistics train and doctrine for a truly expeditionary navy.

171

Creating a Maritime Buffer

The first step in China's naval development is to exert its authority over its EEZ. Basically, Beijing claims the Yellow, East and South China seas. This area is enclosed by what China calls the "first island chain" running from southern Japan through the Ryukyu Islands to Taiwan, then along the Philippine Islands to Borneo and on (almost) to the Strait of Malacca, the choke point for trade from the Arabian Sea and the Indian Ocean to East Asia. But Chinese claims overlap and conflict with those of several other countries, including Japan (over the Daiyoutai/Senkaku Islands), Vietnam (over the Xisha/Paracel Islands) and Taiwan, Vietnam, Malaysia, Indonesia and the Philippines (over the Nansha/Spratly Islands).

Claiming control and exerting control are two very different things. While China claims special rights in the Yellow, East and South China seas, these claims for the most part are not recognized by other countries, and China has found it difficult to exert control in the area. Tensions occasionally flare up as a result, usually involving a naval patrol and fishing or commercial vessels. Boats and ships are sometimes detained, damaged or even sunk. In 2005, for example, Chinese ships opened fire on Vietnamese fishing vessels in the Gulf of Tonkin, leaving several Vietnamese injured or dead. Beijing claimed the Vietnamese fishermen were pirates.

China also has tried more cooperative approaches to reduce direct competition for use and control of the South China Sea, including joint ventures for energy exploration and fishing agreements. Indeed, China has made an effort to shift its image in Asia from that of a "rising China" that threatens to dominate the region to a "cooperative China" that could be an economic partner. In the process, it has managed to reduce tensions with its neighbors and support a rising tide of Pan-Asianism that portrays the United States and the West as bigger threats to the region than China.

China's efforts to create a maritime buffer also extend into the realm of "international law warfare," part of the "unrestricted warfare" paradigm expounded by two senior colonels in the People's Liberation

COMPETING CLAIMS IN THE WATERS NEAR CHINA

—— Chinese sovereignty claim

MONGOLIA

RUSSIA

Beijing ★

NORTH KOREA

Sea of Japan

SOUTH KOREA

CHINA

JAPAN

East China Sea

Daiyoutai/ Senkaku Islands

TAIWAN

PACIFIC OCEAN

LAOS

Xisha/Paracel Islands

South China Sea

Philippine Sea

CAMBODIA

VIETNAM

Nansha/Spratly Islands

PHILIPPINES

MALAYSIA

INDONESIA

| 0 mi | 500 |
| 0 km | 1,000 |

Copyright STRATFOR 2010   www.STRATFOR.com

Army in 1999. They advocated using a broader spectrum of national power — such as leveraging the U.N. Convention on the Law of the Sea (UNCLOS) — to compensate for Chinese military shortcomings in relation to the United States. Regarding the UNCLOS, China is trying to work with other East Asian powers to coherently redefine certain legal distinctions in UNCLOS, like the EEZ and what international activity is acceptable within it. An EEZ currently is defined as an area running 200 nautical miles from a country's coastline within which the country has rights over exploration and extraction of mineral resources, although ships of other countries may pass freely through the area for peaceful purposes and to carry out certain economic and scientific activities (e.g., laying undersea cables). Not every country abides by the UNCLOS or agrees with the definition of an EEZ, and China would like to make it more difficult — legally — for U.S. warships and intelligence gathering platforms to operate within it or approach its coastline.

Despite these cooperative moves, Beijing never stopped its more direct military actions, and it has actually stepped up patrols in the waters out to the first island chain. In 2008, China more than doubled its submarine patrols, according to U.S. Naval Intelligence estimates, with several forays into and around Japanese waters.

On March 8, 2009, a PLAN intelligence collection ship along with several other Chinese-flagged patrol vessels and trawlers confronted the USNS Impeccable some 75 miles off Hainan Island, claiming the U.S. ship was carrying out unlawful military activity. The confrontation topped off days of escalating Chinese activity around U.S. surveillance ships, a maritime parallel to the more aggressive air interdictions that led to the collision between a Chinese Jian-8 fighter and a U.S. EP-3E Aries II surveillance aircraft in 2001. In both cases, it appears the United States was monitoring Chinese submarine developments off Hainan.

China's latest move to assert itself in its claimed EEZ came on March 10, when the China Yuzheng 311, China's largest ocean surveillance vessel, set sail from Guangzhou on its maiden voyage to patrol China's claimed waters in the South China Sea. The ship is a 4,450-ton former navy support vessel transferred in 2006 to the South China Sea Fishery Administration Bureau under the Ministry of Agriculture, now tasked with asserting Chinese claims to contested fishing grounds, islands and reefs in the South China Sea. The bureau plans to launch a 2,500-ton maritime surveillance vessel in 2010 that will carry a helicopter to enhance patrol capabilities.

Expanding Green Water

Aggressive rhetoric and patrols by a single ship or two are insufficient to make China's claimed EEZ an effective buffer, however. This leads to the second step in the PLAN strategy: establishment of logistics bases and ports in strategic locations to push the navy's zone of operation farther from the mainland. In 1996, there were calls for the PLAN to develop at-sea replenishment capabilities in order to extend the navy's reach. Four years later, the Chinese navy was conducting operations with smaller missile boats much farther from shore to test alternative ways of expanding the range of naval operations with existing hardware and in accordance with current doctrine. While China began work on a logistics capability for extended overseas operations in the 1990s, it was not a capability that could be quickly and easily implemented. As a stopgap measure, China simply began moving its coastline farther out.

Beijing did this in part by building docks and facilities in the Nansha/Spratly Islands. This led to a flare-up in tensions in 1998 between Manila and Beijing over Chinese construction on Mischief Reef in the Spratlys, with Manila attempting to draw the United States into the spat. In addition, China began expanding its relations with various Pacific island nations in order to gain access to monitoring and port facilities that could extend the PLAN's reach farther east, along routes heavily traversed by the U.S. Navy and global maritime commerce.

China also began looking west, developing port facilities between the Strait of Malacca and the Arabian Sea. Operating primarily under bilateral trade-promotion agreements, China funded the dredging and improvement of deepwater ports in Sittwe (Myanmar), Chittagong (Bangladesh), Gwadar (Pakistan) and Hambantota (Sri Lanka), creating a string of ports along the northern edge of China's vital supply lines and trade routes from the Middle East through the Indian Ocean. Each of these ports can in some ways be seen as an extension of China's shoreline, serving as repair and logistics hubs and thus extending the range of a green-water navy that still needs an umbilical connection to the mainland. Several of them would also be critical as ports for replenishment ships to sustain Chinese blue-water forces in the Indian Ocean and Arabian Sea — just as the United States relies on friendly ports in the region to supply its own blue-water fleet.

Asymmetrical Counters

The third step in China's naval development is to find ways to counter the U.S. Navy's technological dominance while China's naval evolution is under way. In its simplest form, this would build on the previous steps with the deployment of tracking stations and anti-ship missile installations on China's string of maritime stepping-stones. This could enable China to delay (or at least complicate) a U.S. naval response to a conflict between China and Taiwan, for example, or to deter or complicate any U.S. attempt to blockade Chinese ports or interdict trade routes.

More ambitiously, China has added asymmetrical countermeasures in the form of Russian-built destroyers and submarines armed with anti-ship missiles, already laying the groundwork, in a sense, for building out a new blue-water fleet as well as for countering the U.S. presence on the open seas. China has acquired four Russian-built Sovremenny-class guided missile destroyers, each carrying eight SS-N-22 "Sunburn" supersonic anti-ship missiles (of which China is the only export recipient). Designed by the Soviets to better penetrate the defenses of U.S. carrier battle groups, these missiles have been carefully studied by Chinese engineers, who undoubtedly will try to improve upon and replicate them. Although the destroyers are not impervious to American carrier-based aviation, they can be used as part of a sea denial strategy. In addition, Beijing has acquired a dozen Russian-built Kilo-class diesel-electric patrol submarines, which are now being armed with the SS-N-27 "Sizzler" supersonic anti-ship missile — a weapon senior U.S. naval officers are deeply concerned about. These submarines are known to be very quiet and could pose a threat to U.S. carrier and expeditionary strike groups (and the Kilo design is being incorporated into the development of China's latest domestic patrol submarine).

Beijing's current focus on asymmetrical naval warfare includes a novel way of overcoming advanced anti-ship missile defenses: the use of ballistic missiles. These missiles approach from a near vertical trajectory, from which even relatively simple guidance systems are able to distinguish between a modern American carrier's four-and-a-half-acre flight deck and the open ocean. Ballistic missiles are also thought to exceed the engagement envelope for some of the core defensive systems on U.S. warships, increasing the Pentagon's desire to field Aegis-equipped guided missile cruisers and destroyers in the Pacific that have been upgraded to ballistic missile defense capability. China appears to be working with medium-range ballistic missiles, which have a longer range than its more conventional anti-ship missiles.

In addition, China has begun to focus its attention on a key element of U.S. technological superiority: space. Having begun an ambitious space program of its own in recent years, China is looking to enhance its communications, guidance and observation capabilities. It is also looking to space for more overt military applications. China's January 2007 anti-satellite test demonstrated an alternative ability to deal with a maritime threat by disrupting the guidance systems of sophisticated precision-guided weapons. In line with China's 1999 comment that its neutron bombs were more than enough to handle U.S. aircraft carriers, the anti-satellite test was meant to show that China had the options and creativity to narrow the technology gap if push came to shove with the U.S. Navy.

A Toe in Blue Water

The first three steps in many ways are happening simultaneously, and they allow China to increase its range and capabilities while preparing to take the fourth step: building a robust blue-water navy. The crown jewel for Beijing would be its own aircraft carrier, something naval officials continue to discuss despite the cost and difficulties associated with it. (Recently, this ongoing discussion appears to have moved beyond talk to action.) But before an aircraft carrier can be effectively deployed, the PLAN must demonstrate the ability to conduct extended operations far from home. This is where China's recent participation in anti-piracy operations off the coast of Somalia comes in.

China's testing of extended operations abroad could easily lead to concern about Chinese military expansionism and accelerate the development of countercapabilities by China's neighbors. The Somalia operation, however, has given Beijing a chance to conduct a long-term deployment in a welcoming environment where no one is seen as a threat (except, perhaps, by the pirates). Chinese naval officials have made it clear that their December 2008 deployment of two guided-missile destroyers and a supply ship to Somalia will not be a short one, and that they are preparing to rotate a new squadron of similar size into the area in order to sustain the Chinese presence. This will further test their command, control and logistical coordination, as well as afford opportunities to practice underway replenishment and maintenance.

The Somalia deployment must be understood not as a one-off event, but as a fundamental doctrinal shift rooted in geopolitical realities. There is only one way the PLAN is going to gain experience in naval force projection far afield — by doing it. And as Beijing is finding out, the U.N.-sponsored Somalia operation is one in which it can closely observe the behavior of more experienced navies while practicing its own operational procedures in a nonthreatening way.

But in terms of developing a naval force-projection capability, the U.N.-sponsored mission in the Gulf of Aden represents the shallow end of naval conflict — more green water than blue. A robust expeditionary navy must be able to fight peer forces as well as pirates, and the PLAN has a long way to go before it can deploy a credible blue-water fleet. Complex challenges ranging from damage control (even the British Royal Navy had trouble in this essential area during the Falkland Islands War in the early 1980s) to anti-submarine warfare will occupy PLAN planners for decades to come. While China has started to narrow the gap in terms of anti-ship missiles and submarine development, matters as mundane as the shape and machining of a submarine's screw (propeller) are the products of extensive study and investment, and China has much to learn in these areas.

Nothing complicates the PLAN's expeditionary efforts more than China's lack of a naval tradition. By contrast, the modern U.S. Navy is the product of a maritime tradition that predates its own founding and has strong roots in the even more established maritime tradition of the British Royal Navy. More than simply a matter of subtleties like esprit de corps, such tradition goes to the heart of military proficiency.

American and British naval officers and petty officers have trained under the careful tutelage of seniors well-schooled in their art. In the case of U.S. carrier aviation, for example, this oversight can be traced through hard-won operational experience all the way back to the USS Lexington (CV-2), which was commissioned in 1927 and the oldest carrier to deploy fixed-wing aircraft at the start of World War II.

In the Chinese navy, aviators have no such operational depth to tap, nor do they have aircraft carriers from which to fly. Save for perhaps a handful of Russian advisers with limited experience, few if any of Chinese aviators' instructors or landing signal officers have ever landed or "trapped" a fixed-wing aircraft on a carrier flight deck at sea. Pilots must practice the exacting and unforgiving art of carrier-based flight by simulating takeoffs and landings on paved runways on land instead of on a moving ship.

As the Chinese navy ventures into blue water, it is necessarily doing so with less-experienced officers and seamen. This puts it at a distinct disadvantage, and it is easy to see why it has long deferred this course.

Going Forward

In spite of the many hurdles before it, the PLAN and its expeditionary vision should not be discounted. China may not be able to pull a naval tradition out of thin air, but it is in a good position to begin one. As the American historian and theorist Alfred Thayer Mahan argued, a naval tradition is rooted in a commercial maritime tradition, and China has surpassed the United States in terms of the size of its merchant fleet and in its contribution to global civilian shipbuilding.

Ultimately, with an extensive intelligence and espionage capability, firsthand experience with Russian technology (essentially late-Soviet technology, which in areas like submarine propulsion was quite exceptional) and a new focus on gaining operational experience, the PLAN's trajectory is clear. Chinese naval expansion and improvement over the last decade has been nothing short of dramatic, and the factors that have enabled it will only build upon themselves in the coming years.

Of course, modernizing a navy in East Asia will not occur in a vacuum. The PLAN's blue-water plan will inexorably move forward as long as other, unrelated forces do not interfere. Barring significant economic or political crises at home or the emergence of a threat along China's long land periphery, the PLAN is setting the stage to become a much more potent naval force over the next decade. And as China focuses on the seas to defend its vital supply lines, it will inevitably clash with other regional and international maritime powers, most notably Japan, India and the United States.

Obstacles to a New Naval Strategy
April 1, 2009

China has had three core geopolitical imperatives for much of its history: maintaining internal unity in the Han Chinese regions, maintaining control of the buffer regions and protecting the coast from foreign encroachment. To these can be added a fourth imperative, predicated on China's shift from an agricultural to an industrial economy: securing sea-lane approaches to the Chinese mainland and maritime routes of resource acquisition.

It is this fourth imperative that has prompted the modernization and reform of the People's Liberation Army to include a naval expeditionary focus. But such a focus will put China on a collision course with other emerging or established maritime powers. China's supply lines are, for the most part, identical to Japan's supply lines and run through India's maritime domain. Chinese naval expansion also runs square in the face of a key U.S. imperative — preventing any major regional or international naval power from developing and thus challenging U.S. domination of the seas.

India's Imperatives

India, China's neighbor across the Himalayas, is nearly as populous as China but covers a much smaller land mass. While the Indian culture and population have spread throughout history, the subcontinent itself has been fairly isolated by geography, surrounded as it is by the jungles and mountains of Myanmar to the east, the Himalayas and Tibetan Plateau to the north and the deserts of western Pakistan and Afghanistan to the west. The geopolitical imperatives of India have evolved within this "island," though not all have been achieved:

- Achieve suzerainty in the Ganges River basin.

- Expand nominal control from the core of the subcontinent to the natural geographical barriers.

- Expand control past the Ganges River basin to the Indus River basin.

- Expand power into the Indian Ocean basin to deter foreign penetration.

India has not yet achieved its third imperative and thus remains in a constant struggle with neighboring Pakistan, where Indian security focuses most of its attention. However, this has not prevented India from moving on to the early stages of achieving its fourth imperative — developing a navy capable of exerting nominal control over the Indian Ocean basin.

New Delhi has alternately relied on Moscow and Washington to assist in this development, when it isn't trying to develop technologies and training doctrine on its own. Russia poses little threat to Indian naval expansion and has even encouraged it, so long as New Delhi remained close to Moscow. Russia can offer equipment that is far beyond the reach of indigenous Indian development, but it is the United States, which has dominated the Indian Ocean for decades, that India must turn to either as a competitor or as a partner in extending its maritime influence.

Beijing's push into the Indian Ocean has left New Delhi worried about a Chinese strategy of encirclement. China has close relations and/or port and tracking facilities in Myanmar, Bangladesh, Sri Lanka and Pakistan — all India's neighbors and, in Pakistan's case, a direct competitor. While Beijing's move may have more to do with preventing interdiction of its long, vulnerable supply lines that run from Africa and the Middle East through the Indian Ocean to the South China Sea, even moves intended for defense can be interpreted (or used) for other purposes.

The Indian navy sees its own necessary sphere of operations pushing out from the Indian Ocean and Bay of Bengal to the Persian Gulf and east coast of Africa, and west through the Strait of Malacca to the western coast of Australia. Like China, India has a strategic vision based on a combination of potentially vulnerable trade routes and the need to protect the country from seaborne threats.

In many ways, Indian naval development remains in its nascent stage. But a perceived Chinese maritime encirclement of India has spurred a surge in Indian naval investment and driven New Delhi closer to Washington as a strategic naval partner. This, in turn, can be seen by Beijing as a growing threat to its own maritime security, which could accelerate a regional maritime arms race.

Japan's Imperatives

Like China, Japan is a resource-dependent industrialized nation. As an island, however, Japan is more dependent upon resources from overseas than China is and has been for a longer period of time. As a result, Japan is a much more developed naval power, one that was able to strike a serious blow to the U.S. Pacific Fleet at the onset of World War II.

Like any country, Japan has strategic imperatives shaped in large part by its geography. Japan is a collection of relatively resource-poor islands lying off an Asian landmass rich in space and resources. The Japanese imperatives start at the center and move outward, like the layers of an onion.

- Keep the home islands under the control of a central government and unified military.

- Maintain control of the seas around the Japanese islands.

- Become the dominant influence in the land masses abutting the territorial seas, namely the southern portion of far eastern Russia and the Chinese coastline, at least as far south as Shanghai.

- Be the dominant maritime power in the Northwest Pacific, south to Formosa/Taiwan and southeast to Iwo Jima.

- Secure control of access to mineral resources in mainland China/Southeast Asia (and later to the Middle East as resource routes expand).

Even before Japan's consolidation in the 16th century, the Japanese islands were known regionally as a center of trade and pirate activity, with pirates staging raids along the Korean and Chinese coastlines and down into the South China Sea. At the end of the 15th century, Japanese forces, under the leadership of Toyotomi Hideyoshi, led a massive naval and amphibious assault on Korea, with the intent of moving through to Ming China.

Initially, the invasion demonstrated the strength of Japanese naval power, but its end showed the major weakness of a maritime invasion of mainland Asia — the Japanese were outnumbered by the continental Asians. When the Koreans cut the Japanese maritime supply lines, the invasion collapsed. Two and a half centuries later, an insular Japan was forced open by the gunboat diplomacy of the imperial powers, including the United States. In response, Japan underwent a rapid shift in its own military evolution, embracing maritime power as the way to defend its interests and expand its influence.

By the 1930s, Japan's growing need for resources led to the invasion of China and the military drive into Southeast Asia. Once again, Japan found it difficult to conquer mainland Asia; the population was just too large for the Japanese to overcome. At the same time, Japan's expansion into Southeast Asia created the need to control the waters along the vital supply lines, placing Japan squarely on a confrontational course with the United States. The outcome was World War II's Pacific War, which resulted in a U.S. victory and the loss of all of Japan's strategic interests, including sovereignty of the home islands. After World War II, as the Cold War intensified, Washington saw a need for a strong ally in Japan as a way to contain the spread of Communism and Soviet power. Japanese strategic needs were met in a new manner — Washington provided maritime security while Tokyo dealt with domestic issues and focused on economic expansion.

Decades later, Japan transitioned from being a vanquished foe of the United States to being a major economic competitor, underwritten by U.S. naval power. Rising competition, the end of the Cold War and the reduction of U.S. willingness to underwrite the Japanese economy led Tokyo to begin reassessing its own military capabilities, particularly its Japan Maritime Self-Defense Force (JMSDF). Japan would embark upon a revitalization of its own navy and prepare to take more responsibility for its own maritime security. This inevitably will involve a Japanese challenge to China in the East China Sea over territory and undersea resources.

Because Japanese supply routes, particularly for access to Middle Eastern energy sources, are virtually the same as Chinese routes, Japan sees China's maritime defense moves as a potential threat. This is an untenable situation for Tokyo, and Chinese action and Japanese reaction are feeding a regional maritime arms race. Tokyo is re-engaging Southeast Asian nations, reviving ties left dormant when Japan's economic malaise in the 1990s slashed Japanese development assistance money that had been going to the region. Japan also is looking to enhance ties with India and Mongolia — part of a strategy to refocus China's security concerns and perhaps redirect Chinese investments.

Even more importantly, Japan already has what many consider the second-best navy in the world. The JMSDF is well-funded, developing rapidly and fields some of the latest in modern naval hardware. In this competition, as in the competition with the U.S. Navy, the People's Liberation Army Navy is at a profound disadvantage.

U.S. Imperatives

In their naval expansion, China, India and Japan all must deal with the reality of the world's dominant maritime power: the United States. In many ways, U.S. naval expansion beginning in the late 1700s also was an expression of defense, but the degree of expansion over almost two centuries created room for offensive, or "pre-emptive" defense around the globe. A Chinese navy that is aggressively expanding, no matter the reason, poses a potential challenge to the fundamental U.S. interest of maintaining control of the seas.

The strategic imperatives of the United States are rooted both in the relative isolation of the country and in its contact with both the Atlantic and Pacific oceans.

- Allow no power to emerge in the Western Hemisphere to challenge U.S. domination of North America.

- Control the waters of the Western Hemisphere to prevent the approach of foreign military power.

- Dominate the world's oceans to protect global trade and ensure that no power can build a navy to challenge the United States.

- Ensure that no single continental power arises on the Eurasian landmass capable of challenging the United States.

The expansion of the young United States from a colonial holding of Great Britain to a continental nation to the world's sole superpower attests to its focused, if not always overt, efforts to fulfill and maintain these imperatives. Control of the world's oceans remains a major goal of the United States because it provides the ability not only to protect trade, but also, essentially, to attack any country anywhere while preventing any country from attacking the continental United States. U.S. dominance of the seas is thus a core imperative of U.S. strategic defense, and emerging challengers are either confronted or redirected.

World War II saw the clash of the two emerging naval powers in the Pacific — the United States and Japan. Neither could allow the other to become dominant; Japan needed to expand its empire in order to preserve the security of its natural resources, and the United States could not allow Japan to interdict emerging trade routes in the Pacific or threaten the U.S. Pacific coastline. This clash of strategic imperatives drove the two economic partners to a military confrontation at sea, whether they wanted one or not.

After World War II, the United States dealt with the potential emergence of the Soviet Union as a sea power by encircling it through a series of alliances, redirecting Soviet technology and priorities to a land-based defense. The United States also has employed this strategy in space, another potential battlespace where Washington must ensure that it can strike any country anywhere while preventing any country from attacking the United States. At least for the next 100

COMPARATIVE NAVAL FORCE
PROJECTION PLANS

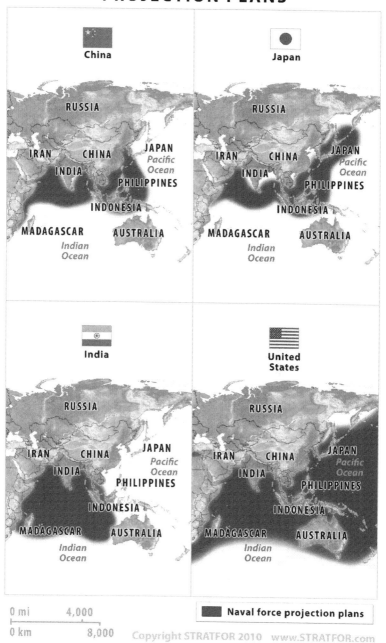

China

Japan

India

United States

RUSSIA

IRAN   CHINA   JAPAN
INDIA   Pacific Ocean
               PHILIPPINES
         INDONESIA
MADAGASCAR   AUSTRALIA
    Indian Ocean

0 mi   4,000
0 km   8,000

Naval force projection plans

years, whether on the sea, under the sea or in space, when an emerging power begins to push out more aggressively, it will meet resistance from the United States.

Chinese naval developments have definitely drawn the attention of the U.S. military, and confrontations and accidents have already occurred as the United States has asserted its claimed right to operate off the Chinese coast for whatever purpose. Beijing will find U.S. resistance not only at sea. Its flirtations in space have drawn serious U.S. responses, and Washington still holds the strategic card of alliance encirclement, which in this case would link Japan, Australia, India and a few key Southeast Asian nations in the effort. Perhaps more troubling for China is the potential for the United States, or possibly even India or Japan, to stir up unrest in China's buffer regions, such as Tibet or Xinjiang.

Strategy of Distraction

Despite the risks, China now considers it necessary to become a naval power, and it has made dramatic progress in doing so. Its interests have become too global for it to focus inward and rely mainly on land-based defense. This recognized imperative, along with China's unwillingness or inability to align with a powerful ally to help guard its interests, is already raising the potential for a maritime arms race in East, Southeast and South Asia, drawing in not only Japan and India, but also South Korea, Malaysia and other Southeast Asian states.

The biggest challenge, of course, will come from the United States. If history is any guide, Washington will work with other countries in the region to enclose China's maritime expansion within the first island chain, from Japan to the Strait of Malacca. And a U.S. strategy of containment may not be limited to maritime activity. As the United States demonstrated in dealing with the Soviets, causing trouble for China along its land periphery could be a useful tool — and China has many internal problems that could be exacerbated by foreign pressure. While China has no choice but to look to the sea, its strategic focus could be forced to turn inward again, as it has been for virtually all of its history.

The South China Sea and Submarine Warfare
June 15, 2009

A towed sonar array deployed by the U.S. guided missile destroyer John S. McCain (DDG-56) was struck June 11 by a Chinese People's Liberation Army-Navy (PLAN) submarine, according to a CNN report citing an unnamed military official. The incident, in which only the array itself appears to have been damaged, took place in the South China Sea near Subic Bay in the Philippines, and Manila was quick to deny that it occurred within its territorial waters. The collision was only the latest in a series of recent naval incidents in the South China Sea between U.S. and PLAN vessels, and it certainly will not be the last.

The McCain, an Arleigh Burke-class destroyer, is equipped with the AN/SQR-19 passive towed array sonar system. The linear array, only a few inches in diameter but nearly 800 feet long, can be towed a full mile behind the ship. Towed arrays are used to expand a ship or submarine's acoustic sensitivity by not only complementing the bow-mounted sonar array but also by providing surveillance at a significant distance from the vessel itself — and the noise of its propellers.

Because the array emits no signal, it would be difficult for a submarine traveling underwater to detect it, although the long tether could get caught in the sub's screw, something that submariners would be careful to avoid. Although warships do not keep the array deployed at all times, it would not be uncommon for them to do so for a variety of training or surveillance purposes, especially in the midst of an exercise. The McCain was reportedly one of four U.S. warships participating with vessels from six regional navies in the Philippine phase of the annual Cooperation Afloat Readiness and Training (CARAT) exercise.

It is neither surprising that the McCain had deployed its towed array nor that the Chinese had a submarine on station to observe the exercises. The PLAN may already be adjusting protocols and guidelines for stalking U.S. destroyers based on this experience with a towed array, which the Chinese believed that American destroyers were no longer using, according to at least one report.

But the bottom line is not the specifics of this incident but that such incidents are increasingly likely to occur between the U.S. Navy and the PLAN as Chinese maritime interests begin to intersect with American maritime interests. Not only does it parallel a series of high-profile incidents back in March, but it also hearkens back to collision between a Chinese Jian-8 fighter and a U.S. EP-3E Aries II surveillance aircraft in April 2001.

The South China Sea has been and will continue to be a focal point for this competition. The bulk of the sea is considered international waters by the United States and the U.N. Convention on the Law of the Sea (to which Washington is a signatory but which has not been ratified by the U.S. Senate). At the same time, Beijing claims most of the South China Sea as Chinese waters, and there are disputes among numerous claimants around its periphery. It is also a heavily trafficked approach to the world's busiest maritime choke point, the Strait of Malacca, through which more than 50,000 vessels transit each year.

Chinese claims overlap and conflict with almost every country native to the South China Sea: Vietnam, Malaysia, Indonesia and the Philippines. Taiwan quietly and much less overtly claims all the same territory that China does. Just north of the South China Sea but still close enough to affect naval dynamics in the region, the Daiyoutai/Senkaku Islands are also an issue between China and Japan. At the same time, claims to disputed territory and seabed beyond the 200-nautical-mile-offshore Exclusive Economic Zone continue to be debated (and in some cases remain to be submitted) under the U.N. Convention on the Law of the Sea.

What all this means is that expanding global interests, increasing resource extraction and international law are all causing long-standing issues in the South China Sea to take on a new urgency — and countries' naval forces are being expanded accordingly.

The latest incident with the USS McCain is a reminder that this competition is also moving beneath the waves — and not just for the United States and China. For many of the smaller nations along the South China Sea fielding naval forces that are relatively ill trained and equipped, the risk of losing surface warships to more modern combatants and land-based maritime strike aircraft in a crisis is real. Although expensive, modern diesel-electric submarines, proficiently operated, are difficult to detect at slow speeds. With their ability to deploy mines, torpedoes or anti-ship missiles, such vessels offer an obtainable capability to project military force and hold maritime territory at risk while retaining an element of stealth. In addition, they offer the capability to clandestinely monitor activity in disputed territory.

Concerned in part with China's overwhelming naval capability, Vietnam, Malaysia and Indonesia are all seeking to acquire new submarines. (Taiwan is also in the market, but international pressure from Beijing has deterred any potential exporter for years.) Singapore has recently acquired two more modern submarines from Sweden. Of these South China Sea countries, only Indonesia, Taiwan and Singapore have any experience operating submarines (Malaysia and Vietnam do not).

Added to this mix are regular operations by U.S. Navy submarines, and although neither Japanese nor Australian subs are known to regularly transit the area, they probably pass through on occasion (as do, perhaps, even South Korean subs). This means that, in the coming years, depending on the particular nature of a crisis, nine countries in or near the region will have the capability to deploy submarines in response. In addition, there are some indications that Hainan Island in the South China Sea will become home to the PLAN's newest ballistic missile submarines, the Jin (Type 094) class.

The deployment of submarines is, of course, only one half of the equation. Anti-submarine warfare is among the most challenging and subtle arts a naval force can master. The South China Sea is relatively shallow and is reportedly a poor environment for detecting submarines — a matter almost certain to be compounded by the noise produced by the steady flow of commercial shipping on the surface.

Most studies and histories of modern submarine warfare have focused on the Cold War competition in the North Atlantic and Barents Sea. The South China Sea is emerging as a new nexus for submarine and anti-submarine operations that presents a profoundly different environment — cramped, shallow and busy with commercial and military traffic. The challenge shifts from identifying a potential target as "ours" or "theirs" to sifting through acoustic libraries to identify a potential undersea target as belonging to one of eight or nine different nations.

The South China Sea will continue to see "incidents" at sea between U.S. and Chinese vessels, and it will become increasingly crowded as more and more countries along or near its periphery deploy submarines. Developments in submarine and anti-submarine warfare in the region certainly bear watching as events unfold.

Fielding a New Anti-Ship Capability
Nov. 18, 2009

The U.S. Office of Naval Intelligence has reportedly found that China is close to fielding an anti-ship ballistic missile, according to a Nov. 17 story broken by Bloomberg. This development has been on the horizon for some time, but many questions remain about this new weapon system and its true capabilities. Despite these questions, the matter is of deep concern for the U.S. Navy as the capability holds considerable promise if China masters it.

Anti-Ship vs. Ballistic Missiles

Anti-ship missiles are generally closer to cruise missiles in configuration and flight profile. There are important reasons for this. Even a large warship is a relatively small target that can maneuver. Whether an anti-ship missile closes to its target while skimming the surface of the water or from a higher altitude, its range can be between one and several hundred kilometers. Consequently, even those that travel at supersonic speeds require some measure of guidance and the ability to refine their course and trajectory as they close the distance to the target ship. Even if the missile's motor has burned out, aerodynamic control surfaces can provide this maneuverability until impact.

Ballistic missiles, on the other hand, are not nearly as maneuverable after launch. Although during the boost phase (the first powered part of flight), various means are used to stabilize the missile and follow the proscribed ballistic path, the weapon is not maneuverable in the same way. Well before apogee (the peak of the ballistic flight path), the missile's motor burns out. Expended stages often fall away, and in single warhead missiles, leave only a small re-entry vehicle (RV) to travel the remainder of the ballistic trajectory. Even modern RVs are not generally guided or maneuverable, so the remainder of the ballistic trajectory is essentially predetermined. In the early decades of the Cold War, large nuclear warheads were necessary to compensate for the resulting inaccuracy.

So the Chinese marrying of the target of anti-ship missiles — small, moving ships — and the un-maneuverable ballistic missile is itself noteworthy. But serious questions remain about the true capability of what now seems to promise to be the world's first deployed anti-ship ballistic missile (ASBM).

ASBM

The Chinese ASBM appears to be based on the DF-21 road mobile medium-range ballistic missile. Fueled by solid propellant, the DF-21 and DF-21A (a refined version) were fielded in the 1990s, and may already be used to carry both nuclear and conventional warheads. The latter could be suggestive of a higher degree of accuracy, since a ballistic missile armed with a conventional warhead on the order of 1,500 pounds with meaningful military capability would require considerable precision. But even if China had achieved an unprecedented degree of accuracy with its ballistic missiles, it would only be relevant for an ASBM if China could pinpoint exactly where a U.S. carrier would be at the exact moment of impact.

But even if the ASBM's time from launch to impact remains consistent with medium-range ballistic missiles, which is well under 10 minutes, U.S. carriers do not tend to sit idle and unmoving — especially in more hostile environments, or when a ballistic missile launch from China's coast has been detected.

All this would suggest that for non-nuclear anti-ship capability, China would require a guided and maneuverable RV. Russia is known to have done work on maneuverable RVs, but with an eye primarily toward evading ballistic missile defenses rather than improving accuracy to the point where a non-nuclear warhead can have utility. China may well have done similar work for the same purpose. Applying that maneuverability to the problem of accuracy and incorporating terminal guidance would require considerable additional work. The 4.5-acre flight deck of a Nimitz-class aircraft carrier against the backdrop of the open ocean certainly makes for an easily identifiable target from altitude. However, marrying guidance with maneuverability at supersonic speeds would be a considerably more advanced capability than lobbing a nuclear warhead in the vicinity of a U.S. carrier strike group (CSG).

In addition, a modern U.S. carrier displaces over 100,000 tons. These are not targets that are likely to be sunk even with a direct hit by a 1,500-pound warhead. If one or several strike the right places on a flight deck, though, they may severely degrade flight operations or possibly achieve a mission kill (prevent the ship from carrying out its primary function even if it does not sink).

In short, several unknowns remain about the true capability of China's new ASBM. In addition to the open question of whether it has sufficient maneuverability and accuracy to be a meaningful threat, there are questions regarding China's ability to pinpoint the location of a U.S. CSG. In all likelihood, this would require space-based sensors to detect approaches from the Mariana Islands. China would also have to reduce considerably the time it takes to feed targeting data from a satellite into a missile at a mobile launch battery on the coast.

Access Denial

The bottom line is that China is using older technology and repurposing other technologies to create new, asymmetric capabilities tailored to the U.S. Navy. By presenting a new threat that approaches from a nearly vertical trajectory at supersonic speeds, a Chinese ASBM would engage a CSG outside what is thought to be the engagement envelope of most of the CSG's considerable array of defensive systems. Though the Aegis-based Standard Missile-3 (SM-3) ballistic missile defense system may be an effective counter, only a small portion of U.S. guided missile cruisers and destroyers — a vast majority of which are currently based in the Pacific — have been upgraded to that capability so far.

China could attempt to use its ASBMs to hold U.S. CSGs at a distance (since their range is approximately 1,500 km, or 932 miles). This distance is at the limits of or even beyond the effective range of carrier-based aviation, particularly a sustained air campaign. Of particular note is the dramatic increase in anti-ship missile range. More traditional configurations are limited to less than one-third this distance. It is this combination of increased range and potential evasion of traditional and refined U.S. shipboard defenses that makes this threat particularly noteworthy.

And though the Chinese may not be able to truly deny the U.S. Navy access to the waters off their coast indefinitely, it can certainly work to keep the United States farther off shore, increase the risks and costs of operating there and slow the American approach in a crisis — which is particularly relevant in a time-sensitive Taiwan scenario. In other words, the fielding of an ASBM capability is completely compatible with Beijing's efforts to attempt to deny the United States access to the Chinese mainland without going to the expense of building a true water navy. And while the Chinese may have considerable work to do in terms of operationalizing the DF-21 ASBM as a meaningful military weapon, it is certainly something that has gotten the attention of the U.S. Navy. Chinese efforts to further refine this new capability will undoubtedly continue apace. This new ASBM — even if it is still being refined — could ultimately prove to be a more significant threat to the U.S. Navy than previous anti-ship missiles.

Espionage with Chinese Characteristics
March 24, 2010

China's intelligence services may not be as famous as the CIA or the KGB, but their operations are widespread and well known to counterintelligence agencies throughout the world. Chinese intelligence operations have been in the news most recently for an alleged cyberattack against California-based Google, but two other recent cases shed more light on the ways of Chinese intelligence-gathering. One involved a Chinese-born naturalized American citizen named Dongfan Chung, who had been working as an engineer at Rockwell International and Boeing. Convicted of espionage, he was sentenced on Feb. 8 to 15 years in prison. The other involved a former U.S. Defense Department official, an American named James Fondren, who was convicted of espionage and sentenced to three years in prison on Jan. 22 after having been recruited by a Chinese case officer.

Together, these cases exemplify the three main Chinese intelligence-gathering methods, which often overlap. One is "human-wave" or "mosaic" collection, which involves assigning or dispatching thousands of assets to gather a massive amount of available information.

Another is recruiting and periodically debriefing Chinese-born residents of other countries in order to gather a deeper level of intelligence on more specific subjects. The third method is patiently cultivating foreign assets of influence for long-term leverage, insight and espionage.

Chinese intelligence operations stand out in the intelligence world most of all because of their sheer numbers. China has the largest population in the world, at 1.3 billion, which means that it has a vast pool of people from which to recruit for any kind of national endeavor, from domestic road-building projects to international espionage. Emerging from this capability are China's trademark human-wave and mosaic intelligence-gathering techniques, which can overload foreign counterintelligence agencies by the painstaking collection of many small pieces of intelligence that make sense only in the aggregate. This is a slow and tedious process, and it reflects the traditional Chinese hallmarks of patience and persistence as well as the centuries-old Chinese custom of "guanxi," the cultivation and use of personal networks to influence events and engage in various ventures.

And though China has long been obsessed with internal stability, traditionally focusing its intelligence operations inward, it is taking advantage of the historic migration of Chinese around the world, particularly in the West, to obtain the technological and economic intelligence so crucial to its national development (and, most recently, to try and influence foreign government policy). To Western eyes, China's whole approach to intelligence gathering may seem unsophisticated and risk-averse, particularly when you consider the bureaucratic inefficiencies inherent in the Communist Party of China's (CPC) administrative structure. But it is an approach that takes a long and wide view, and it is more effective than it may seem at first glance.

A Brief History

China's first intelligence advocate was military theorist Sun Tzu who, in his sixth century B.C. classic The Art of War, emphasized the importance of gathering timely and accurate intelligence in order to win battles. Modern Chinese intelligence began during the Chinese Communist Revolution, when Chiang Kai-Shek's Chinese Nationalist Party (the Kuomintang, or KMT) created its Investigation Section. The Chinese Communists later followed suit with a series of agencies that eventually became the Social Affairs Department (SAD), the party's intelligence and counter-intelligence organ.

The most influential head of the SAD was Kang Sheng, who had become involved in the communist movement while a student at Shanghai University in the 1920s. During the first half of the 20th century, the epicenter for espionage in East Asia was Shanghai, where Chinese agents cut their teeth operating against nationalists, communists, triad gangs, warlord factions and Russian, French, Japanese, British and American intelligence services. Later, Kang traveled to Moscow, where he would spend four years being taught what the Soviets wanted him to know about intelligence operations. Much like "Wild Bill" Donovan of the United States and the Soviet Union's Felix Dzerzhinsky, Kang is considered the father of his country's intelligence services, the first Chinese official to appreciate the practice of global intelligence. Kang also played a leading role in ideological campaigns that served to out "spies" or suspected dissidents and was said to have double-crossed nearly every leader in the early CPC with the exception of Mao.

Following the Communist victory over KMT forces on Oct. 1, 1949, the domestic and counterintelligence functions of the SAD became part of the Ministry of Public Security (MPS), and the military kept its own Military Intelligence Department (MID). Given China's size and its insular geography, its first geopolitical imperative was to maintain internal security, especially along its periphery. China's intelligence services would both police the Han population to guarantee security and monitor foreigners who worked their way in from the coast as the Chinese economy developed. The emphasis on internal security meant extensive informant networks, domestic surveillance and political control and censorship by Chinese intelligence services.

By the mid-1950s, Beijing's Central Investigation Department (CID) had taken on the foreign responsibilities of the SAD. In 1971, in the midst of the Cultural Revolution, the CID was disbanded, only to be reinstituted when Deng Xiaoping came to power in the mid-1970s. Deng wanted China's intelligence services to stop using embassy officials for intelligence cover and wanted to employ journalists and businessmen instead. He later borrowed a centuries-old saying for his policy, "Hide brightness; nourish obscurity," which was meant for the development of China's military capability but could just as well apply to its intelligence agencies. This was a part of China's opening up to the world economically and politically. In the process, Deng's goal was to use intelligence services to enable China to catch up with the West as covertly as possible.

The Ministry of State Security (MSS) was created in 1983 by Deng in a merger of the CID and the counterintelligence elements of the MPS. It is currently the main civilian foreign intelligence service and reports to the premier, the State Council, the CPC and its Political and Legislative Affairs Committee. In China, as in most countries, all domestic and foreign intelligence organizations feed into this executive structure, with the exception of military intelligence, which goes directly to the CPC.

The Chin Case

Since the time of Sun Tzu, perhaps the most successful Chinese spy has been the legendary Larry Wu-Tai Chin (Jin Wudai), an American national of Chinese descent who began his career as a U.S. Army translator and was later recruited by a precursor to the MSS while studying or working in China prior to the Korean War. Following his army service, he joined the CIA as a translator for the Foreign Broadcast Information Service, beginning a 30-year career as a double agent. His most valuable intelligence may have been the information he passed about President Richard Nixon's desire to establish relations with China in 1970, which gave the Chinese leadership a leg up during subsequent negotiations with the United States.

The key to Chin's success may have been his use of third-country "cutouts" (when a case officer travels from one country and an agent travels from another to meet in a third country) and his careful money laundering. Chin traveled to Canada and Hong Kong to pass along intelligence, in meetings that could last as little as five minutes. He was paid significant amounts of money for his espionage activities, and after he moved to Virginia to work for the CIA he became a slumlord in Baltimore, investing his cash in low-income properties.

The Chin case exemplifies, above all, a careful use of operational security, which allowed him to operate undetected (using methods in which the MSS specializes) until a defector exposed him in 1985. Chin had the same handler for 30 years, which means both agent and case officer had a high level of experience and the ability to keep all knowledge of the operation within narrow channels of the MSS. And the Chinese government never acted on Chin's intelligence in a way that would reveal his existence. The only way he could have been detected, other than through exposure by a defector, would have been during his foreign travel or by extensive investigation into his property holdings. Convicted of espionage, Chin committed suicide in his jail cell on Feb. 22, 1986, the day of his sentencing.

Current Organization

Today, China's intelligence bureaucracy is just that — a vast array of intelligence agencies, military departments, police bureaus, party organs, research institutions and media outlets. All of these entities report directly to executive governmental decision makers, but with the CPC structure in place there is parallel leadership for intelligence operations, with the CPC institutions holding

CHINA'S EXECUTIVE STRUCTURE AND INTELLIGENCE SERVICES

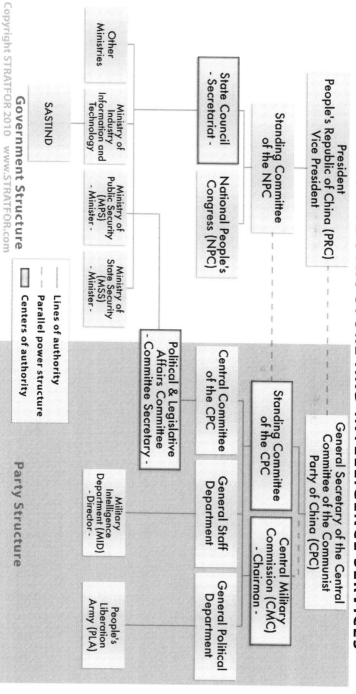

the ultimate power. Beyond the party itself, the opaque nature of China's executive leadership makes it difficult to determine exactly where or with whom the intelligence authority really lies.

The Ministry of State Security

The Guojia Anquan Bu, or Ministry of State Security, is China's primary foreign intelligence organization, but it also handles counterintelligence in cooperation with the Ministry of Public Security (MPS). MSS involvement in domestic operations is widespread through its First and Fifth Bureaus, activities that are coordinated with the MPS. (Due to this overlap, we will discuss domestic operations in the MPS section below.) One target set that clearly falls under MSS jurisdiction is foreign diplomats. Bugging embassies and surveilling embassy employees or those traveling on diplomatic passports is common practice for the MSS. According to one leaked MSS statement, "foreign diplomats are open spies." This is not a false statement, but it does reflect a certain paranoia on the part of the agency and an intention to target such officials. It also underscores the fact that Beijing views all foreigners with suspicion.

As did its predecessor organizations, the MSS follows the bureaucratic structure of the Soviet Union's KGB (the result of founder Kang's formative tour in Moscow), but it operates like no other intelligence agency in the world. We call it espionage with Chinese characteristics. The MSS network is so diffuse and decentralized that each individual asset may be doing nothing particularly illegal — often merely collecting open-source information or asking innocuous questions. But when all the information these assets have collected is analyzed at the Institutes of Contemporary International Relations in Beijing, it can produce valuable intelligence products. Still, it remains to be seen from the outside whether such a process is effective in producing actionable intelligence in a timely manner. For example, in the case of technology theft — a growing focus of the MSS — by the time the intelligence is processed and exploited the technology may already be outdated.

While it is difficult to assess MSS analytical capabilities, much is known about its recruitment and operations. Training for most MSS intelligence officers begins at the Beijing University of International Relations. This is a key difference in the Chinese approach to recruiting intelligence officers. The MSS taps university-bound students prior to their university entrance exams, choosing qualified students with a lack of foreign contacts or travel to make sure they haven't already been compromised. The MSS also places a heavy emphasis on the mastery of foreign languages and operates an intensive language school for officers. To root out possible defectors and moles embedded in the MSS network, the agency runs an internal security department known as the Ninth Bureau for Anti-Defection and Countersurveillance.

These full-time intelligence officers ultimately are charged with managing a legion of agents (also referred to as assets or operatives) who do the actual spying. This is another distinguishing characteristic of Chinese intelligence — the sheer number of temporary and long-term assets spread worldwide in a decentralized network managed by MSS handlers. (The FBI believes there could be hundreds of thousands of individuals and as many as 3,000 front companies operating in the United States alone.) The MSS employs Chinese nationals living abroad, some of whom function as temporary agents and some of whom serve as long-term operatives. For budgetary and security reasons, the MSS prefers to recruit its assets in China, before they venture overseas. It also prefers ethnic Han Chinese because it considers them more trustworthy and easier to control. In recruiting these assets, the MSS relies first on pride in national heritage (known as the "help China" approach), but if more coercion is needed it can always revert to pressure tactics — threatening to revoke their passports or permission to travel granted by sponsoring organizations, promising a dismal future upon their return or making life difficult for their families in China.

One should not assume, of course, that every Chinese national living overseas is a spy working for the Chinese government. Most are not, and many may simply be Chinese students or professionals trying to collect information for their own academic or business purposes, gathering it legally from open sources but also in ways that could be considered illegal. From the targeted country's perspective, the problem with China's human-wave approach to intelligence gathering is that it is difficult to tell if the activities constitute espionage or not.

The MSS divides its operatives into short-term and long-term agents. Short-term agents are recruited only a few days before leaving and are often assigned to infiltrate Chinese dissident organizations. They may be promised financial stipends and good jobs upon their return, or they may be encouraged by the threat of having their passports revoked. Sometimes dissidents themselves are arrested and forced to spy as short-term agents, either overseas or domestically, in order to stay out of jail. Long-term agents are known as chen di yu, or "fish at the bottom of the ocean," what Westerners would call "sleeper agents." Though they likely constitute the minority of Chinese agents, they provide most of the high-value intelligence. Before going overseas, long-term agents with foreign visas are often recruited through their danwei, or traditional Chinese work units, by local MSS intelligence officers. These "fish" are identified, recruited and trained months before departure, and they are deployed mainly to gather intelligence, develop networks and, in some cases, influence foreign policy and spread disinformation in the host country.

The MSS encourages agents abroad to achieve their academic or business goals as well as their intelligence goals, since China benefits either way, and legitimate pursuits provide effective cover for illicit ones. Agents are asked to write letters to their families at home about their arrival in country, studies or work and financial situation, letters that the MSS will intercept and monitor. Long-term agents are generally told to return to the mainland every two years for debriefing, though this can be done in Hong Kong or in

MINISTRY OF STATE SECURITY

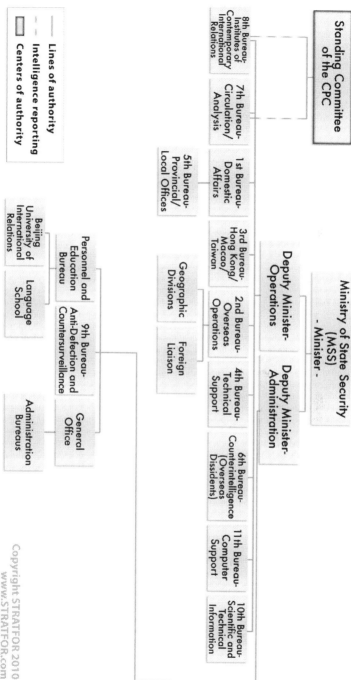

Standing Committee of the CPC

Ministry of State Security (MSS) - Minister -

Deputy Minister- Operations

Deputy Minister- Administration

8th Bureau- Institutes of Contemporary International Relations

7th Bureau- Circulation/ Analysis

1st Bureau- Domestic Affairs

5th Bureau- Provincial/ Local Offices

3rd Bureau- Hong Kong/ Macao/ Taiwan

2nd Bureau- Overseas Operations

Geographic Divisions

Foreign Liaison

4th Bureau- Technical Support

6th Bureau- Counterintelligence (Overseas Dissidents)

11th Bureau- Computer Support

10th Bureau- Scientific and Technical Information

9th Bureau- Anti-Defection and Countersurveillance

Personnel and Education Bureau

Beijing University of International Relations

Language School

General Office

Administration Bureaus

Lines of authority
Intelligence reporting
Centers of authority

third countries. Agents are expressly prohibited from contacting Chinese embassies and consulates, which are known to be monitored by host-country counterintelligence.

It is not uncommon for the MSS to use the more traditional method of diplomatic cover for foreign operations. For example, in 1987 two Chinese military attaches were expelled from Washington, D.C., when they were caught trying to buy secrets from a National Security Agency (NSA) employee who was, in fact, an FBI double agent. While these two agents likely worked for China's Military Intelligence Department (MID), it is believed that MSS agents also serve under similar cover. Since most of its recruitment is done in China, however, the MSS does not likely operate from within embassies. We have noticed a shift in the last 10 years or so, in which Chinese intelligence services have begun accessing non-Chinese agents, usually government officials. For example, a Chinese military attache might establish a covert intelligence-gathering relationship with another military or defense official, and their meetings would appear as part of their normal liaison activities. This is what occurred in the case of Ronald Montaperto, a senior U.S. Defense Intelligence Agency analyst focusing on China. He claimed his meetings with People's Liberation Army (PLA) officers in the 1990s and early 2000s were part of his regular liaison responsibilities. However, Montaperto eventually admitted to orally providing classified information to Chinese military attaches in 2006.

A key MSS target is technological intelligence, which is gathered by ethnic Chinese agents in three primary ways: Chinese nationals are asked to acquire targeted technologies while traveling, foreign companies with the desired technologies are purchased by Chinese firms, and equipment with the desired technologies is purchased by Chinese front companies, usually in Hong Kong.

In the first method, scholarly exchange programs — most often involving recruits from the Chinese Student and Scholar Association — have been the most productive, with the intelligence gathered by Chinese scientists and academics who have been co-opted by Chinese intelligence services. Sometimes technological intelligence is gathered by MSS intelligence officers themselves. The trade-off in using untrained nationals is that the average scientist knows nothing about operational security, and Chinese assets are often caught red-handed. Typically they are not prosecuted, since the fragment of "stolen" information is not valuable in and of itself and is only a tiny piece of the much-larger puzzle.

Two examples of Chinese firms buying U.S. companies are China National Aero-Technology Import & Export Corp. (CATIC) and Huawei. In the first case, CATIC bought the American defense technology firm Mamco Manufacturing, a Seattle-based aircraft parts manufacturer, in 1990. CATIC has a direct connection to the PLA and probably wanted to use the Seattle firm to acquire aerospace technology. The U.S. investigation also found that Mamco technology itself was already under export limitations. Huawei has attempted to buy many foreign firms outright, including U.S.-based 3Com. Huawei established a joint venture with the U.S. anti-virus software company Symantec in 2008, headquartered in Chengdu, China. At this point it only offers software in China, but STRATFOR sources say that if Huawei were to be used for Chinese intelligence, it could easily insert spyware into computer systems subscribing to the service.

In Hong Kong, agents are recruited by the MSS' Third Bureau, which handles Chinese intelligence operations in Taiwan, Hong Kong and Macao. One of their major tasks is purchasing targeted technologies through front companies. These businesses are usually not run by intelligence officers themselves but by people who have connections, sometimes overt, to the MSS. One recent case involved the 88 Queensway Group, named for the address of an office building in central Hong Kong that houses many state-owned Chinese companies, along with the China Investment Corporation, the country's sovereign wealth fund. A U.S. Congressional report claimed a possible link between the building and "China's intelligence apparatus."

An example that reveals a more clear connection between a Chinese front company and Chinese intelligence is the 1984 case involving Hong Kong businessman Da Chuan Zheng, who was arrested in the United States for illegally acquiring radar and electronic surveillance technology for China. After his arrest, he told U.S. customs agents that he had shipped more than $25 million worth of high-technology equipment to China. MSS agents are usually quite honest with the companies they work with regarding the products they are purchasing and why they are sending them to China, though they do use fraudulent documents to get the goods through customs. If the agent is not honest, signs that he is trying to illegally export technology include paying cash when such a sale would usually involve financing and denying follow-up maintenance services.

Another major focus of the MSS is identifying and influencing the foreign policy of other countries — the classic objective of national intelligence operations. Goals in this case are common to all national intelligence agencies — information on political, economic and security policies that may affect China; knowledge of foreign intelligence operations directed at China; biographical profiles of foreign politicians, intelligence officers and others, especially those who deal with China; technological capabilities of foreign countries; and information on Chinese citizens who may have defected.

This challenging mission involves developing relationships with foreigners who could possibly be recruited to spy on their native countries. This process used to involve rather crude entrapment schemes but more subtle methods have evolved. Two relatively simple techniques in China involve entrapment. Intelligence officers will offer classified information to reporters or other foreigners visiting or working in China in what is commonly called a "false-flag operation," then turn around and arrest them for spying. Another approach involves attractive Chinese women — or men — who will approach foreigners visiting China for the purposes of establishing a sexual liaison. French diplomat Bernard Boursicot was recruited in this way by a male opera singer in 1964. He was finally arrested for spying for China 20 years later.

Even the more subtle recruitment methods have obvious signs. A typical approach might begin with Chinese nationals abroad, usually academics, identifying professors, journalists, policy researchers or business people native to the host country who focus on China. Next, these targets receive invitations to conferences at research associations or universities in China that are often controlled by the MSS or MID. The foreigner's trip is paid for but he or she is subject to a packed and tiring schedule that includes bountiful banquets and no small amount of alcohol consumption. The goal is to make the target more vulnerable to recruitment or to cause him or her to divulge information accidentally.

Often the recruitment can be couched in the traditional Chinese custom of guanxi. A relationship is developed between the Chinese host and foreign visitor in which information is shared equally that will inform their respective academic or business pursuits. More meetings are held and information exchanged, and soon the foreigner's family is invited to visit as well. Eventually the foreigner comes to depend on his Chinese contacts for information crucial to his or her work. At first the Chinese contacts (usually intelligence officers) may ask only for general information about the foreigner's government agency, university or company. As the dependence develops, the Chinese contact will begin to ask for more specific intelligence, even for classified information. At some point the contact may even threaten to cut the foreigner off from access to the information on which the foreigner now depends.

The Ministry of Public Security

The Gong An Bu, or Ministry of Public Security (MPS), is the national security organization that oversees all provincial and local police departments. But like any national security service, it also has important intelligence responsibilities, which it coordinates with the MSS. These responsibilities mainly involve dissidents and foreigners in China. This role overlaps with the MSS, and most analysts believe the MPS follows the direction of the MSS. There are likely some disagreements over territory and competition between the two agencies, but they seem to work together better than most modern domestic and foreign intelligence entities.

Domestic intelligence and security begins with the universal Chinese institution called danwei, or the work unit. Every Chinese citizen is a member of a work unit, depending on where they live, work or go to school. The danwei is an institution used by the CPC to promote its policies as well as monitor all Chinese citizens. Each unit is run by a party cadre and is often divided into personnel, administrative and security sections that work closely with the MPS and MSS. Files are kept on all unit members, including information ranging from family history to ideological correctness.

As a member of a work unit, any Chinese citizen can be recruited to do anything on behalf of the state, including reporting on the activities of fellow citizens and foreign nationals in China. In terms of targeting foreigners, this usually happens in venues such as hotels and even dwellings, which are often wired and equipped with monitoring devices by Chinese intelligence services. Some hotels are even owned and operated by the MPS or the PLA.

The MPS and MSS are known to work together, but how effectively they do so is unclear. In 1986, the CPC sent a cable to provincial authorities in Lhasa, the capital of Tibet, directing the People's Armed Police and MPS to target specific dissident groups and to consult with the MSS before taking any action. This reflects standard operating procedure for many provincial and local MPS offices. The MSS has oversight authority, while the local MPS offices are ultimately responsible for public security nationwide.

The MPS tends to recruit many low-skilled agents who are not trained in operational tradecraft or given specific intelligence-gathering responsibilities. Multiple agents are often assigned to

210

the same target and are told to report on each other as well as the target. This allows the MPS to compare and analyze multiple reports in order to arrive at the required intelligence. One major component of the MPS that handles domestic espionage is the Domestic Security Department, which employs a huge network of informants, many of whom can be assigned to intelligence operations (most are used to gather information for criminal investigations) and are paid little if anything at all.

Occasionally, the MPS will recruit higher-level informants who are handled differently. They are often brought out of their home provinces to be debriefed, and they work on specific intelligence assignments that receive financial and technical support. Sometimes these assets, such as ranking members of dissident groups, are arrested and forced to cooperate, but in nearly all cases their missions are afforded a high level of operational security.

Internal intelligence operations tend to be successful at the local and provincial levels but not at the national level. Most dissident groups are infiltrated and sometimes dismantled while still operating locally, and Beijing is fortunate that most groups emerge from single urban populations. The intelligence flow among provinces and from the provinces to Beijing is very weak (unless Beijing specifically asks for it, in which case the information flows quickly). This lack of communication has led to a number of intelligence failures. The Chinese have had very little success, for example, catching democratic and religious activists, particularly foreigners, when they are being spirited out of the country by various indigenous networks. The main problem here is the parallel structure of the party and government. All intelligence has to be reported to the CPC before going to other government offices. Well aware that information is power, the party must stay informed to stay in control, but local party offices are slow to inform the higher levels, and little information is shared in any orderly way between the party bureaucracy and the government bureaucracy. Indeed, such bureaucratic disconnects are the largest exploitable flaw in China's intelligence apparatus.

MPS interaction with foreigners usually amounts to technical and human surveillance. The growing number of foreigners in China, and Beijing's fear of foreign influence, has resulted in more resources being devoted to this surveillance effort. The MPS engages in a considerable amount of mobile human surveillance. Many foreigners, especially journalists and businesspeople, have reported being followed during the workday. The surveillants are easily detected because the government wants the targets to know that they are being followed and to be intimidated. At the same time, the numbers required to surveil many different foreigners mean that many barely trained informants and case officers are deployed for the job.

Military Intelligence Department

The Military Intelligence Department (MID), also known as the Second Department (Er Bu) of the PLA, primarily focuses on tactical military intelligence. Another major priority for the MID is acquiring foreign technology to better develop China's military capabilities. At the top level, the MID has a organizational structure similar to that of the MSS, and it also seems comparable in size.

The bulk of the intelligence it collects historically has been tactical information gleaned from China's border regions, especially its frontier with Vietnam. Much of the information is gathered by PLA reconnaissance units and consists of the usual military intelligence, such as order of battle, doctrine, geography, targets, strategic intentions and counterintelligence. Each military region (MR, roughly equivalent to a U.S. Army corps) has its own recon units as well as a regional intelligence center for analyzing and disseminating the information gathered. The MID also has a centralized tactical reconnaissance bureau, called the Second Bureau, which coordinates the flow of information from each MR.

The PLA has been known to send armed patrols along, and even across, its borders to identify opposing military positions

CENTRAL MILITARY COMMISSION AND MILITARY INTELLIGENCE

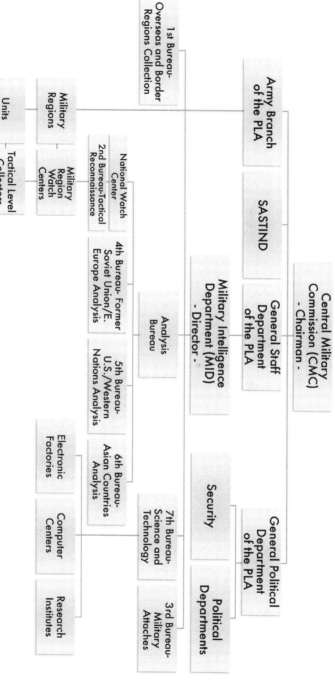

- Central Military Commission (CMC) - Chairman -
  - Army Branch of the PLA
    - 1st Bureau- Overseas and Border Regions Collection
      - Military Regions
        - Units
      - Military Region Watch Centers
        - Tactical Level Collectors
    - 2nd Bureau-Tactical Reconnaissance
      - National Watch Center
  - SASTIND
  - General Staff Department of the PLA
    - Military Intelligence Department (MID) - Director -
      - Analysis Bureau
        - 4th Bureau- Former Soviet Union/E. Europe Analysis
        - 5th Bureau- U.S./Western Nations Analysis
        - 6th Bureau- Asian Countries Analysis
      - Security
      - 7th Bureau- Science and Technology
        - Electronic Factories
        - Computer Centers
        - Research Institutes
  - General Political Department of the PLA
    - Political Departments
      - 3rd Bureau- Military Attaches

and gather other forms of intelligence. Along the full length of China's border with Southeast Asia (and particularly along the Vietnamese border), the MID often recruits residents from the neighboring country and sends them back into the country to gather intelligence. There are at least 24 different ethnic groups from which these agents are recruited along this border, where the groups often comprise isolated communities that are undivided by abstract national boundaries and whose members cross the border at will. Recruitment tactics are similar to those mentioned above for other agencies, including monetary incentives and threats of arrest (or even torture).

The First Bureau of the MID is responsible for gathering human intelligence (HUMINT) overseas and focuses, like the MSS Third Bureau, mainly on Taiwan, Hong Kong and Macao. It is responsible for obtaining much of the technological intelligence used to improve China's military capabilities and for finding customers for Chinese arms exports. To hide any PLA involvement, the MID recruits arms dealers to sell to other countries, which in recent decades have included Iraq, North Korea, Argentina, Iran, Pakistan, Saudi Arabia and Syria. Careful in recruiting these dealers, the MID does extensive background investigations and prefers dealers who already have a lot of experience dealing with China. However, operational security for the actual deals can be shoddy, since so many are uncovered. China's motives for these sales are generally based on profit, in order to support other military operations, though gaining political influence in customer countries can be a contributing factor. Historically, the First Bureau has also been involved in establishing guerrilla warfare schools and assisting with insurgencies in such countries as Angola, Thailand and Afghanistan (in the 1980s and before).

The MID's Third Bureau is made up of military attaches serving in overseas embassies, which are tacitly accepted worldwide as open intelligence collection points. Some Chinese military attaches, not unlike those of other countries, have been caught in covert intelligence activities, including the two mentioned above who were arrested while trying to purchase NSA secrets in 1987. The lack of operational security in such cases involving the MID is noteworthy, including another in 1987 in which MID officers working at the United Nations in New York coordinated with Chinese nationals living in the United States to illegally export U.S. military technology to China (TOW and Sidewinder missiles and blueprints for F-14 fighters). In both of these cases, the officers did not operate using cover identities, nor did they use clandestine communication methods such as dead drops. The military attaches in the previous case even met openly with their "agent" in a Chinese restaurant.

The Third Bureau has improved its methods since the 1980s and appears to have had some success getting deeper into foreign intelligence agencies. In 2006, Ronald Montaperto, then a U.S. Defense Intelligence Agency analyst, pleaded guilty to illegally possessing classified documents and passing top secret information to Chinese military attaches. This is one particular case that deviates from the norm — information was passed within the target country from agent to handler. This is likely a tactical shift in operations involving foreign agents and not ethnic Chinese.

The Fourth, Fifth and Sixth bureaus all handle the analysis of different world regions. Another unnumbered MID bureau disseminates intelligence to military officers and China's Central Military Commission. Unlike Western services, the MID is known to put a great emphasis on open-source intelligence.

MID's "seventh bureau" is the Bureau of Science and Technology. This is where China's vaunted "cyberintelligence" operations are designed and managed with the help of six government-linked research institutes, two computer centers and legions of patriotic citizen hackers. The bureau includes companies that produce electronic equipment — computers, satellites, listening devices and such — for espionage and technical support. Computer espionage is ideally suited to China with its large, technologically savvy population and diffuse intelligence-gathering techniques (assets and methods that have been described in previous STRATFOR coverage).

As part of the CPC, the PLA staffs a large and powerful office called the General Political Department (GPD), which places individuals at every level of the military, including within the MID, solely for the purpose of monitoring and ensuring the ideological commitment of the armed forces. Indeed, the MID is likely one of the Chinese organizations that is more thoroughly penetrated and monitored by PLA/GPD, since a group of well-trained clandestine intelligence officers that are part of the PLA could easily threaten any regime, and specifically the CPC's control of the military. The political department handles counterintelligence cases within its countersabotage department, and prosecutes them as "political" cases. While the obvious purpose of this department is political, it seems to be the main counterintelligence arm of the MID.

While not part of the MID, the Third Department of the PLA is another intelligence organization that handles signals intelligence (SIGINT). It is actually the third largest SIGINT operation in the world, after those of the United States and Russia, monitoring diplomatic, military and international communications — effectively all but domestic intercepts. Although we know very little about this form of Chinese intelligence-gathering, we can only assume that it is likely a key component of China's collection effort, which has made great strides in advancing China's military capabilities and enabling it to keep up with other militaries.

In the past, a major criticism of China's intelligence operations was the time it took to clone a weapons system — gather the information, reverse-engineer the system and put the pieces back together. By the time something was copied from an adversary's arsenal, the adversary had already advanced another step ahead. That does not seem to be such a problem today, especially in those areas involving asymmetrical technologies such as anti-ship ballistic missiles, which China is developing on its own. The PLA's main challenge, one that rests specifically with the MID,

216

is to develop advanced training, manpower and doctrinal capabilities. One recent step in this direction is the PLA navy's anti-pirate mission in the Gulf of Aden, which gives it an opportunity to observe how other countries' exercise command and control of their naval assets, lessons that will be of great value as China develops a blue-water navy. The new challenge is to figure out how to effectively use the technology, not just build it.

Other Intelligence Organizations

A STRATFOR source with experience in counterintelligence estimates that more than 70 percent of Chinese intelligence operations are not directed by the agencies described above but by an array of Chinese institutes, scientific agencies and media outlets that are nominally separate from the MSS, MPS and MID. These entities often compete among themselves, sending agents out on the same missions as part of China's mosaic approach to gathering intelligence. But STRATFOR suspects the level of competition precludes any effective operational integration or sharing of information, a problem that can beset any country's intelligence bureaucracy.

One such agency is the State Administration for Science, Technology and Industry for National Defense (SASTIND), which is separate from the PLA but makes direct recommendations to the CMC for research and planning in military technological development (similar to DARPA in the United States). While it usually relies on the MSS and MID for intelligence gathering, SASTIND will dispatch its own agents to obtain military and technological secrets when a high level of specific expertise is needed. Its scientists are more often involved in open-source intelligence collection, usually when sent to conferences and participating in academic exchanges. Information thus gathered helps the agency set priorities for intelligence collection by the main intelligence services.

Xinhua, or what used to be known as the New China News Agency, has historically been a major cover for MSS officers and agents as well as a collector of open-source material abroad. In this way it functions much like the Foreign Broadcast Information Service for the United States or the United Kingdom's BBC Monitoring. Since its inception, Xinhua has created news publications that aggregate and translate foreign news for general Chinese citizens as well as specific publications for high-level officials. It also produces a domestic-sourced publication for deputy ministers and above that covers internal politics.

Two organizations have historically been involved in covert action, a strategy that China has come to avoid. One is the International Liaison Department, which is controlled by the PLA's General Political Department. Responsible for establishing and maintaining liaison with communist groups worldwide, the liaison department used such links to foment rebellions and arm communist factions around the world during the Cold War. More recently it has used this network for spying rather than covert action.

The other is the United Front Work Department, a major CPC organization that dates back to the party's inception in 1921. Its overt responsibility is to help carry out China's foreign policy with nongovernmental communist organizations worldwide. In addition to being involved in covert action and intelligence gathering, the department has also been active in monitoring and suppressing Chinese dissidents abroad. Its officers typically operate under diplomatic cover as members of the Ministry of Foreign Affairs, a notable difference from China's main intelligence services.

Limitations and Potential

As with any intelligence bureaucracy, especially one in a nondemocratic country, identifying the oversight and management structures of China's intelligence operations is difficult. It is very clear that the Communist Party of China has absolute control over all of the intelligence services, but exactly who is in control is unclear. China's government is known for its opaqueness and bureaucratic infighting, and the leadership of China's intelligence services is no exception. Direct authority lies with the ministers and directors of the individual services, but it appears that more power may be in the hands of the Political and Legislative Affairs Committee secretary and the head of the CMC. STRATFOR sources confirm this, and they also believe the MSS director is the most powerful intelligence leader in the government (but not in the CPC). The ultimate consumers of China's intelligence product are the services' true commanders who, as it happens, constitute the country's most powerful institution — the Standing Committee of the CPC.

The oversight that party leaders have over China's intelligence operations limits the effectiveness of the operations in many ways. In addition to the inefficiencies inherent in China's parallel government-party structures, corruption is likely a pervasive problem throughout the intelligence services, just as it is in other Chinese bureaucracies. There are examples of intelligence officers bringing back scrap metal with U.S. military markings and calling it military equipment — one officer involved reportedly got a commendation for his efforts. Still, cases of corruption in the Chinese intelligence community — despite the central government's current crackdown on the problem — are kept well out of the public eye, and it is difficult to tell the pervasiveness of the problem.

Even harder to identify is China's intelligence budget. It is not intended for public consumption in any form, and even if it were, the numbers would likely be of dubious value. Much funding comes from indirect sources such as state-owned companies, research institutes and technology organizations inside and outside the government. It is important to note that many Chinese intelligence operations, such as MSS front companies or MID arms sales, are self-funded, and some even produce profits for their parent organizations. Chinese intelligence services pay little money for information, especially to ethnically Chinese agents, and thus the Chinese intelligence budget goes a long way.

And in China, it is difficult to say just what "intelligence" is. The Chinese follow a different paradigm. Whereas activities by Western companies involving business espionage would never be coordinated by a central government, in China, business espionage is one of the government's main interests in terms of intelligence. China's intelligence services focus more on business and technology intelligence than on political intelligence, though they are shifting a bit toward the latter. And Chinese companies have no moral qualms about engaging in business espionage whether they take orders from the government or not. As mentioned above, most "intelligence" operations are not directed by the central government or intelligence services but rather by an array of institutes, agencies and media outlets.

Although China follows a different intelligence paradigm that has often shown its rough edges, it is refining its technique. It is training a professional class of intelligence officers beginning even before the candidates enter the university, and it is involving its military — particularly its naval forces — in peacekeeping, foreign-aid and anti-piracy operations worldwide. This is doing much to improve China's international image at a time when the Western world may view China as a threatening emerging power. Meanwhile, China will continue to pursue a long-term intelligence strategy that the West may not consider very advanced, but STRATFOR believes it would be a mistake to underestimate this patient and persistent process. The Chinese may not be that keen on the dead-drops, surveillance and dramatic covert operations that permeate spy novels, but their effectiveness may be better than we know. Larry Chin achieved world-class status as a practitioner of operational security without following Western methods, and there may be plenty of others like him.

CHAPTER 5: INTERNATIONAL RELATIONS

***

Beijing's Obvious Hand
at the U.S. Olympic Torch Run
April 16, 2008

The April 9 Olympic torch relay in San Francisco opened a window into the organizational capabilities of the Chinese government and its intelligence collection apparatus inside the United States. From the coordinating efforts of the city's Chinese Consulate, down through local Chinese business and social organizations, and on to the pro-China supporters who photographed the event, the operation showed an efficiency and organizational capability not seen among the anti-China demonstrators. The run also revealed a high level of sophistication, planning and control in the pro-China camp.

A Day of Confusion

The torch relay in San Francisco proved a mixed bag of anti-China and pro-China demonstrators, as well as spectators simply hoping for a glimpse of the symbol of the Olympic Games. Pro-Tibet and other demonstrators altered their tactics in San Francisco following clashes surrounding the torch run in London and Paris — where pictures of a protester with a Tibet flag trying to snatch the torch from a handicapped torchbearer left the protesters looking worse than China. As a result, the demonstrators in San Francisco planned to impede the progress of the relay rather than attempt to extinguish the torch or interfere with the actual torchbearers. The massive gathering at the beginning of the torch route, and the blocking of a bus carrying Chinese security officials and items related to the torch run, triggered the organizers of the relay to change the route completely. In part, then, the protesters interrupted the relay effectively, though not in the manner they had hoped.

The on-the-fly changes in the torch relay route, which left many spectators waiting down near the piers when the torch was running along the hills several blocks away, allowed the relay to progress relatively smoothly, interrupted only a few times by protesters attempting to block the route or by a few demonstrators bearing little sign of affiliation with the Tibetan or Darfur causes who threw water balloons at the torch. The heavy police and Diplomatic Security Service presence around the torch runners largely kept demonstrators on the sidewalks, while the moving roadblocks and the unclear torch route left demonstrators unsure of where they could amass to intercept it. The security organizers, then, were relatively successful in their efforts to allow all planned participants to carry the torch with minimal interference.

In the end, neither protesters nor security "won" the day. Amid the confusion, however, the groups that showed a very strong sense of organization and planning were the pro-China demonstrators. Their coordination demonstrated the ability of the Chinese government, via its local consulate and its association with overseas Chinese organizations, to rally and coordinate large-scale activities inside the United States — and to use these activities for intelligence collection.

Pro-China Preparation

By 8 a.m. April 9, the pro-China demonstrators were taking up positions along the planned torch relay route, pulling in groups carrying Chinese, U.S. and Olympic flags, and equipped with cases of food and water. However, these were not spontaneous gatherings of overseas Chinese supporting the motherland, as Beijing media have portrayed them. Rather, there was a coordinated effort between local Chinese business and social associations and the consulate to attract, equip, deploy and coordinate the large pro-China turnout. This is in contrast to the Free Tibet, Save Darfur and other anti-China protesters — who often seemed disorganized.

By some estimates, as many as 50 busloads of Chinese from other parts of California were brought to San Francisco. Many of them paid (by some accounts $300 each) to come out for the day in support of Beijing. They were placed in groups along the anticipated torch relay route and given Chinese and Olympic flags, as well as American flags (the latter a tactical move to show they were not anti-U.S., but rather pro-China — a distinction made all the more apparent by the fact that most anti-China protesters did not carry U.S. flags, and some also were critical of the U.S. government).

In addition to those bused in from out of town, many of the local Chinese business and social organizations were involved in fielding groups of pro-China supporters, and these were similarly equipped. Most groups also were supplied with cases of water and food — something not seen among the anti-China demonstrators, who appeared more a gathering of individuals than prearranged groups. One local Chinese organizer was overheard saying they had spent some $30,000 on food and water for the day of the torch run — perhaps not a large amount overall, but a clear investment to ensure that there was group cohesion among the pro-China demonstrators.

In addition to many older overseas Chinese posted along the route, there also were numerous Chinese of college age, many representing several overseas and mainland Chinese student associations. Some carried a large flag representing China's Tsinghua University, which produces many top Chinese officials, and among the others were local chapters of the Chinese Students and Scholars Association. During the run, some of these students challenged the American Free Tibet or Saver Darfur protesters to discussion, asking, for example, whether they had been to Tibet or diverting accusations of Chinese military support to Sudan with counteraccusations of U.S. military activity in Iraq and Afghanistan. In general, the Chinese side kept the confrontations rather civil, seeming to have been well prepared to respond (suggesting they had been provided with materials on how to respond in advance). On numerous occasions, however, the anti-China demonstrators in these one-to-one confrontations would resort to their own chanted slogans or just shout that the Chinese were liars.

The organization of the pro-China contingent was further demonstrated by its self-policing efforts. While the anti-China demonstrators ignored the barriers along the route and moved into the streets, far fewer pro-China demonstrators did so. When one did cross, the pro-China group would shout at them to return behind the barriers and "follow the rules." There was clearly a concerted effort to make the Chinese demonstrators appear as the more controlled, more peaceful and less confrontational participants — part of a broader PR strategy. When confronted by a large group of pro-Tibet demonstrators, for example, the Chinese often simply ignored the repeated cries of "China lies, people die" and instead broke into song, effectively ending the exchange.

Instigation and Intelligence Collection

There was at least one exception to the restraint shown by the pro-China demonstrators, however, suggesting they were not entirely the innocuous gathering they sought to portray. On numerous occasions, individuals or small groups carrying cameras would seek to incite the anti-China demonstrators to acts of confrontation or violence, frequently by parading through the middle of a group of Free Tibet or Save Darfur demonstrators with a large Chinese flag, walking back and forth through the group. In some cases, small scuffles broke out — and pictures were snapped — though the anti-China demonstrators soon deployed individuals to try to keep the two opposing sides separated. The same day, Chinese media ran photos of pro-Tibet demonstrators shoving pro-China demonstrators, "proving" their point that the Tibet supporters are violent.

It was no accident that the photographs appeared so quickly in the Chinese media. In addition to the demonstrators, numerous individuals were sent out with cameras. Although cameras are expected at such an event, many of the photographers were collecting images either for Chinese propaganda purposes or to identify anti-China demonstrators in order to identify pinpoint "troublemakers" who might be planning to attend the Olympics in Beijing. With their pictures on file, Chinese authorities can then either deny their visas or monitor them more closely when they arrive in China.

In addition, Beijing has been trying to locate the organizers of anti-China protests and demonstrations overseas, ones who may be planning action in China, in order to infiltrate their groups and gather intelligence on their planned activities. This is not new for Beijing — as the Chinese Embassy official who defected in Australia a few years ago demonstrated by revealing the details of Chinese infiltration of and spying on Falun Gong supporters in Australia. Beijing also has been seeking out U.S. and other foreign academics for their insights on potential demonstrations in Beijing, hoping to get information about individuals and tactical details of plans in order to pre-empt or at least effectively counter them.

In addition to the intelligence collection efforts and the careful organization and coordination of the pro-China demonstrators in

San Francisco, electronic countermeasures also were used to disrupt the communications and activities of the anti-China demonstrators. In some cases, the cell phones of the anti-China organizers were spammed with prank calls and text messages in order to limit their effectiveness as a coordinating tool — particularly as the torch changed routes. There also were unconfirmed cases of limited cell-phone jamming, likely using the short-range cell-phone jammers that were popular a few years ago. These created intermittent and isolated interference with cell-phone reception, further deteriorating the communications and coordination ability of the anti-China demonstrators.

Beyond San Francisco

Furthermore, China did not limit its activities to San Francisco. It also organized a smaller response to the Dalai Lama's visit to Seattle, Wash., a few days later. Chinese Consul General in San Francisco Gao Zhansheng sent a letter to University of Washington (UW) President Mark Emmert urging him and other UW officials to refrain from meeting with the Dalai Lama or from giving him a platform for political or "separatist" activities. Additionally, the Chinese Students and Scholars Association sent an open letter to the UW leadership and met briefly with Emmert and Provost Ed Taylor, asking them to limit the Dalai Lama's opportunity to use his visit for political reasons. Several hundred pro-China students also staged a demonstration outside the Dalai Lama's speaking venue in Seattle on April 14, using the Internet to coordinate banners, chants and actions.

Throughout the United States there have been reports of other group actions by Chinese students and activists, from Internet-based activity promoting boycotts of French goods following the Paris torch relay to a push to "correct" foreign media coverage of the Tibet riots and the Tibet issue overall. But there also have been more aggressive instances. For example, at least one Chinese student at Duke University received threats after attending a pro-Tibet rally, while others have had their personal information, including their phone numbers and Chinese identification cards, posted on the Internet bulletin board hosted by the university's Chinese Student and Scholar Association (the association denied responsibility, saying those postings were the actions of individuals). The students' concern, however, is that the information will get back to Chinese authorities and thus undermine their future prospects in China or even lead to further harassment of themselves or their families.

China has had a long reach into the Chinese community in the United States for quite some time, and frequently uses this community for espionage, both within the community itself and against American companies, the military and the technology and political spheres. Also, Chinese consulates in the United States have helped facilitate pro-China gatherings in the past. However, while it already was known that China was anxious to restore its image after the Tibet unrest and the trouble with the torch run in London and Paris, the effort and coordination Beijing exhibited in San Francisco, through the consulate and local Chinese business and social organizations, was rather impressive.

There are no estimates of the number of pro- and anti-China demonstrators at the San Francisco event, though the former easily totaled several thousand. Additionally, the actions of the pro-China camp, along with the supporters' placement along the anticipated route, demonstrated a much more centralized and coordinated organization than the anti-China groups — and revealed the depth to which the Chinese government can organize and deploy its overseas population, even in the United States.

A New Approach on African Oil?
Nov. 6, 2009

The ministerial meeting of the Forum on China-Africa Cooperation will begin in Egypt on Nov. 8, with Chinese Premier Wen Jiabao slated to arrive on Nov. 6. This will be the first high-level Sino-African meeting since the 2006 China-Africa summit in Beijing, at which China made significant pledges to Africa including $5 billion in loans and another $5 billion in investment.

China has increased its economic involvement in Africa every year for the last decade. However, in the past year attempts to compete with Western companies for oil deals have met with considerable resistance. China may find it needs to modify its strategy to secure access to Africa's most promising resources.

China's Strategy

China has four strategic imperatives in Africa: gaining access to resources, increasing its political influence, developing outlets for Chinese laborers, and acquiring preferential access to markets. In the past, China has pursued what it considers the most critical of these imperatives — resource extraction — by offering chronically underdeveloped and capital-poor African states huge infrastructure loans and favorable lending terms far beyond what Western companies and institutions are willing to provide, in exchange for access to natural resources, particularly oil.

As international oil companies (IOCs) from the West have already secured some of the most promising oil fields on the continent, China has primarily looked to places where there was little competition, either because the fields were not as productive or because the investments were riskier, both in political and security terms. Because of the quid pro quo structure of these deals — loans for access to oil, China has also frequently been the sole investor in a project, or at least held the majority share.

228

Within this strategy, Beijing has been willing to work with governments that other Western countries prefer to shun for political reasons — such as Sudan — to gain access to natural resources. In the last few years, Chinese companies have signed or attempted to sign exploration contracts in nearly every African country with potential oil resources. China has major and long-standing projects in Angola (which provides 16 percent of China's oil imports, second to Saudi Arabia and barely more than Iran), Sudan (6 percent) and the Republic of the Congo (2.5 percent). On the periphery, China National Offshore Oil Corporation (CNOOC) drilled an exploration well in Kenya in 2009 and gained exploration rights in Somalia in 2007, two countries not known for their oil resources.

This has served Beijing's political and economic interests as well. China has used infrastructure development through loans and investment in a bid to demonstrate its willingness to contribute to the well-being of its African partners, rather than simply take their resources — a significant point for a country that considers itself the leader of the developing world, not to mention a diplomatic tool. The China Development Bank has loaned more than $5 billion to Angola in recent years in return for oil supply guarantees. In 2009, it loaned $420 million to Zambia for Chinese companies to build a power plant and $850 million to Nigeria for a railroad. In return, China also gets political support in international forums like the United Nations from recipient countries.

This approach also takes into account Chinese domestic considerations. Chinese companies have invested in telecommunications and other industries in Africa as part of an effort to open up more markets for their export-based economy. And Chinese-funded and operated projects often bring in Chinese workers, providing employment during an economic slowdown. This can backfire, however, as the countries receiving the loans and investment often have high unemployment themselves, and Chinese workers are hardly considered welcome. In the case of Zambia, China's presence was a significant rallying point for opposition politician

Michael Sata, who came close to unseating the ruling Movement for Multiparty Democracy party in that country's 2006 elections. So while governments in Africa will work with China, at the same time they must manage this relationship closely so that Chinese behavior that accompanies the investments does not trigger a domestic social backlash and cause a government to fall or politicians to lose their post.

Challenges

With a favorable trade balance and massive foreign currency reserves, China was set to take advantage of the financial crisis that began in 2008. The steep drop in commodity prices and Western oil majors' willingness to sell some of their assets in the midst of that crisis provided an opportunity for China to buy up investments. However, as China started to move in on some of the more lucrative assets in Africa, the economic crisis subsided, commodity prices climbed, and the large Western oil majors have proven uninterested in selling.

CNOOC was recently reported to be in discussions on a bid to buy licenses in 23 of Nigeria's oil blocks. Of those 23 blocks, 16 are already leased to Western oil majors and at least 12 appear to be offshore. China's technology is not as advanced as Western oil companies when it comes to evaluating deep-water oil fields. The Western companies have this advantage and already have stakes in many of these lucrative areas. (Shell has claimed it will fight any possible deal.) Nigeria is rumored to be using the increased competition from China to bid up prices on the renewals of the Western IOC blocks.

China has also entered talks this year for two possible bids that compete directly with Western IOCs for African oil. In Uganda, U.K. firm Tullow is developing a Lake Albert region oil project that all three Chinese oil majors have courted. (Eni, Total, StatoilHydro and ExxonMobil are also believed to have entered talks on the field.) In Ghana, a recent $4 billion agreement for

ExxonMobil to purchase a stake in the untapped Jubilee field from Kosmos Energy was said to be blocked by the government. It has been reported in recent weeks that CNOOC and Sinopec — another major Chinese energy company — have made overtures to Accra about purchasing the stake, underscoring the growing competition between Chinese and Western companies.

Some Chinese offers have been rejected outright by African governments. In July, CNOOC and Sinopec pooled their resources to bid for a 20 percent share in a deep-water exploration block in Angola. French company Total would have operated the facilities on the block, but Sonangol, Angola's state-owned company which has a partnership with China's Beiya investment corporation, exercised its right of refusal for the deal. STRATFOR sources say Angola was wary of a growing dependence on China and wanted to keep its assets diversified, and that Sonangol may buy the share itself.

The only successful acquisition Chinese oil companies have had in Africa this year involves the $7.2 billion purchase of Addax by Sinopec. In 2008, Addax blocks produced 108,000 barrels per day (bpd) in Nigeria, 100,000 bpd in Gabon, and 2,100 bpd in Cameroon. It also has access to joint exploration blocks in the Gulf of Guinea, which is believed to hold some of the largest undeveloped reserves in the world. The important tactical point for Chinese oil companies is that Addax gives them access to the offshore technology and blocks that they have been lacking.

A New Approach?

After completing only one major deal in Africa — Addax — in a year that seemed tailored for Chinese success, it has become clear to Beijing that it must adopt a new strategy in order to compete with Western IOCs. The way forward may be to abandon China's past resource acquisition strategy of being the only investor in a project or holding the majority share, to now accepting minority stakes in projects with Western companies in order to gain access to the capabilities they lack. CNOOC is relatively inexperienced in offshore oil extraction and none of the Chinese oil majors are competent in deep-water drilling — where nearly all untapped African oil patches are located.

There are signs this is the tactic China is pursuing. On Nov. 3 China National Petroleum Corporation signed a deal with BP in Iraq for a minority stake, and on Nov. 5 CNOOC bought minority stakes in four Gulf of Mexico oilfields from Statoil. The Chinese oil majors have yet to strike a minority-share deal in Africa, but if they continue with this approach, they stand to gain technology and expertise that may eventually translate into the ability to challenge Western IOCs for more difficult offshore projects. China will continue to bid for less attractive projects, but have found through their inability to strike deals in Africa during favorable conditions that their oil majors must start developing new capabilities in order to stay competitive on resource acquisitions in the long run — even if it means becoming a minority stakeholder to garner that expertise.

A Strategic Pipeline to Central Asia
Dec. 14, 2009

Chinese President Hu Jintao visited Kazakhstan and Turkmenistan from Dec. 12 through Dec. 14, with his trip culminating in the inauguration of the 4,350-mile Central Asia Natural Gas Pipeline, which will ship 13 billion cubic meters (bcm) in 2010 (and up to 30 bcm 2012-2013) from Turkmenistan, through Uzbekistan and Kazakhstan, to China. Once in China, the Turkmen natural gas will travel to booming urban centers to fuel China's rapid economic growth and surging demand.

The pipeline helps China meet two of its national energy strategy goals: providing foreign natural gas supplies as China's consumption increases; and acquiring natural gas imports through multiple land routes so as not to depend wholly on liquefied natural gas (LNG) imports through maritime routes that are potentially vulnerable to outside interference. Even so, China is unlikely to see natural gas provide even 10 percent of the country's energy by 2020.

The pipeline marks a concrete infrastructural link between China and Central Asia as Beijing advances its influence in the region. The pipeline gives the Central Asian states a clear signal that Chinese investment can counter Russia's presence in the region. Nevertheless, Russian dominance remains a reality in Central Asia, and China knows this. Although the Central Asia Natural Gas Pipeline is not currently an object of rivalry between Beijing and Moscow, it could be in the future — which means that China could experience what it means to be on the receiving end of a natural gas pipeline controlled by Russia.

Meeting Rising Demand

Currently, natural gas consumption is a small component of China's overall energy consumption — 3.6 percent, compared to about 70 percent for coal, 18.8 percent for oil and 6.6 percent for hydroelectric energy. Nevertheless, it is rising rapidly — by 25 percent from 2006 to 2007 and by 16 percent from 2007 to 2008, reaching 80.7 billion cubic meters in 2008. This increase is a result of Beijing's pursuit of a national energy strategy that boosts natural gas consumption in order to diversify its energy mix, modernize its energy consumption patterns and reduce pollution (since natural gas emits about half as much carbon as coal). Consumption is expected to grow by about 50 percent between now and 2020, when it could reach around 120 bcm per year — it could exceed 200 bcm per year by 2030.

All sectors are increasing natural gas consumption — residential consumption is one of the fastest growing categories, with per capita consumption increasing by a factor of 10 since 1990.

Currently, industry consumes about 73 percent of China's natural gas supply (with manufacturing consuming 48 percent), while household consumption accounts for 19 percent and power generation 12 percent.

The rapid growth in demand was exemplified pointedly in November, when cities like Wuhan, Chongqing and Hangzhou suffered from shortages due to increased demand with the early onset of winter weather, and were forced to limit industrial gas consumption to ensure residents got enough heating.

To meet this rising demand, China is increasing domestic natural gas exploration and production. Its natural gas reserves are estimated at 2.5 trillion cubic meters. Exploration and new projects are taking place especially in Xinjiang province, where production at the Tarim field currently provides about 21 percent of the country's total consumption, and in Sichuan province, where state firms CNPC and Sinopec are seeking to develop the major Chuandongbei and Puguang natural gas fields, respectively. China National Offshore Oil Corp. has also undertaken natural gas exploration and development in the South China Sea. Nevertheless, domestic production has been falling behind consumption in recent years (with a 4-bcm shortfall in 2008), and China's dependence on external sources of natural gas is set to increase in coming decades; government officials expect a shortfall of 80 bcm by 2020.

As a result, China has turned outward. China began importing natural gas in 2007, when consumption first inched ahead of domestic production. Imported natural gas met 11 percent of China's total natural gas demand in 2008, with LNG accounting for 96 percent of imports. China has invested heavily in building adequate LNG import facilities (located in Guangdong and Fujian provinces and Shanghai, with new facilities to come online soon) to receive exports from Australia, Indonesia, Qatar and Malaysia. China's LNG consumption is expected to grow by 12 percent per year until 2020. To complement these LNG imports, China is seeking imports through land routes by forming pipeline connections with neighbors — not only in Central Asia, but also Myanmar and potentially Russia.

But the growth of natural gas as an energy source is limited. First, inadequacies remain in the pipelines and distribution networks that will continue constraining accessibility and preventing demand growth. China's existing pipeline infrastructure provides the country's major cities with natural gas, but it will not be nationally integrated until several new pipeline projects come online. Beijing is working to redress this problem by expanding and upgrading its pipelines — a plan that has been boosted with fiscal stimulus in 2009.

Domestic price controls present another complication. In general, prices are overregulated, creating a disincentive for natural gas companies to invest in expanding or improving infrastructure since they cannot accurately predict profits. While Beijing is moving toward reforming the price structure and allowing domestic natural gas prices to fluctuate more, to reflect supply and demand, it is also proceeding cautiously so as to ensure that rising prices do not affect households too negatively and that vulnerable sectors are provided with subsidies.

A more important factor limiting natural gas usage in China is the role of coal. China has the world's third-largest coal reserves (about 115 billion metric tons). It has depended on coal for years, with production reaching nearly 2.8 billion metric tons per year and consumption at 70 percent of total energy consumption — in 2008, China made up about 43 percent of global coal consumption. The economy was built on coal and is disproportionately reliant on it. This is especially true for electricity generation, where coal provides three-fourths of feedstock for power generation, compared to natural gas at around 10 percent.

Beijing has had considerable success since 2003 in jump-starting new natural gas-fired power generation projects, but pricing structures and incentives still favor coal. Ultimately, China is unlikely to reach its loftiest goals of having natural gas provide 10 percent of the country's energy by 2020, as it could take most of the next decade to push the share of natural gas to 5 percent of overall energy consumption. It will also be difficult to reach the goal of 30 percent of natural gas going toward power generation, as coal's share of power generation is expected to increase. China's structural dependence on coal will limit the growth of natural gas as an energy source.

Geopolitical Implications

China's reasons for seeking Central Asian natural gas are strategic as well as economic. As China's economy rapidly expands, it consumes more and more energy and becomes increasingly dependent on imports. For example, a chief problem is China's dependency on foreign oil, which has reached 4 million barrels per day (about half of the country's total oil consumption). The risks associated with oil imports include instability in the Middle East (especially when the West is sliding toward a confrontation with Iran that could lead to interruptions in the Strait of Hormuz, through which much of China's oil passes), and vulnerability to the naval supremacy of the United States, which could cut off China's oil imports at will.

China's natural gas consumption is increasing, and LNG is set to account for one-sixth of the country's total natural gas supply in the next decade. Yet LNG import facilities are extremely capital-intensive, and LNG tankers are potentially vulnerable to U.S. naval interdiction. And this explains Beijing's desire to seek sources of natural gas on land, both through developing domestic production and connections with neighboring Asian natural gas producers. Central Asia is the primary target. China has invested heftily in the region, seeing Central Asia as an area that is close, shares a land border and badly needs Chinese cash. To Beijing, Central Asia is a more or less secure source of the commodities China needs — not only hydrocarbons but also minerals and agricultural products like cotton — and a market for Chinese goods.

In essence, the Central Asian pipeline is a major tangible link between China and Central Asia. These states have seen Chinese influence growing in recent years, as Beijing has contributed capital for a level of infrastructure and development these states have never had. Beijing even showed its willingness to come to the financial rescue of Central Asian states during the economic crisis, bailing Turkmenistan out for $4 billion and loaning $3.5 billion for non-extractive purposes to Kazakhstan.

The Central Asian states, for their part, have been happy to oblige. Since the fall of the Soviet Union, the newly independent Central Asian states have sought outside investment to capitalize on their abundant natural resources. Some are also looking for a counterbalance to Russia's predominant influence — especially since the vast majority of their infrastructure and institutions are wedded to Russia through vestiges of Soviet rule. Turkmenistan in particular has suffered, since Russia cut off natural gas imports earlier in 2009, and is looking for a more reliable recipient for its energy exports. Turkmenistan's only other customer is Iran, which is attempting to increase imports to about 14 bcm per year. China — which in a few short years is expected to import 30 bcm annually through the new pipeline — is therefore a godsend for Ashgabat, as it offers a rapidly growing consumer market that is outside of Russia's sphere of influence and manifestly willing to invest the cash to boost Turkmenistan's energy production and build the pipelines.

For China, however, there are liabilities associated with the new pipeline. Becoming more reliant on Turkmen natural gas brings the risk of Russian interference — since Moscow still holds sway over Central Asia's security and political institutions. Beijing got a taste of Moscow's interference when the Russian construction companies responsible for the Central Asian pipeline repeatedly delayed their work. In the future, if Russia should disagree with China, it could pull strings in Turkmenistan (where it outright owns the energy infrastructure) or Kazakhstan to reduce or cut off natural gas exports. Europe has long understood the implications

of depending on Russian or Russian-controlled natural gas —
Moscow has not shied away from politicizing natural gas exports
to pressure Europe. Beijing, however, has not dealt with it before.

Uzbekistan poses another risk for China. It is the only self-
sufficient Central Asian state, and thus is a wild card. Though
Uzbekistan is merely a transit state, the Uzbeks could choose to
cut off the pipes to extract concessions from China, for instance.

Presently, there is little risk that Russia and China will compete
for the same natural gas supplies in Turkmenistan. Russia does not
currently need Turkmen natural gas — low demand in Europe
has lowered Russia's own natural gas exports, obviating the need
to import Turkmen gas for domestic uses. Meanwhile, China's
natural gas consumption is a small enough component of its overall energy mix that it is not a critical vulnerability. But in a few
years, when European demand increases, Russia could begin to
seek more imports from Turkmenistan — potentially competing
with China for the same supplies. Thus, while the Central Asian
natural gas pipeline is not a point of contention between Moscow
and Beijing now, it could be in the future.

China, Myanmar: Re-engagement and Pipeline Politics
Dec. 20, 2009

Chinese Vice President Xi Jinping arrived in Myanmar for his
two-day visit on Dec. 19, after visiting Japan and South Korea on
a tour of Asia. Xi was originally slated to visit Cambodia before
going to Myanmar, but that visit was rescheduled, perhaps due to
the fact that some ethnic Uighurs involved in rioting in July are
now seeking asylum in Cambodia.

China-Myanmar border stability is a priority, but the primary
focus of Xi's trip is to strengthen China's position in Southeast

Asia and address the United States' growing interests in the region. Though the United States' recent moves toward Myanmar have been diplomatic, Beijing perceives them as a threat to Chinese energy security and geopolitical influence over the region.

China has been one of Myanmar's few diplomatic backers since Western countries imposed broad sanctions against the military-ruled country in 1988 following a crackdown on pro-democracy demonstrators. China has been Myanmar's fourth-largest foreign investor, primarily in the energy sector, and depends on the country for access to the Indian Ocean. Bilateral relations, however, were strained in late August when tensions between Myanmar's military and the Kokang ethnic minority's militia pushed thousands of refugees past the border into China's southwestern Yunnan province. Beijing then pressed the country to address the border stability issue, and sent People's Liberation Army Lt. Gen. Ai Husheng to Naypyidaw from Dec. 5-10 to discuss the problem. Xi Jinping's visit will likely include a continuation of these talks in an effort to repair bilateral relations.

Since the election of U.S. President Barack Obama, Beijing has been concerned about the United States' pledge to re-engage with Asia, particularly Washington's intent to move closer to the members of the Association of Southeast Asian Nations (ASEAN). China is afraid U.S. re-engagement in Southeast Asia will undermine its energy security and existing geopolitical influence over the region. As such, the most significant of the U.S. actions, from a Chinese perspective, was Assistant Secretary of State for East Asian and Pacific Affairs Kurt Campbell's trip to Myanmar in early November for talks with the government and the opposition.

Campbell's trip took place just as China's state-owned China National Petroleum Corp. announced Nov. 3 it would begin construction on a 480-mile oil pipeline, and later a natural gas pipeline, through Myanmar. These pipelines are part of China's efforts to diversify its energy import routes, and to decrease the amount of oil imported through the Strait of Malacca from the South China Sea.

China's push to expand land-based energy routes, to increase trade in Central and Southeast Asia, and to pursue seemingly expensive land-based pipeline and rail routes are all largely driven by the country's vulnerable yet critical maritime supply lanes. China's shifts in naval doctrine and the acceleration of development of anti-ship missiles and anti-satellite systems are also part of the same reaction. When Campbell traveled to Myanmar, what Beijing saw was not a visit to pave the way for a less contentious U.S.-ASEAN summit, but rather a concerted effort to undermine Chinese energy security.

Myanmar may have been using Beijing's concern over the growing U.S interest for its own purposes in suggesting that natural gas pipelines to China deliver gas to Yangon first, and that a greater share of natural gas be diverted for domestic use instead of being exported. Xi's visit is intended to better gauge what issues the United States and Myanmar discussed during Campbell's visit in November, and lock down relations between China and Myanmar.

From a broader perspective, Beijing is worried about losing its existing advantageous position over Southeast Asia amid the United States' re-engagement. Since the 1997-1998 Asian economic crisis, China has slowly expanded its economic and political ties with the ASEAN states while Washington, since the end of the Cold War, has been less and less involved. Over the past ten years, though, many nations perceived China's economic growth and expanding influence over the region as a potential threat to their own prosperity and growth. As such, the U.S. shift in policy toward Myanmar, and Obama's presence at the ASEAN summit, have created a new sense of concern in China. While Washington is currently preoccupied dealing with the Iranian nuclear program and wars in Iraq and Afghanistan, Beijing does not want to see ten years of expanding influence and connections in Southeast Asia jeopardized.

U.S., China: Rising Tensions Amid Iran Sanctions Push

Feb. 18, 2010

The United States has intensified its public courting of Beijing's support for a potential sanctions regime against Iran in recent days. U.S. Secretary of State Hillary Clinton visited Saudi Arabia on Feb. 15-16 where she encouraged a deal in which the Saudis would increase oil exports to China to guarantee China's oil supply amid the tensions with Iran. On Feb. 14, U.S. Vice President Joe Biden said he expected the Chinese to provide support for sanctions, while National Security Adviser Jim Jones said the same day that China has supported nuclear nonproliferation efforts against North Korea and that as a "responsible world power" it would also do so with Iran. This followed U.S. President Barack Obama's statement the previous week saying that while the Russians have become "forward leaning" on the sanctions issue, China's support remains a question.

Washington's focus on China over the Iranian issue comes in the midst of a rocky patch in overall Sino-American relations. China has consistently resisted the push for sanctions, as they could put Beijing's energy security at risk and curtail its growing bilateral relationship with Tehran. Ultimately, the Chinese do not have to make a final decision on sanctions until the U.N. Security Council (UNSC) takes a vote. But China has few tools to use against the United States to resist sanctions — and to do so would run the risk of provoking American reactions that China would rather avoid.

The Root of Sino-U.S. Tensions

The Chinese and American partnership has undergone several strains since American financial troubles became global financial troubles in late 2008. Inherent characteristics of the two economies, and their mutual dependence, made it inevitable that economic and trade tensions would arise. China's single-largest customer is the United States, to which it exported $220.8 billion worth of goods and services in 2009, 18 percent of China's total exports. By contrast China is the United States' third-largest export market, importing $77.4 billion in total in 2009. In the process of running large trade surpluses, China has racked up $2.39 trillion in foreign exchange reserves and invested about one third of that into U.S. Treasury debt, thereby helping the U.S. Federal Reserve to maintain low interest rates that perpetuate U.S. consumption of Chinese goods.

U.S.-Chinese economic and financial interdependency has called attention to vulnerabilities and disagreements. The Obama administration slapped tariffs on Chinese-made tires in September 2009, and a host of other disputes have arisen at the World Trade Organization (WTO). While these disputes are mainly political efforts meant to release domestic social pressure, both states are aware that there is potential for protectionist tactics to spiral out of control, making the relationship inherently uneasy and suspicious.

Economic tensions are coupled with military ones. There is already lack of trust between China and the United States on the question of defense. Beijing's military power has increased as its economic success has enabled greater reforms and better weaponry, and Beijing's rising military profile has caused concern among states that doubt its intentions. Meanwhile the United States is the world's leading military power by far, and not only dominates the oceans with naval power (implicitly threatening China's vital supply lines) but also maintains strong alliances with states on the Chinese periphery, including Japan, South Korea and Taiwan, a territory Beijing claims as its own. Military-to-military talks were canceled in 2008 when the Bush administration agreed to a new arms package to Taiwan, and briefly restarted when China canceled them again in 2010 following the Obama administration's approval of the deal.

These broader national security issues have become entangled with the trade spats. China has threatened sanctions on American arms manufacturers for making the weapons that Washington is selling to Taiwan in the most recent U.S. arms package. China's threat to introduce retaliatory sanctions marks a harsher reaction to such arms deals than in the past. On a separate front, a conflict has erupted over China's Internet control policies and American cybersecurity. China has also reacted sharply against American criticism of its policies in dealing with ethnic minorities and separatism in Xinjiang and Tibet, which has created another diplomatic row in light of President Obama's plan to meet with the Dalai Lama on Feb. 18.

Resistance to Iranian Sanctions

While trade and defense tensions have long been present in the Sino-U.S. relationship, the controversy over the Iranian nuclear program — and the U.S. push for sanctions — have introduced a new, urgent and potentially destabilizing element into the dynamic. China has rejected the idea of new sanctions since the Obama administration launched negotiations in mid-2009, and the Chinese have shown increasing displeasure with the U.S. sanctions drive since late December 2009 by postponing and sending lower-level officials to negotiations with the P-5+1 group, which consists of the five permanent members of the UNSC (China, the United States, the United Kingdom, France, and Russia) plus Germany. China's foreign ministry has continued its rejection of sanctions in 2010.

China's position on Iran follows from its concerns for energy security. China imported about 51 percent of its oil in 2009, and Iran was the third-largest supplier, providing about 11.4 percent of its imports — after Saudi Arabia (20.5 percent) and Angola (15.8 percent). While the current batch of proposed sanctions do not target Iranian oil exports, they would escalate tensions in the Persian Gulf overall. China fears that a military conflict could erupt that would threaten supply lines from other Gulf providers, such as Saudi Arabia or Oman, since the Iranian retaliation might target the Strait of Hormuz through which roughly half of China's total oil imports transit. Without a steady stream of Gulf oil, China's ability to maintain economic growth would be threatened. And China is not willing to take such risks with its energy supply.

Moreover, China's exports of gasoline and refined oil products to Iran have grown in recent months. Iran's dysfunctional domestic energy situation forces it to import these goods, and China has excess refining capacity. This growing area of trade would specifically be targeted in international sanctions, as the Americans have long signaled that Iran's dependency on external sources for gasoline is its Achilles' heel. Sanctions against Iran would also interfere with China's investments in Iran's energy sector — including China National Petroleum Corp's (CNPC) planned exploration of Iran's massive South Pars natural gas field in March, as well as deals for oil production involving CNPC in Iran's North Azadegan and Sinopec in the Yadavaran oil field. In other words, while China will not base its decisions solely on its exports to and investments in Iran, those considerations are substantial and will not be ignored.

China also has a reputation to uphold. Especially in recent years, China has positioned itself as a global leader, seeking to complement its economic power with rising military and political status. Beijing has made its voice heard at the United Nations, the G-20 and other global forums as a leader of the developing countries and a counterweight to the developed countries. Simultaneously, China has sought to play a more active role in international security operations, including peacekeeping and disaster relief, and has taken a leading role in the international anti-piracy efforts off the coast of Somalia, all with the intention of enhancing its prestige and developing powers outside the economic sphere. These efforts are also meant to present China as a potential alternative global leader to the United States, and to earn supporters and followers.

A substantial amount of credibility thus rests on China's defending of states like Iran that are antagonistic toward the United States — if China turns its back on Iran, then countries in Latin America, Africa and Southeast Asia that might have thought they could count on Beijing in a pinch will have to rethink their policies. On the contrary, if Beijing can prolong negotiations and delay serious action on Iran, it can extend the time in which the United States is bogged down in the Middle East, winning more room to maneuver toward meeting domestic and international objectives.

Limited Options

Beijing's problem is that it has very few tools with which to influence the United States' behavior in general, not to mention toward Iran. China's only tools to pressure the United States are economic — specifically through trade disputes and purchases of U.S. debt — and they would backfire. Beijing is also not able to directly affect negotiations between the United States and Russia on sanctions. And if sanctions are proposed in the UNSC, China can veto them only if it is prepared for the blowback from the United States.

China's chief weakness lies in the fact that it cannot escape economic troubles until its export sector revives, but the United States has the ability to put pressure on this sector. The Obama administration has shown a willingness to exercise Section 421, an American law that China admitted into its WTO accession agreement in 2001 that gives the United States the right to enact barriers when it perceives that a dramatic increase in Chinese imports into the American market could disrupt domestic producers. The significance of the September tire tariffs was primarily to warn China that Washington is willing to use this prerogative and there is little China can do about it. If Beijing should seek to retaliate through its own tariffs, it risks provoking a trade war with the United States that it could not win, since its economy is too fragile to sustain the shocks that could be caused by a more aggressive use of Section 421, or more drastic measures.

Even China's great advantage of being the United States' primary creditor does not provide as much leverage as one might think. At the latest tally (in December 2009), China held around $755 billion in U.S. Treasury debt, about 6 percent of total U.S. government debt. Slowing or stopping the purchase of U.S. Treasury bonds could have an effect on the U.S. economic recovery, were it feasible for China to do so. But selling off large chunks of American debt would not only require finding lots of very rich buyers, but would leave Beijing with nowhere to invest its surplus dollars month after month, since the other deep debt markets are unsafe (Japan), vulnerable to exchange rate risk (Europe) or too small (everyone else). Investing that much cash into commodities would both roil global debt markets and drive commodity prices sky high. Even if Beijing could successfully diversify away from U.S. debt, the move would cause interest rates to rise in the United States and disrupt U.S. consumption patterns crucial for China's economy (and global economic stability).

A Russian Turn?

Recently, prominent Russian authorities have made statements implying that Moscow was becoming more willing to endorse sanctions. As long as Russia appears intransigent on the U.S. call for sanctions, it provides China with diplomatic cover. But if a Russian shift is in fact under way — and there is no hard evidence yet that the United States has offered the concessions necessary to win Russia over — then it will have an impact on China's strategy.

Moscow is critical to the efficacy of any sanctions regime because it can circumvent sanctions by means of its communication and transportation routes through the Caucasus and Central Asia to Iran. Without Russia, international sanctions will not work. Unlike Russia, however, China is not capable of making or breaking sanctions covertly through its participation or lack thereof — its links to Iran go over sea routes, making them vulnerable to American naval power (while the land routes from China to Iran are logistically unfeasible and still hinge on Russian influence). Finally, the United States and European allies are not likely to bring sanctions to a vote at the UNSC unless they have already gained the assurances they need from Russia — and China has no ability to impact these negotiations.

If a resolution authorizing sanctions goes to the UNSC, China will have to determine whether to approve, abstain or to exercise its veto (and China has only vetoed sanctions once, sanctions against Zimbabwe in 2008). Voting for sanctions, China will be stuck with enforcing them (and all that enforcement entails) and managing the domestic and international blow to its reputation for caving to American demands despite its much-vaunted rising-power status. Still, this is a path that China has taken before, and is also likely to take in the event that sanctions are watered down. But even if China abstains from voting to register its displeasure, it will be bound by law to enforce the sanctions, or else it will be publicly exposed for undermining them and subject to a harsh reaction from the United States.

Alternately, if the Chinese were to veto a sanctions resolution, they would risk marginalizing the UNSC's role in dealing with Iran. The United States has shown before that it is willing to act with an international coalition outside of the United Nations, and Iran presents just the type of scenario in which the United States can do so with broad international support, including all the leading European powers and possibly even Russia. Since the UNSC is a key arena for China in attempting to expand its global influence, Beijing would suffer the effects of both isolating itself from the American coalition and seeing the influence of its UNSC seat dwindle.

Looking Ahead

With little impact on the international negotiations, and limited ability to challenge the United States, Beijing can only attempt to play the diplomatic game and stall. The Russians have not yet signed onto sanctions, and as long as they remain in limbo, Beijing does not have to commit. Nevertheless, exposure to the United States is the reason that China's Communist Party leadership has become consumed with furious internal debate over the country's path forward. Beijing is fully aware that the United States plans to withdraw from the Middle East in a few years, which raises the frightful question of where the superpower will focus its attention next. China is afraid that it is the next target, and sees renewed U.S. attention to Southeast Asia as the beginning of a full-scale containment policy. The problem for China is that to decrease its vulnerability to foreign powers will require difficult reforms, and at a time when the Communist Party is approaching a leadership transition in 2012 and the course ahead is uncertain. With these considerations in mind, China must weigh whether it can afford to break with the United States now over Iran, or whether it could better spend its energies fortifying against what it sees as a likely onslaught of geopolitical competition from the United States in a few short years.

Crunch Time in U.S.-Chinese Relations
March 30, 2010

U.S.-Chinese relations have become tenser in recent months, with the United States threatening to impose tariffs unless China agrees to revalue its currency and, ideally, allow it to become convertible like the yen or euro. China now follows Japan and Germany as one of the three major economies after the United States. Unlike the other two, it controls its currency's value, allowing it to decrease the price of its exports and giving it an advantage not only over other exporters to the United States but also over domestic American manufacturers. The same is true in other regions that receive Chinese exports, such as Europe.

What Washington considered tolerable in a small developing economy is intolerable in one of the top five economies. The demand that Beijing raise the value of the yuan, however, poses dramatic challenges for the Chinese, as the ability to control their currency helps drive their exports. The issue is why China insists on controlling its currency, something embedded in the nature of the Chinese economy. A collision with the United States now seems inevitable. It is therefore important to understand the forces driving China, and it is time for STRATFOR to review its analysis of China.

An Inherently Unstable Economic System

China has had an extraordinary run since 1980. But like Japan and Southeast Asia before it, dramatic growth rates cannot maintain themselves in perpetuity. Japan and non-Chinese East Asia didn't collapse and disappear, but the crises of the 1990s did change the way the region worked. The driving force behind both the 1990 Japanese Crisis and the 1997 East Asian Crisis was that the countries involved did not maintain free capital markets. Those states managed capital to keep costs artificially low, giving them tremendous advantages over countries where capital was rationally priced. Of course, one cannot maintain irrational capital prices in perpetuity (as the United States is learning after its financial crisis); doing so eventually catches up. And this is what is happening in China now.

STRATFOR thus sees the Chinese economic system as inherently unstable. The primary reason why China's growth has been so impressive is that throughout the period of economic liberalization that has led to rising incomes, the Chinese government has maintained near-total savings capture of its households and businesses. It funnels these massive deposits via state-run banks to state-linked firms at below-market rates. It's amazing the growth rate a country can achieve and the number of citizens it can employ with a vast supply of 0 percent, relatively consequence-free loans provided from the savings of nearly a billion workers.

It's also amazing how unprofitable such a country can be. The Chinese system, like the Japanese system before it, works on bulk, churn, maximum employment and market share. The U.S. system of attempting to maximize return on investment through efficiency and profit stands in contrast. The American result is sufficient economic stability to be able to suffer through recessions and emerge stronger. The Chinese result is social stability that wobbles precipitously when exposed to economic hardship. The Chinese people rebel when work is not available and conditions reach extremes. It must be remembered that of China's 1.3 billion people, more than 600 million urban citizens live on an average of about $7 a day, while 700 million rural people live on an average of $2 a day, and that is according to Beijing's own well-scrubbed statistics.

Moreover, the Chinese system breeds a flock of other unintended side effects.

There is, of course, the issue of inefficient capital use: When you have an unlimited number of no-consequence loans, you tend to invest in a lot of no-consequence projects for political reasons or just to speculate. In addition to the overall inefficiency of the Chinese system, another result is a large number of property bubbles. Yes, China is a country with a massive need for housing for its citizens, but even so, local governments and property developers collude to build luxury dwellings instead of anything more affordable in urban areas. This puts China in the odd position of having both a glut and a shortage in housing, as well as an outright glut in commercial real estate, where vacancy rates are notoriously high.

There is also the issue of regional disparity. Most of this lending occurs in a handful of coastal regions, transforming them into global powerhouses, while most of the interior — and thereby most of the population — lives in abject poverty.

There is also the issue of consumption. Chinese statistics have always been dodgy, but according to Beijing's own figures, China has a tiny consumer base. This base is not much larger than that of France, a country with roughly one twentieth China's population and just over half its gross domestic product (GDP). China's economic system is obviously geared toward exports, not expanding consumer credit.

Which brings us to the issue of dependence. Since China cannot absorb its own goods, it must export them to keep afloat. The strategy only works when there is endless demand for the goods it makes. For the most part, this demand comes from the United States. But the recent global recession cut Chinese exports by nearly one fifth, and there were no buyers elsewhere to pick up the slack. Meanwhile, to boost household consumption China provided subsidies to Chinese citizens who had little need for — and in some cases little ability to use — a number of big-ticket products. The Chinese now openly fear that exports will not make a sustainable return to previous levels until 2012. And that is a lot of production — and consumption — to subsidize in the meantime. Most countries have another word for this: waste.

This waste can be broken down into two main categories. First, the government roughly tripled the amount of cash it normally directs the state banks to lend to sustain economic activity during the recession. The new loans added up to roughly a third of GDP in a single year. Remember, with no-consequence loans, profitability or even selling goods is not an issue; one must merely continue employing people. Even if China boasted the best loan-quality programs in history, a dramatic increase in lending of that scale is sure to generate mountains of loans that will go bad. Second, not everyone taking out those loans even intends to invest prudently: Chinese estimates indicate that about one-fourth of this lending surge was used to play China's stock and property markets.

It is not that the Chinese are foolish; that is hardly the case. Given their history and geographical constraints, we would be hard-pressed to come up with a better plan were we to be selected as Party general secretary for a day. Beijing is well aware of all these problems and more and is attempting to mitigate the damage and repair the system. For example, it is considering legalizing portions of what it calls the shadow-lending sector. Think of this as a sort of community bank or credit union that services small businesses. In the past, China wanted total savings capture and centralization to better direct economic efforts, but Beijing is realizing that these smaller entities are more efficient lenders — and that over time they may actually employ more people without subsidization.

But the bottom line is that this sort of repair work is experimental and at the margins, and it doesn't address the core damage that the financial model continuously inflicts. The Chinese fear their economic strategy has taken them about as far as they can go. STRATFOR used to think that these sorts of internal weaknesses would eventually doom the Chinese system as it did the Japanese system (upon which it is modeled). Now, we're not so sure.

Since its economic opening in 1978, China has taken advantage of a remarkably friendly economic and political environment. In the 1980s, Washington didn't obsess overmuch about China, given its focus on the "Evil Empire." In the 1990s, it was easy for China to pass inconspicuously in global markets, as China was still a relatively small player. Moreover, with all the commodities from the former Soviet Union hitting the global market, prices for everything from oil to copper neared historic lows. No one seemed to fight against China's booming demand for commodities or rising exports. The 2000s looked like they would be more turbulent, and early in the administration of George W. Bush the EP-3 incident landed the Chinese in Washington's crosshairs, but then the Sept. 11 attacks happened and U.S. efforts were redirected toward the Islamic world.

Believe it or not, the above are coincidental developments. In fact, there is a structural factor in the global economy that has protected the Chinese system for the past 30 years that is a core tenet of U.S. foreign policy: Bretton Woods.

Rethinking Bretton Woods

Bretton Woods is one of the most misunderstood landmarks in modern history. Most think of it as the formation of the World Bank and International Monetary Fund, and the beginning of the dominance of the U.S. dollar in the international system. It is that, but it is much, much more.

In the aftermath of World War II, Germany and Japan had been crushed, and nearly all of Western Europe lay destitute. Bretton Woods at its core was an agreement between the United States and the Western allies that the allies would be able to export at near-duty-free rates to the U.S. market in order to boost their economies. In exchange, the Americans would be granted wide latitude in determining the security and foreign policy stances of the rebuilding states. In essence, the Americans took what they saw as a minor economic hit in exchange for being able to rewrite first regional, and in time global, economic and military rules of engagement. For the Europeans, Bretton Woods provided the stability, financing and security backbone Europe used first to recover, and in time to thrive. For the Americans, it provided the ability to preserve much of the World War II alliance network into the next era in order to compete with the Soviet Union.

The strategy proved so successful with the Western allies that it was quickly extended to World War II foes Germany and Japan, and shortly thereafter to Korea, Taiwan, Singapore and others. Militarily and economically, it became the bedrock of the anti-Soviet containment strategy. The United States began with substantial trade surpluses with all of these states, simply because they had no productive capacity due to the devastation of war. After a generation of favorable trade practices, surpluses turned into deficits, but the net benefits were so favorable to the Americans that the policies were continued despite the increasing economic hits. The alliance continued to hold, and one result (of many) was the eventual economic destruction of the Soviet Union.

Applying this little history lesson to the question at hand, Bretton Woods is the ultimate reason why the Chinese have succeeded economically for the last generation. As part of Bretton Woods, the United States opens its markets, eschewing protectionist policies in general and mercantilist policies in particular. Eventually the United States extended this privilege to China to turn the tables on the Soviet Union. All China has to do is produce — it doesn't matter how — and it will have a market to sell to.

But this may be changing. Under President Barack Obama, the United States is considering fundamental changes to the Bretton Woods arrangements. Ostensibly, this is to update the global financial system and reduce the chances of future financial crises. But out of what we have seen so far, the National Export Initiative (NEI) the White House is promulgating is much more mercantilist. It espouses doubling U.S. exports in five years, specifically by targeting additional sales to large developing states, with China at the top of the list.

STRATFOR finds that goal overoptimistic, and the NEI is maddeningly vague as to how it will achieve this goal. But this sort of rhetoric has not come out of the White House since pre-World War II days. Since then, international economic policy in Washington has served as a tool of political and military policy; it has not been a beast unto itself. In other words, the shift in tone in U.S. trade policy is itself enough to suggest big changes, beginning with the idea that the United States actually will compete with the rest of the world in exports.

If — and we must emphasize if — there will be force behind this policy shift, the Chinese are in serious trouble. As we noted before, the Chinese financial system is largely based on the Japanese model, and Japan is a wonderful case study for how this could go down. In the 1980s, the United States was unhappy with the level of Japanese imports. Washington found it quite easy to force the Japanese both to appreciate their currency and accept more exports. Opening the closed Japanese system to even limited foreign competition gutted Japanese banks' international positions, starting a chain reaction that culminated in the 1990 collapse. Japan has not really recovered since, and as of 2010, total Japanese GDP is only marginally higher than it was 20 years ago.

China's Limited Options

China, which unlike Japan is not a U.S. ally, would have an even harder time resisting should Washington pressure Beijing to buy more U.S. goods. Dependence upon a certain foreign market means that market can easily force changes in the exporter's trade policies. Refusal to cooperate means losing access, shutting the exports down. To be sure, the U.S. export initiative does not explicitly call for creating more trade barriers to Chinese goods. But Washington is already brandishing this tool against China anyway, and it will certainly enter China's calculations about whether to resist the U.S. export policy. Japan's economy, in 1990 and now, only depended upon international trade for approximately 15 percent of its GDP. For China, that figure is 36 percent, and that is after suffering the hit to exports from the global recession. China's only recourse would be to stop purchasing U.S. government debt (Beijing can't simply dump the debt it already holds without taking a monumental loss, because for every seller there must be a buyer), but even this would be a hollow threat.

First, Chinese currency reserves exist because Beijing does not want to invest its income in China. Underdeveloped capital markets cannot absorb such an investment, and the reserves represent the government's piggybank. Getting a 2 percent return on a rock-solid asset is good enough in China's eyes. Second, those bond purchases largely fuel U.S. consumers' ability to purchase Chinese goods. In the event the United States targets Chinese exports, the last thing China would want is to compound the damage. Third, a cold stop in bond purchases would encourage the U.S. administration — and the American economy overall — to balance its budgets. However painful such a transition may be, it would not be much as far as retaliation measures go: "forcing" a competitor to become economically efficient and financially responsible is not a winning strategy. Granted, interest rates would rise in the United States due to the reduction in available capital — the Chinese internal estimate is by 0.75 percentage points — and that could pinch a great many sectors, but that is nothing compared to the tsunami of pain that the Chinese would be feeling.

For Beijing, few alternatives exist to American consumption should Washington limit export access; the United States has more disposable income than all of China's other markets combined. To dissuade the Americans, China could dangle the carrot of cooperation on sanctions against Iran before Washington, but the United States may already be moving beyond any use for that. Meanwhile, China would strengthen domestic security to protect against the ramifications of U.S. pressure. Beijing perceives the spat with Google and Obama's meeting with the Dalai Lama as direct attacks by the United States, and it is already bracing for a rockier relationship. While such measures do not help the Chinese economy, they may be Beijing's only options for preserving internal stability.

In China, fears of this coming storm are becoming palpable — and by no means limited to concerns over the proposed U.S. export strategy. With the Democratic Party in the United States (historically the more protectionist of the two mainstream U.S. political parties) both in charge and worried about major electoral losses, the Chinese fear that midterm U.S. elections will be all about targeting Chinese trade issues. Specifically, they are waiting for April 15, when the U.S. Treasury Department is expected to rule whether China is a currency manipulator — a ruling Beijing fears could unleash a torrent of protectionist moves by the U.S. Congress. Beijing already is deliberating on the extent to which it should seek to defuse American anger. But the Chinese probably are missing the point. If there has already been a decision in Washington to break with Bretton Woods, no number of token changes will make any difference. Such a shift in the U.S. trade posture will see the Americans going for China's throat (no matter whether by design or unintentionally).

And the United States can do so with disturbing ease. The Americans don't need a public works program or a job-training program or an export-boosting program. They don't even have to make better — much less cheaper — goods. They just need to limit Chinese market access, something that can be done with the flick of a pen and manageable pain on the U.S. side.

STRATFOR sees a race on, but it isn't a race between the Chinese and the Americans or even China and the world. It's a race to see what will smash China first, its own internal imbalances or the U.S. decision to take a more mercantilist approach to international trade.

U.S., China: Conflicting Interests in Southeast Asia
Aug. 12, 2010

The United States and Vietnam launched a round of joint activities Aug. 8 as part of a commemoration of the 15th anniversary of normalized U.S.-Vietnamese ties in 1995. The United States sent nuclear-powered aircraft carrier USS George Washington to Da Nang, Vietnam, on Aug. 8 to host talks with Vietnamese officials, and the guided missile destroyer USS John S. McCain arrived Aug. 10 to lead the first-ever joint naval exercises over four days, covering search and rescue, damage control, maintenance, emergency repair and firefighting operations. At the same time, the Vietnamese Foreign Ministry confirmed that Hanoi has entered bilateral negotiations with the United States over a civilian nuclear cooperation agreement, which has been rumored to involve the United States giving its blessing for Vietnam to enrich uranium on its own soil.

The meeting comes amid heightened tensions over the U.S. presence in China's near abroad. In recent months, the United States has sped up its re-engagement with Southeast Asia, stirring anxieties in China about U.S. intentions. While the United States will not necessarily maintain its current rapid pace, it appears committed to sustaining this policy in the coming years, contrary to previous bids to rejuvenate its interaction with the region after the post-Cold War hiatus. The American goal is to reassert leadership gradually in the region in economic, political and security affairs. By doing so, the United States would update its strategic posture, increase competition with China and give Association of Southeast Asian Nations (ASEAN) states more confidence and freedom to maneuver on pursuing their interests in the presence of greater powers.

Forms of Re-engagement

The high-profile U.S.-Vietnamese visit and exercises are taking place after a series of recent U.S. moves to increase its stature in the region. In July, U.S. Secretary of State Hillary Clinton visited the ASEAN foreign ministers' summit and emphasized that the United States is genuine about implementing its Southeast Asia re-engagement policy, starting with closer ties to ASEAN.

Clinton pointed to a critical dimension of the policy when she declared that freedom of navigation in maritime Southeast Asia is in the "national interest" of the United States and all states with an interest in stable seaborne trade. She also called for an international resolution mechanism for handling territorial disputes in the South China Sea between China, Taiwan, Vietnam, the Philippines, Malaysia, Indonesia and Brunei. Clinton's comments drew sharp rebuttals from Chinese officials and state press, highlighting China's policy that the South China Sea is a sovereign area of "core interest" like Taiwan or Tibet and that territorial disagreements should be handled through bilateral negotiations. Subsequently, China's People's Liberation Army Navy launched large-scale military exercises in the sea. Clinton's comments also provoked debate across the region, with the Philippine foreign secretary stating publicly that the United States has no reason to get involved in regional boundary disputes, which rightfully belong to China and ASEAN alone. The statement should not be taken to mean that the Philippines, a U.S. ally, will not play a supportive role in the policy, but it does indicate the ambivalence that Southeast Asian states feel toward the prospect of becoming contested terrain between the United States and China.

The United States has a Pacific coast and an extensive and longstanding interaction with the Asia-Pacific region, including Southeast Asia. Fundamentally, U.S. global power rests on its control of the oceans, which enables it to protect its own shores and intervene selectively abroad to prevent the rise of regional powers. Maritime Southeast Asia is essentially a bottleneck — marked by the Strait of Malacca, the South China Sea and other minor routes — through which all commercial and military vessels must pass if they are to transit between the Indian and Pacific oceans. The United States thus seeks to ensure that there is freedom of navigation on international waters, that shipping routes remain open and stable and that no foreign power could seek to deny access to the U.S. Navy. This drives the United States to pursue security ties with regional players, to stem militancy and piracy and to preserve the broader balance of power.

Moreover, Washington has an interest in cultivating strong economic ties with Southeast Asia, which has a population of 500 million; produces natural resources and offers low-cost, labor-intensive manufacturing; and is hungry for investment to fuel its rapid development. The financial crisis has inspired the United States to expand these ties both to increase its exports and to tap into new sources of growth. Essentially, the region's economic power is large and growing, and the United States already has a history of trade and security ties with several states. After having played an extremely limited role in the region following the conclusion of the Cold War, the United States is seeking to revive those ties and form new relations with non-allies to reflect changing realities — namely China's economic and military ascent and increasing assertiveness in the region, especially in the South China Sea.

American engagement with the region is focusing specifically on reinforcing its freedom to operate in international waters and updating relations with official allies like the Philippines and Thailand, strengthening bonds with partners like Singapore, Indonesia, Malaysia and Vietnam, and forging new ties with states formerly shunned, like Cambodia, Laos and, to a lesser extent, Myanmar. By re-establishing diplomatic relations with Myanmar in 2009, the United States paved the way to improve its interaction with ASEAN as an organization. U.S. President Barack Obama met with the ASEAN heads of state and Secretary Clinton signed the Treaty of Amity and Cooperation in 2009. The United States also established the Lower Mekong Initiative to help Vietnam, Laos, Cambodia and Thailand with a range of environmental, social and infrastructural issues and pledged to send a permanent ambassador to the ASEAN Secretariat in Jakarta.

Meanwhile, the United States has stepped up bilateral relations with the ten ASEAN members, including, among other things, pursuing the aforementioned naval and nuclear deals with Vietnam, restoring full military relations with Indonesia to pave the way for enhanced training and assistance, opening up the annual major Cobra Gold military exercises to Malaysia, holding military and security training with Cambodia and opening diplomatic visits with Myanmar and Laos. The United States has also sought to participate in the East Asia Summit, a security grouping that it previously showed little interest in, and has begun negotiations to create a new regional trade bloc called the Trans-Pacific

Partnership (TPP) that will include among its ranks Singapore, Vietnam and Brunei.

China's View

From the U.S. point of view, this policy not only does not require China's approval but also is not inherently aggressive toward China. Asserting the need for stability and right of safe passage on international waters can be expected from the naval superpower. Moreover, it falls in line with the 1982 U.N. Convention on the Law of the Sea (UNCLOS), and although China understandably criticizes the United States for not yet ratifying the treaty (which the U.S. Senate does not appear likely to do soon, though it has broad support and was nearly put to vote as recently as 2009), Washington nevertheless argues that it adheres to the principles of the UNCLOS anyway since they are based on older international maritime norms.

On the issue of a multilateral mechanism for resolving territorial disputes in the South China Sea, the United States argues that such disputes pose a risk to international maritime security and that U.S. support for such an initiative merely means supporting a binding agreement based on principles of the ASEAN-China 2002 Declaration on the Conduct of Parties in the South China Sea while maintaining its customary neutrality in specific disputes. Similarly, with the Lower Mekong Initiative, the United States claims it intends merely to assist with water resources management and similar issues among states bordering the Mekong. However, China patently rejects what it sees as the "internationalization" of the South China Sea's territorial disputes, as well as the idea of the United States insinuating itself into bilateral arguments about China's hydropower projects and their effect on the Mekong's water levels as a means of setting the smaller countries against Beijing.

The problem for China is that the reassertion of American interests runs directly counter to its national interests and policy for the region, but will prove tough to resist. China has been enjoying stability on its borders with Southeast Asia and rapidly expanding economic ties with these states over the past two decades (and notably after the ASEAN-China free trade agreement took full effect in January). Following a tumultuous 20th century, China's strength is growing on the back of a surging, albeit imbalanced, economy, and its leaders feel it has only recently met crucial strategic objectives. Namely, it has achieved regime stability and unity in the Han core and has secured its important buffer zones, though it knows this achievement is resting on a shifting foundation and is dangerously at risk from a range of internal and external forces. Still, to maintain and extend these strategic successes, Beijing needs to focus on certain external objectives.

Chief among these objectives are resource security and national defense as they relate to Southeast Asia. As China's economic dependence on the international system has grown, it has become more reliant on overseas trade, in particular for Chinese exports to consumers and imports of raw materials. Many essential inputs, especially oil from the Middle East and Africa, require transit through Southeast Asia. Long maritime supply lines are inherently vulnerable to disruptions of various kinds, from piracy to terrorism. But there is the added fear that as China becomes stronger, the United States will become more aggressive, and the U.S. Navy — or even other rival navies like that of Japan or possibly India — could someday take hostile action against China's supply lines. Because China's social and political stability currently rests on maintaining economic growth, Beijing must think of ways to secure supplies and minimize risks. It has sought to do so in part through continuing to develop domestic natural resources, reducing imbalances and inefficiencies in domestic consumption and pursuing land supply routes through Central Asia and Russia and a hybrid sea-land energy route through Myanmar.

Nevertheless, seaborne supplies remain critical, and the chief focus thus becomes the South China Sea. In addition to modernizing its navy, China has concentrated more of its naval resources and strategy on the Southern Fleet based on Hainan Island, the launching platform for projecting naval power farther abroad, from its neighboring seas to the Indian Ocean, the Middle East and East African coast.

Separate from supply line concerns, the South China Sea has inherent value because it holds discovered and potential natural resources, including fishing grounds, oil, natural gas and other mineral deposits, thus intensifying the sovereignty disputes over the Paracel and Spratly islands. In fact, China has already threatened to retaliate against foreign companies cooperating with Vietnam on offshore oil exploration in the sea.

Even aside from the economic and commercial importance of the sea, Beijing has security reasons for reasserting its sovereignty there. Beijing wants to be capable of denying foreign powers the ability to approach the Chinese mainland or assist China's enemies in the region in the event of conflict. Taiwan remains a longstanding target due to the sovereignty dispute, and Vietnam is a traditional adversary and has aggressively resisted China's South China Sea strategy, including through the pursuit of Russian submarines and fighter jets.

The U.S. thrust into Southeast Asia thus inherently poses a threat to China's naval strategy and "core interest" in the South China Sea. China sees greater U.S. involvement as a deliberate attempt to take advantage of its new international dependencies, thwart its expanding influence and form a containment ring around it that can be used to suppress it, or even someday cut off its critical supplies or attack. Moreover, it raises the specter of deepening American involvement in mainland Southeast Asia that could serve as a tool to pressure China on its southern borders, as England and France did in the 19th and early 20th centuries at the height of European colonial power.

Conflicting Interests

The conflict between U.S. and Chinese strategic interests is therefore apparent, but not necessarily urgent. The U.S. re-engagement policy is gaining some momentum, but the United States will not necessarily permanently maintain this accelerated pace. U.S. efforts to reignite interest in Southeast Asia have moved haltingly throughout the past decade. Constraints on the American side as it attempts to extricate itself from Iraq and Afghanistan and develop balances between powers in the Middle East and South Asia suggest limitations on the amount of energy the United States will be able to devote to the policy.

What is clear is that the United States, despite delays, obstacles and other foreign policy priorities, is serious about re-engagement and will remain committed to a gradual process in the coming years. This will create new points of stress and rising competition with China for influence in the region. While neither side is looking to ignite hostilities, previous incidents show that there is potential for mistakes and confrontation. These include the EP-3 incident in 2001, a Chinese submarine surfacing near the USS Kitty Hawk in 2007 and minor confrontations and collisions between Chinese ships and the USNS Impeccable and USS John McCain (the same ship that visited Vietnam in mid-August) in 2009.

Ultimately, however, the United States has the upper hand. It has greater trade and security ties in the region as well as allies like Japan and Europe that also have strong economic ties with ASEAN states. The ASEAN states also have an incentive to attract a distant superpower to give themselves leverage against a potentially threatening and overbearing regional power — especially given the disadvantages of falling on the superpower's bad side. And Beijing's ability to compete will continue to be limited by its fragile domestic economic and social stability, given that its political and economic elite are in the midst of deep debates about the future of the country as they vie for better positioning in the generational leadership transition taking place over the coming years. Nevertheless, the United States will be limited in its engagement by the need to maintain bilateral relations with China, by the ASEAN states' need to maintain a balance in their relations with China and their divisions between themselves, and by Washington's own decisions and constraints regarding foreign policy priorities.

Overall, the effect of U.S. engagement will be gradually to modernize its strategic footholds in the region, put China on edge about U.S. intentions and give ASEAN states more freedom to maneuver for themselves. This will allow them to hedge against China, but it also will give them the opportunity to play the two countries — and Japan and other interested players — against one another, all while they continue to compete amongst themselves. Beijing can be expected to criticize the American strategy vocally when it takes notable steps, such as naval training with Vietnam, as well as to attempt to accelerate and leverage its own involvement in the region to pursue its interests.

China is not without options. Through its massive economic demand for Southeast Asian goods, aid with little political requirements attached and ability to give out state-supported credit and provide infrastructure construction, it will be able to lure ASEAN states into tighter relations. Its growing economic and military heft will be useful in deterring these states from becoming tools of the United States. Still, since Beijing knows it sits at a disadvantage to Washington if the policy is pursued aggressively, it will be particularly vigilant in watching the pace and means by which the United States pushes forward, especially focusing on military and security cooperation and issues in the South China Sea. China's vulnerability will make it more reactive to perceived threats, and Southeast Asia will likely become the scene of new flash points in the ongoing saga of U.S.-Chinese tensions.